The
Sacred Harp

A Tradition and
Its Music

BUELL E. COBB, JR.

THE
UNIVERSITY OF GEORGIA
PRESS
ATHENS

Copyright © 1978 by the University of Georgia Press
Athens 30602

All rights reserved

Set in 12 on 14 point Kentonian type
Printed in the United States of America

Library of Congress Cataloging in Publication Data

Cobb, Buell E., Jr.
    The sacred harp.
    Includes index.
    1. The Sacred harp, a collection of psalm and hymn
tunes, odes, and anthems. 2. Hymns, English—History
and criticism. 3. Church music—Southern States. I. Title.
ML3111.C6   783.6'7   77–6323
            ISBN 0–8203–0426–3

Contents

Illustrations follow page 70

Preface

Much of this study of the Sacred Harp depends upon the scholarship of George Pullen Jackson, who in six books and several articles over a span of two decades almost single-handedly reconstructed an entire chapter of American musical and cultural history. I have made use of much of the research represented in those publications and have followed to some extent their organization. And throughout the book in general, even when I have not credited Jackson specifically, my indebtedness to his work will be apparent. Jackson introduced the Sacred Harp to the world in 1933 with *White Spirituals in the Southern Uplands*. Several other studies followed. *The Story of the Sacred Harp* (1944) was a brief summarizing account for the layman and for the Sacred Harp singers themselves, who Jackson hoped would be proud to learn of the depth of the tradition they upheld.

A few of the older Sacred Harp singers have related Jackson's eventual disappointment that the body of singing folk did not respond more actively to his publications, that they did not appear more interested in investigating the remarkable historical process he had traced. The singers shared with Jackson, as he of course knew, an intense pride in the durability and richness of the tradition he described. And they genuinely appreciated then, as they do today, all expressions of interest and help in making their singing life more accessible to the world around. But, plainly, these people would rather make music than read about it.

Nevertheless the story of this tradition deserves to be told. And my approach to this work is not only to pay tribute to the tradition and the people of the Sacred Harp but to set down, in a more complete form than has been done before, the inner workings, the local variations, and the style of that tradition for those who know it only at a distance.

In so doing I have necessarily gone over ground that has already been covered. I have reviewed, for example, aspects of the musical history leading up to the Sacred Harp that are now rather generally known in the belief that some discussion of these is essential to fill out the picture. But I have not given, in any depth at least, a technical analysis of the music. Others, who are referred to in the text, have accomplished much in this regard already, and more will yet be done. My interest in the music is less with the printed form than with the music as *rendered*, the living tradition.

The Sacred Harp embodies many contradictions and variations, and I have tried to give an account of the differences between the various groups that sing this spirited music. But for the most part I have kept my focus on the "Denson-book" singers, the best known and most influential of the singing groups.

For some of the works quoted here, particularly the handwritten documents, I have regularized the spelling and punctuation, except when these were too picturesque, or otherwise significant, to be altered.

I am grateful to the *Virginia Quarterly Review* for permission to reprint passages from my article "The Sacred Harp: Rhythm and Ritual in the Southland," which appeared in the spring 1974 issue of the journal.

Acknowledgments are due the Sacred Harp Publishing Co. for permission to reproduce many songs from the Denson Revision of the songbook, and to H. J. Jackson for permission to use "Florida Storm" from *The Colored Sacred Harp*. A research grant from West Georgia College, where for seven years I was a member of the English faculty, made possible the publishing of the music and other illustrative material in the book.

I must also express gratitude for the help and encouragement I received from many people. I should thank first of all Daniel Brittain, who generously assisted me as a consultant through much of the process of completing this work. His expertise and his understanding of the tradition were necessary supports on which I leaned. I am grateful to Dr. Eugene Current-Garcia and other members of the Auburn University Department of English who guided my master's thesis, out of which this study grew. I am also greatly indebted to Daniel W. Patterson, who corrected mis-informations in the manuscript and suggested new directions for parts of the book. John S. Ramsey devoted much time to helping me collect and verify data and should be thanked for patient and thorough assistance. Kenneth H. Thomas, Jr., graciously provided me with the hitherto unknown genealogical information about E. J. King and followed up that initial bequest with continued research, which he also made available for the writing of that sec-tion of the book. Harry Eskew, additionally, made suggestions which I have been able to use.

Compiling the entries for the list of singings at the end of the book represented a formidable challenge which could not have been successfully undertaken without the help of many people, too numerous to name, who gave or relayed information, passed on to me pamphlets of minutes, or, in many cases, scratched their heads and somehow came up with the dates and locations of dozens of singings not elsewhere recorded.

I should mention the generosity of Hugh McGraw, who helped in many ways, not the least of which was making available for long periods of time many of the old books and records from his considerable collection. Raymond Hamrick also is due thanks for similar aid in lending source materials and for unfailing good ad-vice and encouragement. Others of the Sacred Harp following to whom I owe special thanks are Ruth Denson Edwards, W. A. Parker, and L. L. Welborn, all of whom were valuable sources of information.

I am grateful also to Max Peterson and Randall and Betty Sea-bolt, good friends who shared the travail of this project and read portions of the manuscript with insight and shrewd suggestions. And to my wife Mary I owe the deepest gratitude.

1
The Tradition

Sometimes the best way to get somewhere—as any Sacred Harp singer knows—is to travel indirectly. And perhaps the best way to begin a definition of Sacred Harp singing, to differentiate it from other existing traditions of religious song, would be to re-peat an analogy offered by an old-time Sacred Harp singer and let his statement, by indirection, point the way. This elderly singing-school teacher, from a small Alabama town, directed his attention first to modern music: "Now all this other stuff," he said with a chuckle, "is more like *aspirin,* or *calamine.*" He had in mind near-by rivals seven-shape and gospel music, but he left room in his generalization for any other music similarly padded with acci-dentals—ear-ticklers, "painkiller." Sacred Harp singers, on the other hand, "sing by *feelings.* And we don't need sharps or flats either." What the old singer meant and what may serve here as an introductory description of the southern tradition he represents is that the Sacred Harp is—in tone, in musical effect, in the themes the songs focus on—an emotive and yet a disciplined music, aus-tere and uncompromised.

As this spokesman implied, staunch Sacred Harp singers from rural Georgia to Texas have not been drawn to various fads of music, secular or sacred, because they cannot respond deeply to a music so diluted. Instead they follow a need that other kinds of music and fellowship do not satisfy. And for this, on warm Satur-days or Sundays in the year, they drive for distances, sometimes across state, to meet at country churches or occasionally a county courthouse. Here at a kind of democratic songfest, in a ritual much older than any of the participants, they re-create from the tune book *The Sacred Harp,* harmonized melodies that are for them the purest sounds they have ever heard. Even they are aware, it might be admitted, of the frayed voices in their midst. But they make no pretensions to angels' song. They speak with pride of "earthly tones."

The older generation of singers, like the old singing-school teacher above, have observed in their own lifetime much of the shift in taste among the singing folk in the South, the evolution from this once widely popular four-shape music into successive stages: the seven-shape books like William Walker's *Christian Harmony,* with a more modern sound, and then the pervasive gospel music, a further development mixed with elements of jazz and ragtime. But Sacred Harp singers are not impressed by this ostensible show of progress. For at least one of them, the analogy is a simple one: "When they change music, it's just like somebody being operated on; it just gets weaker and weaker every time."

Whatever the state of "modern" music and however generally the world seems to have passed the Sacred Harp by, "weak" could never be used to describe any representative example of this kind of singing. Of course the demise of the shape-note phenomenon has long been predicted, and in truth the singing has already failed in many areas. But the Sacred Harp has been and is a sturdy tradition, self-sustaining and efficient, one which has overcome most of its own problems and outlasted most of its detractors.

The strength of the tradition is paralleled by the strength of the music and its participants. To sing as these people sing requires stamina. Their sessions normally last from nine or ten o'clock in the morning until two or three in the afternoon, and so driven are they that most of them put in at least four full hours of singing.[1] Settling back to the severity of their wooden benches, they whip their voices up to a volume that billows and almost deafens, ringing off the dusty pine walls. Foot-stamping is impulsive and irresistible, and the arms of the singers swing up and down, keeping rigorous hold on the rhythm.

Before the words are sung, the participants run each song through with its *fa sol la*'s, to all appearances using their solmiza-

tion like some unknown tongue to insulate and heighten their experience. A cooling breeze would otherwise be welcome to the
singers, crowded around an open square, row on row, but they
know that a sustained draft of wind would soon shut off their
voices, and so they often leave the doors closed, only stirring the
air occasionally with cardboard fans. They may sing, before they
finish, upward of a hundred songs from the over five hundred entries in their stout, oblong book. And they do not go until they are
drained, their voices hoarse—until they simply are not up to any-
more of a good thing.

Sacred Harp has never been a "performance" kind of music.
The singers are not arranged in a line or a semicircle facing the
audience. Instead the circle or square is closed, and the singers
face each other. Front-row privileges are accorded to visiting singers, and shy beginners are urged to come up and join the group.
"Up front's where all the racket is," one singer offers as a friendly
inducement, and even reluctant novices are drawn from the back
by that kind of incontestable logic. Although those who come only
to listen are left to fend for themselves on the benches that are
left, the Sacred Harp folk are not unmindful of listeners. They
yield to requests for songs, favorites such as "Murillo's Lesson,"
or "Rocky Road," and frequently a leader will select "Amazing
Grace" with the explanation that "everybody in the house can
sing on this one." It is also true that some of the most devoted
supporters of the Sacred Harp never sing at any of the sessions
they attend. Yet it is the act of participating that constitutes the
true appeal of this music.

Sacred Harp music is ultimately group singing. Solos and quar-
tets would be totally out of place at a Sacred Harp gathering. And
small groups of singers who represent their tradition by singing at
folk festivals or church programs understand, although the audience may not, that what they are doing is at best a kind of substitution. Still, the songs of the Sacred Harp are not entirely laid
aside between the occasional public meetings when there are several singers on every part. In the late afternoon, couples sit on the

home porch and thumb through the book, lightly harmonizing to tunes their grandparents knew. These are the songs they sing to themselves as they work and the songs they hear at leisure from the tape recordings made at Saturday or Sunday's convention. Truly, these people carry their songs with them wherever they go. When one federal judge in the 1960s ruled to restore the rights to one of the revisions of the Sacred Harp song book to its original body of owners—after an individual had gradually asserted control over the book rights—he announced his verdict and then called the courtroom party of petitioning singers into his chamber. "Now let me hear one of those tunes," he said. Someone sounded a pitch and the singers launched into a characteristic song, "Ragan": "Hallelujah, hallelujah, / I belong to this band, hallelujah."

The song book which gives its name to this tradition was first compiled in 1844 by two Georgians, Benjamin Franklin White and his assistant editor, E. J. King. But although the book itself is only 134 years old, the unaccompanied singing style of the Sacred Harp has preserved folk elements—melodies, performance practices, a basic harmony, and even a life style—of early America and the Old World. In a limited sense, the Sacred Harp is a final stage of the singing-school movement which began in New England in the eighteenth century and gradually spread into the West and South.

Itinerant singing masters of colonial America taught young men and women part-singing with a musical scale represented by the sequence of syllables then popular in England: *fa sol la fa sol la mi fa*. Later, as an aid to sight reading, a system was invented which gave each of the four syllables of the scale a distinct shape. (The standard symbols were a triangle for *fa,* a circle for *sol,* a rectangle for *la,* and a diamond for *mi,* the leading tone.) *The Sacred Harp* was one of the last of many tune books published in this four-shape notation. A synthesis of the earlier oblongs and the tradition they created, this volume supplanted other four-

shape books and eventually overshadowed subsequent publications
of the same genre in the seven-shape notation.

Deemed quaint or obsolete by a world whose standards have
been progress and change, the Sacred Harp tradition has nevertheless remained virtually intact from the time it became a popular movement in the South almost two decades before the Civil
War. The acceptance and preservation of the tradition by successive generations have been due in part to singing schools, a week
or two of annual singing instruction in a little-changed set of
"rudiments" by traveling singing masters. Although nondenominational, the tradition has shared a natural alliance with the Primitive Baptist church, many of whose members also sing from the
old book. Now, as a century ago, "fasola" singing, as it has come
to be called, is a way of life for thousands of rural southerners.
Independent and thoroughly democratic, the Sacred Harp remains
today a vigorous tradition of time-honored song, a living vestige
of the past.

Other forms of the original shape-note systems still in existence
are Joseph Funk's *Harmonia Sacra* (which appeared in 1832 as *A
Compilation of Genuine Church Music* in the four-shape note
system; in 1851, with three shapes added, as *The Harmonia Sacra;*
and in 1876 and up until the twenty-third edition in 1972 as *The
New Harmonia Sacra*); William Walker's *Southern Harmony*
(first published in 1835) and *Christian Harmony* (first published
in 1866); and W. H. and M. L. Swan's *New Harp of Columbia*
(first published in 1849). Of these only the *Southern Harmony*
uses the four-shape system found in the *Sacred Harp,* and for decades the sole community in which this book survived as the center of a living tradition is the township of Benton, Kentucky,
which has one annual singing. The *Harmonia Sacra,* the oldest
shape-note book still in active use, is the source of seven yearly
singings at Mennonite churches in the Shenandoah Valley of Virginia, an area of historical musical activity from the early nineteenth century on. The seven-shape *New Harp of Columbia*

persists in at least eight counties in eastern Tennessee around Knoxville, with annual singings in Baptist, Methodist, and Pres-byterian churches. The *Christian Harmony* is found in communi-ties in Mississippi, Alabama, Georgia, and the Carolinas. In robust quality of singing, it alone rivals the Sacred Harp, and that only in areas where Sacred Harp followers join in the song making.

Shape-note singing was from the start a practice of the Scots-Irish, English, and German folk who settled the upland stretches of the Southeast. And the Sacred Harp was for some time an in-stitution of the white southerner alone. For as long as a hundred years, however, the volume of songs has been enjoyed by groups of black singers in southeastern Alabama, northwestern Florida, eastern Texas, northern Mississippi, and, since the turn of the twentieth century, in and around Union County, New Jersey, where blacks brought the singing with them from the South. Black and white groups have traditionally remained segregated, and the different singing styles which have developed through this separa-tion make the prospect of a consolidation remoter still.

Behind the structure of this tradition are hundreds of singings and conventions in scattered areas of the region—principally in Alabama, Georgia, Florida, Mississippi, and Texas, with a few in Tennessee. Here at community and regional gatherings on ap-pointed dates throughout the year, the Sacred Harpers convene to sing for a day or two from one of the three revisions of their book now currently in use. These are referred to simply as the Denson book, the Cooper book, and the White book.[2]

The revision with the smallest following today is the White book: *The Sacred Harp*, "Fourth Edition, with Supplement," a 1911 revision by B. F. White's son, James Landrum. The singing from this book has been less representative of the central tradi-tion because the book contains so many gospel-hymn songs or tunes arranged in close harmony. About nine annual all-day sing-ings are held from the White book, most of them around the east Atlanta area with a few in the northwest corner of Georgia, remnants of the old North Georgia-Tennessee Sacred Harp Singing Convention.

The Cooper book, the B. F. *White Sacred Harp,* is published by the Sacred Harp Book Company of Troy, Alabama. First copyrighted in 1902, this revision by W. M. Cooper of Dothan, Alabama, has gone through many editions up to the present. Singings from the book are found (along with those in New Jersey) in a wide strip along the southern coast from Florida to Texas, including the western sections of Florida, the lower sections of Alabama and Mississippi, Texas, and, perhaps still, parts of Louisiana and Arkansas. Since there has never been any central organization or even a common means of communication for this segment, the singers who use this book are divided into many area groups, each managing a number of singings in its territory and most publishing a separate directory of singings. Although it is impossible to say exactly how many singings from the Cooper book are held each year, the number of annual sessions is over one hundred and fifty, in addition to about fifty monthly night singings. Included in this number are all black Sacred Harp singings except those in north Mississippi, where the Denson book is favored.

The sphere of the Denson book comprises the heartland of fasola singing: Georgia and the north and central portions of Alabama, as well as community areas in Mississippi and Tennessee. More activity occurs within this section, both in singing and in publishing, than in the others combined. The Denson book was based on the 1911 *"Original Sacred Harp,"* known as the James book in honor of its editor, Joe S. James. The James book was the standard revision for most of Alabama and Georgia until the 1930's. In 1933 the Sacred Harp Publishing Company, organized by Thomas J. Denson, purchased legal rights to the *Sacred Harp* from the James family. Under the leadership of Denson and his son Paine, the Sacred Harp Publishing Company brought out the *Original Sacred Harp (Denson Revision)* in 1936. New editions with revision followed in 1960, 1966, and 1971. The James book was used for singings in central and south Georgia up through 1975, when the singers in that area made the changeover to the Denson book.

Today over three hundred annual singings take place in the Denson-book territory, along with over one hundred monthly sing-ings. A few pamphlets with a separate listing of singings are pub-lished in this division each year, but most of the sessions are re-corded, with dates and locations, in the *Directory and Minutes of Annual Sacred Harp Singings*, a publication financed and dis-tributed by the participants at the singings listed in the directory.

During the days when the various revisions were appearing—1902, 1911, 1936—there were many more Sacred Harp singings, and in a broader area, than there are today: how many more it is impossible to guess. Even today there are about five hundred an-nual singings altogether (many of these two-day or even three-day sessions), as well as approximately two hundred regularly sched-uled night singings or fifth-Sunday singings (see Appendix A for list of singings). The sessions proceed much the way they did a century ago, and, except for the songs that are sung, they vary little from one area to the next.

Customs and Techniques

As each session gets underway, the singers take their places ac-cording to a square-shaped seating arrangement which divides the four harmonic parts: tenor, bass, treble, and alto. The seating ar-rangement, by part, is a carry-over from the days of the old singing schools. So is much of the terminology used during the session. Each leader, for instance, directs the "class" (the singers) in one or two songs, which are referred to as a "lesson." And, as in the singing schools of the eighteenth and nineteenth centuries, it is not the upper voice part, the treble in this case, that carries the melody but the tenor. Both the melody and the treble part, however, are sung by men and women (an octave apart). The bass is sung by men exclusively and the alto, almost always by women.

Before singing the text to each song, the singers heartily vocal-ize the syllables representing the notes according to their shape. Through the use of these four shaped notes, the Sacred Harp folk can read music impressively well. But their strength is also their limitation. They cannot successfully sing music they are unfamil-iar with unless it is transcribed in shaped notes, for they cannot otherwise conceive of the pitches. The "solmization," then, once served a purely practical purpose: to "put the tune in mind" for those just learning to sing. But in time the singing of the notes became a ritualized part of the song service, used with familiar as with less well-known melodies. Except in the case of long anthems, to which the singing of syllables might become burdensome, or songs used during the "memorial lesson" (songs to commemorate the deceased of the past year), when the jangle of *fa sol la*'s might seem frivolous, it would be unthinkable to these musicians to leave off "the notes."

This solmization—performed to a music which combines folk melodies, harmonies reminiscent of organum, and fuging patterns long since obliterated from congregational song—distinguishes the Sacred Harp from the gospel singing movement, whose commer-cialized blare has obscured the unique idiom of the Sacred Harp from the outside world. Many popular gospel song collections in the South, commonly referred to as "little-book" or "new-book music," continue to appear in shape notes—seven rather than four—but these shape notes are never vocalized except rarely in learning exercises. There are other differences more basic, if less obvious. Unlike the gospel music tradition, which fosters quartet and solo performances with everyone else listening, Sacred Harp music is music of participation in which everyone is encouraged to sing and even the harmonic parts are relatively independent and melodic. And unlike gospel music, which fashions new songs in increasingly modern harmonic and rhythmic dress, the Sacred Harp has restricted itself largely to melodies which were transcribed in the 1800s, even the 1700s, many of which had been orally transmitted for centuries before that time.

The songs from the book, then, are traditional. But the Sacred Harp, at least into the present, is not a bodiless, theoretical system of music. It is much a part of its own locale. Most of all, it is deeply rooted in a social pattern, a set of comfortable, efficient rituals that have gradually sifted down over the decades into a way of life that seems as natural to its followers as it seems extraordinary to those who stumble upon it from without.

The typical meeting place of the singing—a country church, perhaps of Primitive Baptist, Missionary Baptist, or Methodist denomination and borrowed for the occasion—will usually be a simple, boxlike structure that stands in a cluster of trees close by a graveyard. The locality is significant; the singers are never farther than this from a sacred context and from tradition itself, the pattern of lives of their parents and friends now gone. Inside, the church is often bare of decoration, with perhaps only a podium at the far end and rows of benches that the singers arrange in the age-old formation. Seats for the listeners are left in two aisles facing the singers. The benches to the front are divided among the four parts in a square shape, an open space left in the middle for the leader.

After a sufficient number of singers have arrived at the church, the singing is opened with a song directed by the retiring chairman. Then after a prayer, usually led by the chaplain, a new slate of officers is summarily elected. The officers next appoint an "arranging committee," whose task will be to determine the order of leaders, for the most part by calling out in turn everyone they see or know. Unless the singing is especially weak in attendance, in which case leaders may be called upon more than once or may be allowed three songs at a time, the sole policies governing the proceedings are that each leader come before the group only once and that he be allotted for his "lesson" two songs of his choice, provided they have not been previously sung. Neophytes and young children are often given special immunity from this last restriction, since they would not be expected to have ready standbys if their favorites had already been taken. But any other singer arriving late and selecting a song already performed would quickly be informed that "that one's been used." Also each leader, even if he normally sings another part, traditionally sings the melody line while leading.

Purists prefer that both of the songs in their lesson be in the same mode (or what they assume to be the same mode), either major or minor. And singers occasionally give a token nod to this custom even when they decide not to follow it: "I'm going to mix my lesson" or "Now I want to change music." But the practice is not at all binding, and in some communities, and by some singers in any area, it is ignored altogether. Beyond the special appeal of a song, a leader's choice often depends in part on his competence or his confidence in leading. If he is not sure of his leading ability, he may rely on a good "class song" that the group needs no real direction in, or he may venture a more unfamiliar song or a difficult anthem if he knows it well or is confident of his ability to carry the class along.

The chairman presides loosely over the whole session, announcing the several five-minute recesses at the proper time (normally one at the end of every hour), the dinner hour, and, if the singing is to have one, the memorial lesson, usually just before or after the dinner recess. The only other interruption in the singing itself is just before the closing song and prayer when the representatives of other singings in the area rise and announce their own sessions for the coming weeks. With the exception of these few interruptions, the day proceeds in such a fashion—song upon song, leader after leader—that at the close most or all of those present who would lead have been called on and eighty or ninety songs have been sung.

The sonorousness of the singing is always a surprise for visitors, even for those who have heard recordings. The four-part music is loud and full beyond any newcomer's expectation. At times the air is so dense with sound, it seems, as the singers sometimes say, "you could cut it with a knife." Back from the group, one hears voices that stray from the mark. (This is democratic music; any-one can sing without audition.) But in the center, in the midst of the terrific volume, it is as if the imperfections are burned away. When the singing is at its best, the timbre of voices on each part seems to fuse, and the chords that come through then are rich and true.

In the early morning before the volume has risen to its eventual heights, the more solemn hymn tunes are likely to be sung. By mid-morning the rhythm and volume have picked up, and the se-lections come chiefly from the revival spirituals and fuging songs (often referred to as "class songs" or sometimes "convention music"). With these the strong rhythm is underscored by the pat-ting of feet on the wooden floor.

One of the revelations for a new observer of Sacred Harp sing-ing is the art of leading, as perfected and demonstrated by many of the singers. Though the 1869 edition of the *Sacred Harp,* like other books of the time, had advised that "all affectation should be banished" in singing and leading, and though the most popular revision of the book still frowns on the " 'winding,' 'grabbing' and 'snatching' methods of some leaders," the techniques of lead-ing vary greatly from the simple movements directed in the rudi-ments. The singers apparently discovered long ago the infinite variations that could be worked around the up-and-down beats of the right hand with which they are taught to lead. The fuge songs offer still further possibilities. At some point the custom was insti-tuted of motioning-in each of the parts as they commenced their share of the polyphonic sequence. While the conservative leader might stand in one spot and draw in the parts with direct hand beats, many other singers are more demonstrative, circling the open space as they step from one part to the next in perfect rhythm and weaving in the hand movements that are an expression of each singer's individual style.

At black singings from the Cooper book, the leader's square is widened beyond the dimensions provided elsewhere, and the singers take advantage of the added space. The leader at these singings may often stand while directing the class through the singing of the notes, but someone will say "step it off" as the words are begun, and the leader will comply, marching back and forth across the front of the tenors, marking the beat with every step. Here the leader's movement to signal the entrance of the parts has lost some of its original function, and the "stepping it off" is fostered for its own sake.

Undeniably, some degree of showmanship occurs in the leader's space in any of the Sacred Harp areas. Most of the singers hold the book with one hand when leading, leaving the other hand free to designate the beats. But others, singing from memory and directing the class with both hands, relinquish the book altogether or hand it to someone else after singing "the notes." Apparently because of the custom of directing with one hand only, those who lead without a book in some areas draw one hand behind their back. This may only be a natural reaction to avoid feeling awkward. Still, the others sing out with confidence when the leader appears to know what he is doing, and this particular posture amounts to a demonstration of poise, as if the leader were saying, "I can lead this class with one hand tied behind me." One Georgia singer, proudly remembering her brother, a long-time singing-school teacher, could say no more about how he excelled at leading a class than "And oh, when he laid that hand behind that back! . . . ," her sentence breaking off in admiration.

Much of the technique of leading is absorbed through experience at the singings. But the fundamentals of leading and singing, of reading the music and keeping time, are inculcated by a hardy rural institution that has remained much the same for over a hundred years—the singing school. It was after crop lay-by time in July and August, when the crops were "in the ground," that the big singing conventions and singing schools from the Sacred Harp were first held. (From this precedent, the summer months remain the period of greatest singing activity today.) In the nineteenth century and in the first decades of the twentieth, singing "profes-

sors" taught a twenty-day school at local church-houses for room
and board and wages. The singing teacher would likely use one
household as his home base but would often stay at other resi-
dences in the community too. And each day from eight until four
he instructed his charges in the rudiments.

The singing-school pupils were taught the major and minor
scales and the three modes of time and their variations. They
learned the markings they might encounter in the music and prac-
ticed singing and leading songs from the book. But there was a
point at which further instruction in musical theory began to yield
diminishing returns. The *Sacred Harp* rudiments at the beginning
of the book were of course available to those who were interested
in knowing more of the mechanics about chord structure and
other such matters. And toward the end of the school the professor might lead his students into discussion of keys and of how to
place sharps and flats. Such information would be important for
composing, but even the singing teacher would admit that it was
not really useful in helping these beginners to sing.

For convenient instruction, Tom Denson, the most popular of
all the singing professors, carried a portable blackboard of cloth-
like material, painted with the clefs and scales, which could then
be rolled up "like a window shade" for handy use. On this home-
made screen, thousands of singing adepts, including the oldest
generation of the Sacred Harp folk today, first learned their "*faw
sol law*'s."

After the novices had completed their twenty-day school, they
were anxious to attend a real singing or convention and to take
their places among the regulars. Often the whole class arranged to
attend a singing together. Although this experience was bound to
have been exhilarating for them, it must also have given the youngsters some dismay. At the actual singing they found the few songs
they had become familiar with lost in an endless succession of more
difficult tunes. Having mastered the simple intervals and rhythm
of the singing-school standard "Sweet Canaan," they wondered
how they would ever work their way through the whirl of parts

in "Bear Creek," one of the favorite fuging pieces. With time, of course, they would feel competent enough to sing out even on anthems like Billings's famous "Rose of Sharon," but it might take several stints in singing school or much individual practice to attain that level of proficiency.

Today the appearance of the singing school has changed somewhat, as the singers' style of life in general has evolved. The classes are now almost always taught at night, and they last for no longer than a week or two. If the teacher lives too far away to drive over for each night's session, he stays, as his forebears did, with families in the church community that hosts the school. The pay is usually from fifty to one hundred dollars per week, and since the teachers today do not depend upon the schools for a livelihood, some merely take up a collection rather than request a fee. Normally the schools are not publicly advertised but are announced for several months in advance at the church or at singing sessions in the area.

The method and content of the instruction have changed little since J. P. Reese held his sober singing schools in Coweta County, Georgia, in the 1870s and Tom Denson became a legend as a singing professor in north Alabama in the early twentieth century. Today, as earlier, the teacher works from a blackboard, drawing the scale and then pointing out the notes with a stick as the novices stretch their voices to reach the pitch. The students rehearse, by motion of the teacher's stick, the leap of intervals from the key note to the fourth, the fifth, the third. Sometimes the teacher will point out, note by note, a pattern of intervals and surprise the class into singing a tune it is already familiar with. To accustom them to singing in harmony, the teacher may have the girls sing the scale up and down and the boys follow, in canon, a few notes behind. Most of the youngsters begin on the tenor part and move to other parts in later singing schools or at the actual singings as their sight reading improves and their voices naturally sort themselves into higher or lower ranges.

Each child, or set of children in a family, is expected to practice leading by coming before the group and directing it in a song. The teacher watches as the leaders keep time and is quick to intercept their hand motions if they miss the beat. Gradually the youngsters acquire the necessary techniques. To continue beating time at the end of the chorus, for instance, sends the class back through a repeat. The hand raised in air, however, indicates that the leader is perhaps out of breath and that once through will do.

The singers recognize the importance of the singing schools to the continuation of their music, and they are willing from time to time to make up a collection and arrange for someone to teach the young in their community. Active singers in each area also try to make an appearance at the schools and lend their support by rounding out the parts. Some attend every night. Still, to look out over the intent faces of the young enthusiasts and hear their first attempts at the scale requires the stoutest optimism. The incipient songsters range from the musically apt to the hopelessly tone-deaf. As their voices reach for the top of the scale, the spread of tones grows to a proliferation of discord, the most scattered of the pitches sounding as loudly as the truest tone. But the singers can smile with pride on these fledglings and their awkward excursions into the rudiments: a few out of this number will learn to soar.

Attitudes and Values

Beyond the singing and related activity, a real sense of fellowship is evident at the singings, an emotional bond compounded of mutual affection and appreciation and the knowledge that all are joined in a common cause. At each recess and at the noon hour the singers visit among the crowd, talking with friends and shaking hands with acquaintances. Dinner-on-the-grounds, a folk tradition worthy of comment on its own, is a great social hour as well as a communal feast. To the back or to the side of the church local singers bring their boxes of food—meats, vegetables, cakes, pies, and bread—and the crowds wander along the tables filling their plates at will, the ladies inviting favored singers to dip into their baskets of chicken or sample their fried apple pies. Some things in life remain fairly constant, and the singers' appreciation of good food seems to have changed little from a century ago when a correspondent to the *Carroll County Times* of Carrollton, Georgia, gave this description of the dinner hour, highlighting a singing gathering at New Hope Church, just west of town: "At 12 o'clock an intermission of sixty minutes was given for dinner. Repairing to a clear, bubbling spring near by, we did ample justice to a large basket of substantials and delicacies, provided for the occasion; refreshing ourselves with repeated glasses of lemonade and making a dessert of a variety of confectioneries."

Altogether, the tradition is a curious blend of the sacred and the secular: from the hybrid origin of many of the songs themselves to the actual singing, whether in the "meeting house" or at a county courthouse. Noticeably, every session is opened and closed with prayer. For some of the singers this may be only a token gesture; for others the prayer is a meaningful moment, serving to tie all the individual expressions of song together and proffer them as a tribute to God.

But there is a sense of pleasure for its own sake here too. This is foot-tapping music. And the singers grin or nudge their neighbors when the singing is particularly good. The tenors eye the "tribble" admiringly when they can clip along at ease on a tune that runs high. Or both commend the bass class when it hits the fuging songs with heft. Sometimes a leader, after finishing one song, will mop his brow with his handkerchief, then look across the page and say, "Now let's get that other one." And even though Sacred Harp singers are known for vocalizing the shape-note sounds, one of their number will occasionally insist that they sing not so much by note as "by letter." "We just open our mouths," the explanation goes, "and let 'er fly."

Good-natured banter often fills the break between songs. When

Mrs. Ruth Denson Edwards steps cautiously back from the leader's spot at a convention to her seat with the altos, her cousin, "Uncle Bob" Denson (the two of them the last of the old-time singing Densons), can't resist a tease. "That was good leading," he says, ". . . for *you*." "It was good for *anybody*," she retorts with mock seriousness. And George Mattox, the irrepressible leader of the singings in Tennessee, urges Georgia and Alabama singers to attend an upcoming session with a traditional spiel on Tennessee hospitality: "We may not have much to eat, but we'll have plenty of Hardshell coffee. We'll treat you so many different ways, you're bound to like some of 'em."

Still, for all their joking, the hearty meals they partake of, their enjoyment of the music itself, the singers are sobered to the realities their songs teach. And they are plainly moved from time to time by the power of this music and its words. A story is told of an old shape-note singer often kidded about his strong preference for "minor" music over major. When a friend quizzed him one day about whether he thought there would be any minor music in heaven, he had to concede: "I guess not," he said after a pause, "but it'll sure help you get there!" As some of the singers express it, if they did not believe in the moral power of the singing —did not feel its effects when they are together—they would not devote themselves so completely to this tradition. In a letter to the *Atlanta Journal and Constitution Magazine,* Lonnie Rogers, a leading singer from Roopville, Georgia, summed up the chief characteristics of a singing session as "love and fellowship, religious spirit and thankfulness. . . . These songs mean a lot to us; they are our way of getting closer to God." And one lifelong Sacred Harp devotee justified her involvement with a single phrase. "It'll do to die by," she said with a smile that did not lessen her seriousness. Such testimony, after many years of observation of Sacred Harp practices in Mississippi, led the late John Quincy Wolf to realize, as he put it, "that *Sacred Harp* singing is an expression of the highest and noblest thoughts and feelings of which these people are capable—of what they believe and love and are in their best moments; in short, that perhaps more than anything else it is an expression of their total ideals and total sensibilities."[3]

George Pullen Jackson, who first brought attention to the phenomenon of the Sacred Harp and other fasola traditions in his 1933 *White Spirituals in the Southern Uplands,* thought at one time that the early American folk-hymns were put together primarily by the Methodists. Eventually he came to change his position enough to call the Sacred Harp tunes "Old Baptist music." In his *Story of the Sacred Harp* (1944) Jackson described in simplified terms the process by which the early Baptists and Methodists began to sing religious poetry to previously unwritten and secular music.[4] Still, though many of the singers today are Primitive Baptists, Missionary Baptists, or "just plain ole Baptist," Sacred Harp singing is interdenominational, as it has always been, with a good smattering of Methodists and other groups represented.

B. F. White himself, the author of the song volume, established this posture very early in the tradition. Joe S. James, the chairman of the revision committee for the 1911 *"Original Sacred Harp,"* says in his *Brief History of the Sacred Harp* (1904) that White was a Missionary Baptist, but that he was "liberal in his views" and "worshipped in the various churches: the Primitive Baptist, Presbyterian, Lutheran, Methodist, Christian." (One of White's chief goals was to see his book taken up by the average churchman, and how much of his demonstrated catholicity was shrewd business practice is difficult to say.) At any rate, James further adds that the many revisionists who assisted White with the book over a period of several decades belonged to "different denominations," that they were, quite simply, "religious men who sprang up from among the common people."[5]

For some time, it is true, a rapport has existed between the Sacred Harp and the Primitive Baptists. These fundamentalists, like the Sacred Harp folk, sing without accompaniment. Also the

Primitive Baptists have often used the *Old School Hymnal* and Cayce's *Good Old Songs,* repositories of many of the standard Sacred Harp songs, and Lloyd's *Hymns,* a book of texts that are usually sung to the old tunes from the *Sacred Harp* and other early shape-note collections. But in general what Earl Thurman, longtime secretary of the Chattahoochee Musical Association, said about that convention could be said about any other Sacred Harp organization or group of singers: "The Association has never concerned itself with dogmas, doctrines, or articles of faith. Participation in its activities is open to all, regardless of church affiliation." At the singings today the only references to religious differences take the form of ribbing between Baptists and Methodists or between "Regular" and "Hardshell" Baptists. And if any religious biases are carried into the singing, as Thurman has said, "feelings of prejudice and intolerance melt away under the spiritual warmth of songs like the immortal 'Ballstown' ":[6]

> Great God, attend, while Zion sings
> The joy that from Thy presence springs;
> To spend one day with Thee on earth,
> Exceeds a thousand days of mirth.

A few scattered Primitive Baptist congregations today use the *Sacred Harp* in their services. But otherwise, apparently, the Sacred Harp is not anywhere involved in regular church worship. The failure of the book to be adopted by a single one of the southern churches must have been a major disappointment to the authors and revisers of the original *Sacred Harp* volumes. White had advertised the *Sacred Harp* as being "well adapted to churches of all denomination" and had stated in the preface to the book that "the compiler . . . being necessarily thrown among churches of various denominations, and all the time observing their wants in that of a variety of church music, has in this work endeavored to supply that deficiency which heretofore existed, by placing all the church music within his reach, in one book. That such a compilation is needed, no person of piety, observation, and taste, will

deny." But the books soon to be officially adopted by the churches
were those with the "improved" music tailored to fit the newly
available pianos and organs. The music editors for the new hymnals lived in the city, removed from the southern rural songster and
from his taste and affection for the "good old tunes." Also Charles
Ellington has suggested that the very adaptability of the *Sacred
Harp* to "churches of all denomination" may have been another
reason why it was not accepted by any of them. "Sentiments expressed in *Sacred Harp* texts," Ellington writes, "were suited to
both Baptist and Methodist persuasions, but *Sacred Harp* did not
contain hymns which particularly supported the dogma of either
denomination."[7]

Even so, throughout the century and a quarter of its history a
close relationship has remained between the Sacred Harp and
many small community churches. In earlier days most of these
churches were serviced—and many still are today—by circuit-
riding preachers. The meeting house was used for only one or two
Sundays a month, leaving the church building available for season-
al or annual singings on a few of these open dates. The annual Sacred Harp singing thus became a part of the life of the church and
its community. Many southern rural churches still hold an all-day
Sacred Harp singing once a year even though they now meet regularly all other Sundays.

In the preface to his 1844 volume White had also stated that
"while the churches may be supplied from this work, others have
not been forgotten or neglected; a great variety will be found suited to singing-schools, private societies, and family circles; in fact,
the Sacred Harp is designed for all classes who sing, or desire to
sing." Very nearly these same claims had been made by every tune-
book author of the time. But if the Sacred Harp was never officially accepted by the churches, it did become and has yet remained,
as White hoped, a music for the people, for those "who desire to
sing." Into the beginning of the twentieth century, J. S. James
could say, "no song book, taken as a whole, so stirs the hearts of
the people as does the Sacred Harp."

The Texts

That the book did stir the hearts of the people is testimony in large measure to the power of the music itself. It also has much to do with the message which the songs contained, with the style and fiber of the verse. As varied as they are in some ways, the texts in the *Sacred Harp* tend to fall into two general categories: verses of the eighteenth-century English hymnists (Isaac Watts, Charles Wesley, John Newton, William Cowper, and Philip Doddridge) and texts either taken from or influenced by the camp-meeting spirituals of the nineteenth century. In all cases the arrangers of the Sacred Harp songs took the liberty of affixing any available text to any type of tune: hymn, fuging song, or revival spiritual.

The favorite hymn writer represented in the *Sacred Harp* is Isaac Watts. Over sixty texts in the volume can be attributed to this English hymnist, as well as portions of a number of other songs of the camp-meeting variety which have combined verses of the universally known hymns with local refrains. In incorporating so many of Watts's hymns, the *Sacred Harp* was again following a traditional tendency, for Watts was by far the most popular sacred writer of the eighteenth century, his hymns being sung exclusively in many churches. But even Sacred Harp writers up through the mid-twentieth century have preferred the verses of Watts over all others. There are two likely reasons for this. First, the democratic Watts wrote to the level of the common man, and second, his hymns emphasize dramatic images (as shown by the verse from the song "Montgomery" below) which would appeal to a people whose inclination in music and theology was always for a suffusion of emotive power:

> Early my God, without delay,
> I haste to seek thy face;
> My thirsty spirit faints away
> Without thy cheering grace;

> So pilgrims on the scorching sand,
> Beneath a burning sky,
> Long for a cooling stream at hand,
> And they must drink or die.

Along with the verses by Watts and the other eighteenth-century English writers—and sometimes merged with them—are many others which were born of the American camp-meeting movement of the early nineteenth century. Some of these, linked with vigorous melodies, floated from camp meeting to camp meeting and were transcribed at last for the *Sacred Harp* by B. F. White, E. J. King, Leonard P. Breedlove, J. P. and H. S. Reese, T. W. Carter, and Edmund Dumas.

One distinct quality of many Sacred Harp songs and of revival spirituals particularly is their subjectivity, as illustrated in the songs "Jackson," with a text by Jesse Mercer:

> I find myself out of the way,
> My thoughts are often gone astray,
> Like one alone I seem to be,
> Oh, is there any one like me?

and "The Grieved Soul":

> Come my soul and let us try
> For a little season,
> Every burden to lay bye,
> Come and let us reason.
>
> What is this that cast thee down?
> Who are those that grieve thee?
> Speak and let the worst be known.
> Speaking may relieve thee.

Texts with such sentiments could not easily find their way into congregational hymnals of today. But songs which spoke as these did for the individual, for his doubts and despondencies as well as for his affirmations, were surely responsible for much of the popular appeal of the *Sacred Harp* in the era in which it flourished in the South.

Some of the Sacred Harp texts, like the one to the tune "Ado- ration," express delight in the world as the visible immanence of God:

> Lord, when my raptured thought surveys
> Creation's beauties o'er,
> All nature joins to teach thy praise,
> And bid my soul adore.

But far more characteristic of the songs is the theme of world- rejection. Life, from this perspective, is experienced as a span of troubles and trials, hardships and griefs. Those making their way through such a wilderness, who "still your bodies feel," are en- couraged to "struggle on for the work's most done," to "look be- yond this vale of tears to that celestial hill." Typical refrains of the camp-meeting songs express this looking beyond: "Then my troubles will be over," "I have but one more river to cross, / And then I'll be at rest," "I am on my journey home," and "I am bound for the promised land." They speak of being "done with the world . . . And I don't expect to stay much longer here" or "And I don't care to stay here long."

Like most other tune books of its era, the *Sacred Harp* sounds the theme of death or mutability again and again in its songs. In- variably the theme occurs as a warning, often made ominous by the intensity of its imagery:

> Your sparkling eyes and blooming cheeks
> Must wither like the blasted rose;
> The coffin, earth, and winding sheet
> Will soon your active limbs enclose.

It would of course be a mistake to suggest that all or even most of the Sacred Harp songs have doleful lyrics (as it is often mistaken- ly assumed that most of the melodies are in a minor key). Indeed,

few sacred songs can surpass the joy in anticipation of heaven expressed in many of the Sacred Harp tunes. But the songs which do
place emphasis on "fleeting time" or "conquering death" constitute a substantial and significant minority. This view of the im-
permanence of earthly pleasures and the assurance that "Religion
is a fortune, / And heaven is a home" combine to give a strong
message of where the individual should situate his values.

Another motif which runs throughout the book is that of parting, echoed in titles such as "Farewell," "Farewell to All," "The
Minister's Farewell," "Farewell Anthem," "The Teacher's Farewell," "Sister's Farewell," "Never Part," "Can I Leave You?",
"A Parting Prayer," "Parting Friend," and "Parting Friends" and
in texts of as many other songs. For the singers, this emphasis is
also appropriate. The tradition of the Sacred Harp exists through
intervals of space and time, is experienced as convenings and sep-
arations, group happenings eagerly anticipated and wistfully concluded. The fact of parting and the hope of reunion are the
common bond of Sacred Harp followers. And as yearly reunions
inevitably come to represent the spiral of life itself, the singers
are made to reflect on the last farewell—and on a time when "parting will be known no more."

The closing of traditional Sacred Harp conventions is often sol-
emnized by the taking of "the parting hand" and the singing of
these words:

> My Christian friends, in bonds of love,
> Whose hearts in sweetest union join,
> Your friendship's like a drawing band,
> Yet we must take the parting hand.
>
> Your company's sweet, your union dear,
> Your words delightful to my ear
> Yet when I see that we must part
> You draw like cords around my heart.

This tension between the necessity of parting (or the desirability

of leaving this world) and the pain that it brings is the recurring
theme of the parting songs:

> But when I come to bid adieu
> To those I dearly love,
> My heart is often melted—
> It is the grief of love.

As a music book of the people, the *Sacred Harp* inevitably lent
itself to narrative interests. Many of the songs recount char-
acters and situations from the Bible: "David's Lamentation,"
"Weeping Mary," "Blind Bartimeus," "Babel's Streams," "The
Prodigal Son," "The Converted Thief," and "Hebrew Children."
There are also songs of sailors in storm and shipwreck, of a dying
gold miner on California's coast, and of "The Dying Boy," a song
written from a time when the "Fever" took many of the Sacred
Harp number. An engaging entry is "The Bride's Farewell":

> Farewell, mother, tears are beaming
> Down thy pale and tender cheek;
> I in gems and roses gleaming,
> Scarce this sad farewell can speak.

> Farewell, mother, now I leave you,
> Griefs and hopes my bosom swell;
> One to trust, who may deceive me:
> Farewell, mother, fare you well.

The theology represented in the book is heterogeneous, and
there is a wide range of styles in the "poetry." But the feeling in
the Sacred Harp has always been that there is something here for
everyone. As the singers are quick to say, there is enough spiritual
substance contained in this oblong volume to make a sermon in
song.

The inherently religious nature of the songs is further pointed
up by the biblical verse or phrase affixed below the title of most of
the songs in the James and Denson books. These verses were added
in the ambitious 1911 James Revision, the editors making an effort

to place the text to every song in a biblical context. For the song "Fleeting Days," for instance, the verse quoted is from the Book of Job: "He cometh forth like a flower, and is cut down." The camp-meeting favorite "The Promised Land" has as its inspirational heading a verse from Isaiah: "Thine eyes shall behold the King in his beauty: they shall behold the land that is very far off." In some songs, particularly in texts by Watts or Billings, which were often paraphrases or reconstructions of biblical passages, the compilers simply linked the texts with the verses on which they were modeled.

Below most of the songs the editors of the James revision also added brief commentary about the authors of text and tune, whenever such information was known. The content and style of these notes, which were carried over into the Denson edition (with some additions and deletions), richen the character of the book. Most of the notes were penned by Joe S. James, the great promoter of Sacred Harp music in Georgia around the turn of the century. As Jackson has said, James was a lawyer "of the old-time rural type," and the sketches he provided are rooted in a rural archaism which sometimes achieves poignance, more often a lighter charm. On page 338 of the James and Denson books, one discovers the appropriateness of the title of "Sawyer's Exit," a song borrowing the folk melody "Old Rosen the Bow." The words to the tune, the note explains, were composed by the Reverend S. B. Sawyer on the day he died, "with a request that they be applied to the melody and published, and on completing the words his spirit took its eternal flight." About the song "Morning Sun," the reader is told that "the run of this tune is fine." And of L. P. Breedlove, the composer of "Mercy's Free," the note below the song reads, "he was one of the old-time singers fifty or sixty years ago. Several claims are made about him being dead, but nothing definite about it."

True to the narrative bent of the songs in general, the footnotes pause to give concrete particulars about the life and death of many of the songwriters. John Leland, a Baptist minister from Massa-

chusetts and the author of some of the most durable texts in the
volume, is remembered for his unusual preaching tour in 1801:
"The farmers of Cheshire, for whom he was pastor, conceived the
idea of sending the biggest cheese in America to President Jeffer-
son. Mr. Leland offered to go to Washington with an ox team
with it and preach along the way, which he did. The cheese
weighed 1,450 pounds. He died with great hope of rest in the glory
world." Major B. F. White, the compiler of the book and the composer of "Baptismal Anthem" (under which this note appears),
"met with an accident by falling on Spring Street in Atlanta,
from the effect of which he died in eight days." And about U. G.
Wood, composer of the music to "Antioch," it is recorded that
"B. F. Wilson in leading this tune in the various Musical gatherings in Georgia, stated that Mr. Wood, whom he knew intimate-
ly, was a good man, fine singer and director of music, and that he
was killed by a falling tree or limb."

The information about the songs and the songwriters is plainly
outdated and often faulty. In James's day, linking old tunes with
their composers was anything but an exact science. (One of the
choicest errors in the *Sacred Harp* and other nineteenth-century
tunebooks was the ascription of tunes by the songwriting Chapin
clan of the Shenandoah Valley to F. F. Chopin.) But to the Sacred Harp singers, James's commentary remains the central source
of information about the persons who gave them their music. For
the most part, those singers who are interested in such history read
with little skepticism these biographical sketches written in the
early 1900s. And they enjoy, scarcely less than does a newcomer
to the book, the eccentricities, the alternately terse and rambling
style, of the footnotes.

The tune names of the songs are another source of historical
interest and general perspective. The titles of many of the songs
are abstractions from the texts: "The Last Words of Copernicus,"
"War Department," "Vain World, Adieu," "The Midnight
Cry." But many other songs go by proper names, following the
old English practice of assigning to a song a tune name. (Tune

names were practical at a time when popular tunes were often matched with various texts.) Such songs are named for states ("Georgia," "Alabama," "Florida," "Virginia," "Arkansas," "Louisiana"), counties ("Cleburne," "Union," "Jackson"), cities or towns ("Greenwich," "Nashville," "Cusseta," "Columbiana," "Abbeville"), and churches or communities ("New Harmony," "Prospect," "Corinth," "Antioch," "New Hope," "Sardis," "Holly Springs") which the composer wished to honor. Tunes named for individuals or families include "Seaborn," "White," "Dumas," "Jester," "Coston," "Ogletree," "Morgan," and "Horton." The Sacred Harp volume has thus become a record of the singing eras which formed and sustained it, particularizing on almost every other page a place or a figure of the past or present tradition.

Today the Sacred Harp does not hold the important social position it did in the days of Joe S. James. The scope of this tradition has dwindled from a whole region to these scattered bands of followers, altogether perhaps no more than a few thousand. But the singing is no less vigorous for that. If no longer a prominent part of southern culture, the Sacred Harp has persisted as a subculture of its own, drawing on the strength of family ties and on the appeal of a music and a system unreformed by time. "I belong to this band," one of the favorite refrains in the book, could serve as the theme song for these shape-note practitioners. Their conventions often occur only short distances from some of the largest southern cities. But in their singing practices and ritualistic music, the Sacred Harp folk are separated from the life around them by centuries; and in other ways—in their attitudes and values, their joy in group singing—by more than years.

2

The Music

Singers of the Sacred Harp have never been fond of the term "folk music" when applied to their singing. It is an appropriate designation nevertheless. The music does exist almost wholly in a folk context, and its tradition was made possible from the beginning by the oral preservation of singing techniques, rhythms, and melodies from other lands and other times, as well as from the America of the eighteenth and nineteenth centuries. This oral heritage includes revival spirituals of the early nineteenth century and ballads and dance tunes of colonial America by way of the British Isles. William Walker spoke for many of the shape-note writers when he prefaced his popular 1835 *Southern Harmony* with the statement, "I have composed the parts to a great many good airs, (which I could not find in any publication, nor in manuscript) and have assigned my name as the author." And as Constance Rourke has said, "the composer in an earlier day was often literally one who only put a piece together."[1]

George Pullen Jackson, who chronicled the various fasola traditions in several books and articles beginning around 1933, has detailed the history and characteristics of many of the folk melodies which were harmonized and notated in the *Sacred Harp* and other early tune books. A well-known example is the lovely hymn "Wondrous Love," one of the oldest ballad tunes preserved in the *Sacred Harp*. Jackson probed the origins of this tune in an article entitled "The 400-Year Odyssey of the 'Captain Kidd' Song Family—Notably Its Religious Branch."[2] The Captain Kidd song, Jackson related, made its public appearance as a twenty-two-verse ballad, "Captain Kid's Farewel to the Seas," distributed on May 23, 1701, in London, the day the Scottish pirate was executed. But the melody accompanying this particular text originated much earlier, the broadside instructing that the ballad was to be sung to the old tune "Coming Down." The song was evidently a great favorite of the people through subsequent generations: Jackson found twelve variations among the camp-meeting hymnals of the nineteenth century. In the *Sacred Harp* the antique melody appears richly harmonized, the parts intertwining with near-perfect grace (see Appendix B).

There are many more examples. The somber words of the Sacred Harp "Plenary" (beginning "Hark! From the tombs a doleful sound") share their melody with "Old Grimes Is Dead," as well as the better-known "Auld Lang Syne."[3] "To Die No More" in the *Sacred Harp* is set to the tune of the traditional "Three Ravens" or "Three Crows."[4] "Primrose Hill" is the melodic offspring of the old game tune "Needle's Eye."[5] And the list goes on and on. There is indeed a wealth of folk melody in the "spiritualized" music of the Sacred Harp.

Down through the ages religious music and literature have of course drawn substance from secular sources. Still it might be surprising that one of the popular forms in the Sacred Harp repertory is a dance or fiddle tune. Protestant sects of the eighteenth century had long condemned dancing as the Devil's sorcery, and it would seem that songs which taught the feet to betray Christian sobriety would have been stricken from the song books of the colonial Americans. But this was not the case. The *Sacred Harp,* like the tune books that preceded it, contains a number of irrepressible dancelike melodies, some of which had been used for centuries and were then transformed with the addition of sacred texts.

The typical tune of this type in the *Sacred Harp* is characterized by a succession of eighth notes running a sprightly course through the two accented beats of a six-eight rhythm. It must have been obvious to the early tune-book compilers that such energy needed to be harnessed for higher purposes. Thus were Old World tunes with a distinctly secular past made respectable in the sacred song books of the eighteenth and nineteenth centuries.

This lively form is represented in the *Sacred Harp* by, among others, "The Old-Fashioned Bible," which must have come to the tune-book writers, Jackson says, as "a set of the familiar jig-tune called St. Patrick's Day in the Morning."[6] The familiar Celtic dance rhythm may be observed here in the dactylic meter which matches the accented pattern of the music step for step: "How *pain*-ful-ly *pleas*-ing the *fond* re-*col*-*lec*-tion of *youth*-ful con-*nec*-tions and *in*-no-cent *joy*." Another example in the volume is "The American Star," a patriotic song which commemorates the "spir-its of Washington, Warren, Montgomery." The thoroughly Yan-kee text accompanies a popular melody which had existed in both the Scottish and Irish folk traditions.

The history of such folk-tunes only partially reveals the tradi-tion behind Sacred Harp music. Though now furnished with har-mony, many of the melodies of the Sacred Harp are in "gapped" modal scales (bare of chromaticism), a recurring characteristic of primitive music. The old folk modes represented in the volume are the Ionian and the Aeolian (comparable to the major and minor diatonic scales) and, less commonly, the Mixolydian (lowered sev-enth) and the Dorian (minor third and seventh, major sixth). Jackson explained that the modality of many of the Sacred Harp tunes arises from certain melodic characteristics which antedate the use of traditional harmony: "The folk-tunes of America are not, in the main, built upon scales of the diatonic major and minor systems which, as is well known, have assumed their present form under the demands of *harmony;* but on a modal system which grew out of *melodic* exigencies long before harmony made its con-quest of the music of western civilisation." Nor do these folk tunes, he continued, "make use of all the tones of even these modal scales. They often employ but five or six of the seven avail-able tones, leaving characteristic gaps in such scales."[7]

In general, pentatonic major songs in the *Sacred Harp* skip the fourth and seventh degrees, less commonly the third and seventh, and the five-tone minor songs skip the second and sixth degrees.

Six-tone major tunes usually omit either the fourth or the seventh interval, and corresponding minor tunes usually omit the sixth or the third. The Sacred Harp predilection for these "gapped" melodies is evident in the list of eighty tunes which Jackson represented in his *White Spirituals* as those occurring most often in all the early tune-book collections, including the *Sacred Harp*. By Jackson's reckoning, fifty-eight of the eighty tunes are of this elliptical nature, twenty of the six-tone scale and thirty-eight of the five-tone scale. The other twenty-two—with but a few exceptions, Jackson maintained—are not those composed by southerners or other unschooled American melodists, but instead, those which were drawn from art sources.[8]

The compilers of these tune books drew no distinctions, indeed recognized none, between the full-scale and the gapped melodies they gathered for their collections. Further, they assumed that all of the tunes belonged to either the major or the minor mode. Thus when they attempted to transcribe a piece of "unwritten music," they often erroneously printed a Dorian melody as Aeolian, forcing the sixth to appear a minor rather than a major interval. Happily, the singers have never let notation get in their way in singing. Whenever they perform a song so written, they sing (unknowingly) the major sixth rather than the minor interval. Jackson pointed again to "Wondrous Love" as an example of a melody already existing in the oral tradition which had been incorrectly notated in the tune books as Aeolian but was restored in performance to its original Dorian character by the singers' raising of the sixth in the tenor line. This practice is followed wherever the sixth is encountered in a "minor" song, not just in the melody line but in all harmonic parts, even in the songs purposely composed as minor. (In Daniel Read's fuging tune "Greenwich"—reproduced in Appendix B—the singers assert the Dorian mode over the notation not only by the raising of the sixth in the tenor and treble parts but by the altos' rendering of the sharped seventh as a natural.) Jackson surmised that the folk singer does not like "the step from the strong perfect fifth of his scale to the flatted sixth, or vice versa, and that he feels only the whole step there as normal."[9] The singing practices of the Sacred Harp bear out this supposition.

The average Sacred Harp singer cannot "hear" the flatted sixth, just as he cannot conceive of other accidentals. His approach to melody is essentially modal rather than chromatic. And thus for these singers the danger of encounters with "modern harmony" —as represented by gospel music, and even the later editions of William Walker's *Christian Harmony,* if not by the schools, the recording industry, or the piano—is the possibility of their acquiring a sense of pitch they do not naturally possess. The true folk singer's sense of melody and harmony (that is to say, his sense of modality) is a kind of musical innocence. Once it is lost—as with any other kind of innocence—it cannot be restored.

As noted above, however, the transcribers of the Sacred Harp tunes—the original compilers and the later revisers—knew nothings about modes, though they may well have sung in them. At least at one point, a Sacred Harp reviser recognized the singers' raised sixth for what it was, but even that single recognition was overturned by a later revision. In the 1911 James book (the standard edition of that time) J. T. White's "Jordan's Shore" was "rearranged by Geo. B. Daniel." Along with other revisions Daniel added a sharp at each point where the sixth was notated. In so doing, of course, he was not altering the real tune but only officially making the modification the Sacred Harpers insisted on in their singing. In the 1966 Denson Revision, however, the music committee, reviewing the tunes for errors, decided that the sharped sixth was not proper here and removed it. At least this move had the virtue of consistency. Now all of the tunes of this type, as written, keep the sixth as a lowered tone, while all of the tunes *as sung* maintain the sixth as a raised interval.

Whether the singers render the tunes as Aeolian or Dorian, the high percentage of "minor music" in the Sacred Harp (roughly two songs out of five) is an anachronism. Minor hymns had accounted for a similar percentage of colonial church music, but they

passed out of vogue as inevitably as the style of life in general
changed. Gradually the minor tunes were deleted (with the exception of some "high church" music) from the repertoire of congregational singing. Even the traditional folk-hymn "The Promised
Land" had to be majorized to fit the cheery optimism of the gospel
sound. The southern tune books, however, retained the minor-
modal melodies and today these tunes thrive in the Sacred Harp,
where for generations many singers have preferred them to the
major songs. The singers would not approve of the stubborn di-
chotomy which holds that major songs are happy and minor songs
are sad. And they could point to spirited melodies like "Alabama"
and "Delight" for illustration that minor songs can effectively express a joyful sentiment: "Thou art my sun and thou my shade, /
To guard my head by night or noon."

It is generally accepted that the instinctive harmony for the
gapped scales like those in the Sacred Harp is quartal rather than
tertian. Just so, the early Sacred Harp writers leaned toward the
interval of the fourth (or the inverted fourth, the fifth) rather
than the third as the harmonic basis for their songs. In Sing to Me
of Heaven: A Study of Folk and Early American Materials in
Three Old Harp Books Dorothy D. Horn observes that in the pentatonic tunes in the Sacred Harp collections, "thirds and sixths are
treated very much as dissonances are treated in traditional tertian
harmony; they are 'prepared' and 'resolved.' "[10] In avoiding the
third, a relatively modern development in the history of harmony,
many of the shape-note tunes are rooted in a very old harmonic
tradition. The ancient Greeks recognized only three intervals as
consonances—the fourth, the fifth, and the octave. And written
music extant from the medieval period reveals this same pattern
of preparation and resolution for the "dissonant" third.

The increasing importance of the alto part in the Sacred Harp
around the turn of the twentieth century brought an inevitable
increase in close harmony, resulting in a shift in much of the harmonic structure from quartal to tertian. But the percentage of
harmony in the Sacred Harp based on the intervals of the fourth

and the fifth is still significantly higher than that of any generally known community or congregational singing today. And if they were able to verbalize their musical preferences, most of the "faso-la" people would probably still subscribe to the sentiment expressed by Johannes de Muris in the fourteenth century, that "the Octave, the Fifth, and the Fourth" have "a *nobler* effect on the human mind than the Third and Sixth . . . not to mention the rest of the intervals."[11]

The Sacred Harp singers may not be aware of the technical differences in spacing or in voice leading between their music and that of congregational singing elsewhere, but they do distinguish what they are pleased to call "dispersed harmony" from the close harmony (where the upper three voices are spaced as closely to-gether as possible) of other religious song. According to one spokesman, remembering the definition as it was passed down to him, "dispersed harmony" occurs whenever "a chord exceeds two octaves or the alto goes above the 'soprano.' " This is not a com-plete definition, but it does point to the two essential characteristics of the Sacred Harp dispersed harmony. The first characteristic is that the upper members of a chord are often dispersed rather than grouped closely. The Sacred Harp composers and singers like the effect of the upper three voices spread over a range of an octave and a third or a fourth, a trait which occurs with regularity throughout the music. Another feature of Sacred Harp composi-tion is the crossing of voices, an inevitable result of the contra-puntal nature of the songs. From the definition given above, this procedure is apparently most obvious to the present-day Sacred Harp theorists when the alto crosses the tenor, as in the final ca-dence of most of the major tunes where the tenor descends to the tonic and the alto rises to the third. In many of the songs either the bass or the alto is likely to go above the melody line, the bass crossing the male voices of the tenor or the alto crossing the fe-male voices of the tenor. But the crossing of tenor and treble lines is even more consistent and occurs repeatedly in many songs, the treble being generally more melodic than the bass and alto and having a greater range than the alto.

The crossing of voices of course necessitates the printing of each part on a separate staff. In the four-part tunes the staves are assigned in order, from the bottom upward, to bass, tenor, alto, and treble. (When there is no alto line, the altos traditionally double the bass.) The three or four staves for each line of music and the greater width of the page itself, for easy reading, account for the unusual appearance of the hymnal. In order to squeeze in several verses, however, many of the songs list different verses under each part, a system which makes for difficulty when a singer is unfamiliar with either words or music and must look for the words considerably above or below the line of music to be sung.

Although these pages contain references to the "harmony" of the Sacred Harp songs, the tunes in the typical four-shape hymnals—as Charles Seeger and Irving Lowens have remarked—do not, in the strictest sense, represent a harmonic style.[12] The voice pattern is largely contrapuntal, so that in almost any representative song each voice attains something of the independence of counter-melody. Speaking of the New England prototypes of the tunes in the Sacred Harp volume, Irving Lowens explains that "we hear them today as a succession of vertical chords, but they were originally experienced as a fabric of interwoven melodic flow. The ideal toward which these composers reached was to make each individual melodic line as interesting as expressive, and as graceful to sing as the other. Of course they did not always succeed, but the vertical aspects of their settings were merely an incidental product of the conjunction of horizontally conceived lines."[13]

This emphasis on the linear aspect of the music leads to a certain amount of dissonance. But it is clear that in songs in which dissonances appear, as in "The Converted Thief" or "Columbus," melodic independence of the parts outweighs harmonic considerations. An example of an attempt to curb this tendency involves the alto line of the old standard "Amazing Grace" (or "New

Britain," see Appendix B). In the 1911 James book and the 1936 and 1960 editions of the Denson book, an A in the alto part coincides with a G in the bass in the first beat of the tenth full measure. When so many "discords" in other songs go unnoticed by the singers as they pursue their individual parts, it must have been a shrewd pair of eyes that happened to light on the page at that spot, discovering the patent dissonance. Or this may have been one of the more obvious dissonances to hear in performance, given the length of the note. Through whatever means the chord came to be exposed, the fivemember revision committee of the 1966 Denson edition removed the A, substituting a G in its place. Custom, however, is stronger than any law of harmony, and the altos at the various singings, who may or may not have had the substitution pointed out to them, still sound the A in that measure, just as if it were printed. As can be seen by observing the flow of the line, the A makes much better sense melodically, and the altos, even if unknowingly, have confirmed its rightness.

Nonharmonic tones occur with frequency throughout the music of the Sacred Harp, for the most part as passing tones and accessory tones—"melody helpers," as they are called in the rudiments which preface the Sacred Harp. The neighboring or accessory tone, according to the rudiments, "moves up or down a degree on the scale to a tone not belonging to that chord, and immediately moves back again to the original tone." It naturally provides the variety characteristic of good melody. Passing tones, as the name implies, are the tones used by the singer to pass from a note to the next significant interval. Because of their dissonant effect, they are unaccented and quickly passed over.

Approximately a third of the Sacred Harp volume is made up of the celebrated "fuging tunes," a form carried over from colonial singingschool days. Adapted from the popular polyphony of England and imbued with a distinctly American flavor, the fuging tunes compensate for "harmonic ineptitudes" with rhythm, colorful style, and interest for each singing part (for examples, see "Northfield" and "Alabama" in Appendix B). In his 1866 Chris-

tian Harmony William Walker defined the "fuge" as "a composition which repeats or sustains, in its several parts, throughout, the
subject with which it commences, and which is led off by one of
the parts." This imitation by the successively entering parts is
more often rhythmical than melodic. Usually the "fuge" section is
enclosed by homophonic passages at the beginning and the end. A
phrase of several measures (from four to as many as fifteen) with
some melodic completeness precedes the fuge passage, which usually introduces another or slightly different theme. At the end of
the song, by means of pauses or notes held over by the beginning
voices or to a shortening of the musical phrase by the later parts,
all voices join again in rhythmical unison. The contrast of the fugal
adventurings in each part with the strong sense of a "coming
home" when all the parts resume the common metrical pattern
and join once more in semiharmonic alignment makes for stirring
and interesting song.

Just as characteristic of the song book, if less numerous than the
fuging tunes, are the show pieces of the *Sacred Harp,* the odes and
anthems. These are works of considerable length (from two to six
pages) with changes of meter and usually one- or two-part voicing
for any or all of the parts. Several of this type—"The Farewell Anthem," "Ode on Science," Billings's "Easter Anthem" (see Appendix B)—had appeared as standard pieces in the shape-note
hymnals of the early nineteenth century. And to these in the Sacred Harp repertory were added anthems by B. F. White, E. J.
King, James Denson, M. Mark Wynn, and in the twentieth century by Paine Denson and A. M. Cagle. Today, however, there
are not so many accomplished singers in the Sacred Harp as there
were a hundred years ago, or even forty years ago, and the singers
of the present are less familar with most of the anthems than their
predecessors were. In some areas only a handful of these more difficult pieces are ever used. In other areas, in the Denson segment at
least, some effort is being made to reclaim the more obscure anthems. At a recent session of the two-day Chattahoochee Convention in western Georgia, for example, fourteen different odes and

anthems were sung. But few singers in any area will undertake the leading of any but the most common of these except when there are several skilled singers on hand to carry each part.

The Singing Style

Some branches of the American shape-note tradition are represented today only in history books. But the Sacred Harp does not yet exist in the abstract alone. It is a living thing, re-created anew by the singers who convene around the open square to tune their voices to its ancient chords. And the fact that it is living necessarily stretches its definition. The patterns of melody, the unusual harmonies, the solmization and the texts do not alone comprise the effect, the Sacred Harp sound. One must still account for performance practice, for style—what the singers do with the music and the texts.

For all their reverence for the book and convention, for the written and notated page, the music of the Sacred Harp singers is very much an oral tradition. In performance, the natural impulse is just as commanding as the printed instruction. It could be said that this tendency is the saving prerogative of those who follow the tradition—the license, freely indulged, to let the natural feeling (or what is convenient or practical) supplant a stubborn or defective rule, to let the spirit triumph over the letter.

Even in the matter of composition, the Sacred Harp often does not follow its own rules. Most of the writers of the fasola songs have ignored the standard nineteenth-century musical theories echoed here and there throughout the rudiments section of the later editions of the book, their tunes generously employing discords and parallel fifths and octaves, all of which are expressedly banned in the rudiments. For example, the "rudiments" of the Denson book includes the following statement under the heading "Major and Minor Chords": "If the third is omitted from a chord there is no way to tell whether it is major or minor. Some of the music in the Sacred Harp has only three parts and much of it was written without regard to what has been stated about the use of the third. The harmony in such music might be improved." In spite of the nudging of such criticisms, nothing is more character-istic of Sacred Harp writing than the open fifth. The open chord abounds in both major and minor songs, and fully all of the minor tunes fix their final chord with the third conspicuously—one might say almost defiantly—absent.

With regard to such matters—the avoidance of the third, the pitching of songs higher or lower than keyed on the page—it is a mixture of common sense and natural inclination that prevails, an approach the singers adopt with admirable simplicity. As one pert, elderly lady said, after leading a song that does not mark its chorus for repeating as most of the others do, "Now I know enough about music to know that that didn't have any repeat sign on it. But I wanted to repeat it, so I did." The point of view may have been summed up best by one old black singer who is in charge of setting the pitch for the singing in his community. "Anybody who don't know more than's in the rudiments," he wisely observed, "ain't learnt but mighty little."

One of the more obvious manifestations of the tendency to give way to the natural impulse is the ornamentation the singers bring to the written page. Jackson felt that the flourishes which the Sacred Harp singers add to the notated forms of their songs not only were the product of a singing manner brought over from the British Isles but were characteristic of the embellishment any folk singer would naturally draw into a melody. Throughout his works he referred to songs in the shape-note hymnals which gave every indication of having been taken from folk sources except that they were melodically spare and stiff. True folk singers, he theorized, would not have produced or cherished melody so bare of orna-mentation. Later hearing many of these songs performed at Sacred Harp singings, Jackson found that his initial assumption had been right, that the singers were adding to the notated form of the song and thus were probably restoring the tune to its original form in

the oral tradition before it had been faultily recorded by some un-
skilled arranger.

As Jackson speculated, the pull of the oral tradition is still
strong for the Sacred Harp singers, who are accustomed to modi-
fying in the notated songs any elements that are stiff or unnatural
for their group singing. There are, for example, the songs in which
the singers unconsciously restore melodies to their original modal
nature, which the arranger had failed to recognize. In other cases,
the arrangers have made unhappy rhythmical strictures (notes
unnaturally long usually) which the singers correct instinctively
and unflinchingly.

Grace tones, universally used in Sacred Harp circles, constitute
another aspect of the singing style not encompassed by the book
itself. Generally defined, grace notes are of two kinds: (1) anticipations and passing tones and (2) the optional flourishes which
garland the central notes of the melody. The most consistent and
obvious use of grace notes in Sacred Harp singing comes under the
first category: notes that help the singer to "feel out" the melody.
The passing tones supplied by the singers, like the ones written in
the music, prepare for a subsequent note by sounding the intermediate tones. They are usually heard as the intervening tone
when a singer moves from one note to another a third above or
below. Anticipations occur when a note on the first or fifth degree
of the scale is preceded by a note written one step above or below
(occasionally a third above). In this case the singer pulls away
from the first note, sounding an anticipation of the next tone.

In this respect, the tonic and dominant operate like magnetic
poles. Each draws a preceding note to itself if that note comes
within its range (i.e., one step above or below, sometimes a third
above). The magnet image comes to mind especially on the minor
songs when the la tone is preceded by the sol a step below. It is not
so much that an anticipated la is sounded then as that the sol pulls
up to the other note, the singer even changing his pronunciation
of the syllable as he slides from sol to la.

The purely ornamental grace notes appear more often in the

slower tunes where the folk singer has more opportunity to em-
bellish. This ornamentation occurs naturally wherever the fasola
style exists, but it is much more evident in the songs of the black
Sacred Harp singers. In most respects the black singers follow the
discipline of the Sacred Harp less rigorously than does the white
segment; they are more improvisational, altering or adding to the
musical line—though for the most part unconsciously. On slow,
emotion-charged songs (the Cooper book's "My Span of Life,"
"Amazing Grace," and "My Native Land"), the music is transformed by these singers through ornamentation and exclamation
into something considerably different from what is notated.

In departing from the written music, individual singers of the
black Sacred Harp groups create new harmonies and sometimes
blue notes. Although some tunes are performed with a staccato
effect, other songs are much more fluid, and individual singers may
lavish a central note with a cluster of grace notes. One specific
effect fostered by the black singers in southern Alabama is that of
adding an upper neighbor tone between repeated tones at cadence
points. That is, when a phrase ends with two or three successive
notes on the same pitch, many of the singers—and on any of the
parts so written—will insert a grace note one or two steps higher
just before sounding the last tone. In minor songs this grace note is
usually a minor third above the repeated tones, usually the first
and fifth degrees of the scale. In the major songs the tenor—usually ending on the first degree—goes up a third, but the parts on the
fifth—the treble and alto usually—move up only one step before
returning to sound the final note.

Notable examples of tunes performed with this mannerism are
"The Old Ship of Zion," "The Morning Trumpet," "Ragan," and
"Sweet Morning." In some of the songs only one or two of the
parts will have the repeated tones. And wherever these occur, apparently, the grace note is employed. Easily fallen into but not
consciously produced, this twist at the end of the musical line has
become a natural part of the singing style of the black Sacred
Harpers in Alabama.

Many of the songs to which grace tones seem such an inevitable part had already existed in the oral tradition before they were brought into the shape-note hymnals by William Caldwell, William Walker, White and King, and the others. In taking down these tunes, the song compilers reproduced only a skeletal form of the tune. As Jackson has said, had the tunesmiths tried to inscribe the many flourishes and grace notes that doubtless clothed the songs in the oral tradition, "the singers would not have been able to see the melodic woods for the notational trees."[14] With the basic melody or harmonic part before them, the singers supply the grace notes wherever these seem natural or wherever they are accustomed to hearing them sung.

Grace notes had been a common melodic practice of the folk in early American times and had won approval from that giant of early American music, William Billings. In the quaint colloquy between "Scholar" and "Master" that serves as the section of rudiments in Billings's *The Continental Harmony*, the scholar asks, "Sir, I should be glad to know whether the grace of transition should be always used in tuning thirds up and down?" The master replies, "Where the time of the notes will admit of it, I am very fond of the notes being graced by sounding the intermediate note, which serves for a stair for the performer to step up or down upon." Grace notes and other melodic accessories had thus been condoned from time to time in the musical tradition out of which the Sacred Harp emerged. Their appearance in the Sacred Harp singing today reveals not a degeneration of the musical form represented in the book but rather a continuation of a mode of singing instituted long ago in the oral tradition for which the book itself is in many ways only a formal guideline.

In general, then, it is ultimately not the printed page that is important in the singing. Many of the singers, steeped in these melodies from childhood, sit with their books on their laps but with their eyes gazing elsewhere. Many do not use a book at all. To some extent this is because of the gradual memorization of parts, but the evidence of the singers' restoration of modal qualities to songs otherwise notated, their corrections of printed rhythmical impediments, and the systematic endowment of the basic melodies with nonharmonic tones reveal that there are everywhere glimmers of a living oral tradition in the Sacred Harp.

Of the several components of the musical style in evidence at fasola gatherings, the one most likely to come under criticism by first-time observers is that of intonation. Listeners with a trained ear frequently remark that the pitches are "off" somewhat, that it all sounds a bit out of tune. (Indeed, individual singers here and there do sing "out of tune," as anywhere.) Yet this particular intonation is too consistent and universal to be dismissed as merely the failing of undisciplined voices. Instead, the intonation is an integral, perhaps intentional, part of the Sacred Harp sound. Like other elements of the music, it is often tinged with a yearning quality. Some black Sacred Harp singers sing with a good bit of vibrato, but most white singers project their tones straight, with scarcely ever a trace of vibrato. And surely one of the resulting effects is to give an even more "open" quality to the open chords so characteristic of the music.

In a descriptive sketch of an encounter with Sacred Harp singing, Donald Davidson once noted the intonation of the singers and speculated wistfully on its origin: "Perhaps their manner of intonation was itself traditional and went back no telling how far, to some time when music was in truth wedded to immortal verse."[15] Davidson's conjecture is of course beyond proving, but the particular quality of the Sacred Harp sound may well be traditional.

Joseph Yasser theorized that representative folk music is often not reconcilable with the fundamental tempered scale and pitch system because the folk singers and musicians center their notes differently:

The fact that every tone, musically speaking, must have—and, indeed, usually has—a certain breadth in musical performances (unless produced on instruments with fixed intonation), may explain how it is that the folkloristic musical material collected in a given region with what would appear to be scientific accuracy does not seem always to adhere to the fundamental scale on which this material is ordinarily based, but occasionally manifests various acoustical deviations from it, which some theorists are even inclined to view as independent scales. It is very likely that the breadth of the *same* tones, when reaching the limit at some points of the melodic line, is responsible for the impression that *entirely different* tones, absent in the fundamental scale, are struck by the performer, or even . . . by a great number of performers.[16]

A scale or pitch system based on variant folk sounds, then, might very well legitimize the different intonation of the Sacred Harp.

In the singing performance, it is the alto part that most obviously produces flatted tones, and, as the alto part centers on the interval of the third in the harmonic structure, it is the third that receives the flatted effect most often. The third was a harmonic necessity virtually forced upon the Sacred Harp by the introduction of the alto part, and it should serve theoretically to sweeten or soften the spare chord structure of the Sacred Harp—make it sound less primitive. In that respect, could the flatted quality of the third be a compensation in a way for the interval itself?

On the subject of the rendering of the third by folk musicians, Cecil Sharp has said,

It must be understood that the third is not a fixed note in the folk-scale, as it is in both of the modern scales. The English folk-singer varies the intonation of this note very considerably. His major third is never so sharp as the corresponding interval in the tempered scale, to which the modern ears are attuned. On the other hand, it is often so flat that it is hardly to be distinguished from the minor third. Frequently, too, it is a "neutral" third, i.e., neither major nor minor, like the interval between the two notes of the cuckoo's song, when the Spring is waning. Apparently, the folk-singer, not having any settled notions with regard to the pitch of the third note of the scale, varies it according to the character of the phrases in which it occurs.[17]

As indicated here, the flatness of key tones inclines them to the minor. To the Sacred Harp singers, in fact, flatness is equated with "minor," for the singers often have reference to something other than just the characteristics of the minor key when they use the term. Jackson recorded this statement from a Southern Harmony singer: "there is a lot of miner [sic] music in the Southern Harmony and it suits my voice the best but I can sing either major or minor."[18] When this shape-note singer spoke of "miner" as suiting his voice best, he evidently had reference to something other than the scale which differs from the major only by lowering a couple of notes by a semitone. He must have had reference to the kind of sound, the intonation, which the minor keys encourage.

This may in part explain why the Sacred Harp people by and large have not responded favorably to recordings of their songs by trained choirs. L. L. Welborn, an elderly singer from Cullman, Alabama, explained the difference in the sounds this way: "Their minor chords are not minor. They sing to a metallic key notation—the piano, you see. We sing *vocally*—in tune with *each other*." The Sacred Harp singers, as this spokesman indicated, spurn the "metallic" sound of the tempered pitch system, favoring instead a really "minor" quality which is based upon the pristine musical patterns of the untrained human voice and which is discovered and confirmed by singing "in tune with each other."

Some elements of the Sacred Harp sound that mark it as a vestige of an old tradition also alienate many listeners who are not oriented to this mode of singing. Jackson countered criticisms to the music by arguing that it was "songs for the singers, not for the listeners." First of all, he explained, it was difficult for the listener to distinguish any tune because of the contrapuntal nature of the music. Then too, in accord with another long-standing custom, the melody is given to the middle part rather than to the highest part, as in conventional practice today.

But if the melody of a song does not always come through clearly on a first hearing, the beat of the music certainly does, for a deeply sensed rhythm is also a distinguishing characteristic of the Sacred Harp sound. The strength of the harmonic parts is one feature developed to compensate for the absence of instrumental accompaniment; the pulsating, metronomic rhythm is another. Although some of the songs in the volume are in "triple" time, the

majority of the music is in either "common" or "compound" time
and can be interpreted by means of the simple down and up beat
of the hand by which the singers are taught to "beat out" each
measure. (Triple meter is indicated by "down, down, up." The
first down beat falls half the distance of a beat in duple meter, the
second beat goes the rest of the way down, and the up beat returns
the hand to the original position.) Textual misbarring and the
division of time into two accented beats per measure—whether
the song is fast or slow, 4/4 or 2/4—combine to give the Sacred
Harp the rhythmic gait that is peculiarly its own.

In the matter of beating time, the Sacred Harp for the most part
differs from the later developments of seven-shape and gospel singing. The editors of the 1909 *Union Harp and History of Songs,*
who were also the editors of the 1911 *Original Sacred Harp*
(James book), observed in the opening pages of their hymnal that
when four shaped notes were used there were usually two beats
to the measure and when seven-shaped or round notes were used
there were generally four beats. With some exceptions, this distinction has remained until the present. In his rudiments B. F.
White had designated that all modes of common and compound
time should be directed with but two beats to the measure, and
the majority of the Sacred Harp singers have always followed this
usage. Only in Mississippi and a few areas of north Alabama and
north Georgia (the result of trafficking with "round head" and
seven-shape music) has there been any sympathy for keeping time
with four beats.

The Sacred Harp singers talk a great deal about "accent," about
the placement and the relative strength of the beat that surges
through their music. They feel that the strength and the exactness
of the beat are most important in making their singing effective.
Thus the arms that wave up and down during the singing are a
means of maintaining, and communicating, a common beat, as
well as the irresistible expression of "feeling the music." But there
is some disagreement from group to group over what tempos best
allow true "accent," as well as melody and harmony. Other than

the several revisions of the *Sacred Harp* used in different areas, nothing separates the Sacred Harp folk so much as differing attitudes toward tempo.

As a rule, Sacred Harpers get by with little bickering, but they admit that the question of tempo has been an irritant for several decades. They too have their generational differences: the young often favor faster tempos; the older singers prefer to let the words they sing go by a little slower. How fast the songs should be rendered is a question sometimes vigorously contested between Georgia and Alabama singers, between fasola adherents in one community and those in another. A. M. Cagle and Earl Thurman, two leaders of the Sacred Harp in the middle of this century, held that the controversy arose with the influence of Tom Denson, the great singing-school teacher whom Thurman called "the most dynamic figure that ever trod the Sacred Harp highway." According to these sources, the singers under the tutelage of Tom Denson in the first few decades of the 1900s preferred a livelier rendering of the music than had been traditional. B. F. White had listed, under the discussion of "moods of time" in the rudiments section prefacing the original book, the amount of time each measure should be given, according to its time signature: 2.5 seconds, for example, to a measure of 4/4 time. Cagle's remembrance, as relayed by Raymond Hamrick of Macon, Georgia, was that the revisers of the 1936 Denson book had by that time become so uncertain over the question of tempo that they deleted all reference to the matter in their revision, leaving the choice of tempo to the individual leader.

In his history of the Chattahoochee Convention, Thurman conceded that "some of the older singers . . . were inclined to think 'Uncle Tom' was a little too fast in rendering this music" but added, "if they could observe some of our present day leaders they would consider Tom Denson a very deliberate leader." Thurman recalled Denson at a singing in Carroll County, Georgia, in the early 1930s giving a talk on the proper method of rendering Sacred Harp songs and closing with a remark on tempo. Uncle Tom's

words, "accompanied by gestures that only he could make," Thurman wrote, were " 'You can rush it to death, or you can
D....R....A....G.... it to death.' " Denson's advice was to
avoid either extreme, for singing either too fast or too slow was
destructive of the "general musical effect" that should be produced in Sacred Harp song.

In the succeeding decades singers have found the middle ground
Denson was advocating difficult to achieve. And in general they
have leaned toward a faster rendition of the music. Even Jackson,
who had defended the characteristic "trotting movement" of the
singing in his 1933 *White Spirituals,* became worried that the
Sacred Harpers were "rushing their music to death." Raymond
Hamrick, a singer and close observer of Sacred Harp practices,
tested the tempo at some of the singings for over a decade, and his
statistics chart the striking rise of speed in most of the singing
groups and the subsequent return to a more moderate tempo. Hamrick records that a reasonable estimate of the time given 4/4 music
in the early fifties by the fastest of the singing groups was one
second per measure, a speed that might have left the average New
England singing master a little dizzy. The pace has slackened some
since that time, however, and Hamrick notes that most of the
singings today run a measure of time at a tempo of 1.4 to 1.7
seconds. A contributing influence may have been the popular record albums of the last decade by the Sacred Harp Publishing Company. Each of these recordings displays representative tunes sung
at a moderate speed by a select group of singers.

Even though the tempo of individual songs in any of the singing
areas may vary considerably from that of other songs with the
same time signature, a few distinctions can be drawn between the
groups sometimes divided over the matter of tempo. In general,
Alabama singers sing at a faster clip than Georgia, Mississippi,
and Texas singers, the black singers in northern Mississippi especially preferring a slower pace and the Sand Mountain area singers
of north Alabama having the greatest reputation among the other
groups for galloping speed. The Cooper book singings are more

difficult to compare. This segment performs some tunes as fast as
do any of the other groups; other songs they sing as slowly as do
their lower-Georgia counterparts. The black singers who use the
Cooper book like a slow, bouncy beat—except on some 3/4 music
which they sing faster than any of the other groups. Thus uniformity of tempo is yet beyond the grasp of the singing folk, and
the largest singing conventions, which bring together people with
varied singing styles, sometimes prove a source of frustration for
that very reason (though not enough to make the singers stay
away). These vocalists take their music seriously, and most of them
like a song the way they are used to hearing it sung.

The late John Quincy Wolf has quoted one singer with strong
feelings about the tempo differences—J. Boyd Adams of Varda-
man, Mississippi. "The main difference," Adams says, "is that
those to the east of us sing 4/4, 6/8 and other time controls as if
they were all 2/4 and therefore allow insufficient time for accent
or proper breathing. This practice, I believe, impairs harmony,
though I must add that they are artists and sing so well that I must
compliment them."[19] It is no wonder that the singers of the Sacred
Harp in Mississippi have developed or held to different preferences
in matters such as tempo, for the Mississippi singers are set off
from all other Sacred Harp folk by a striking distinction. Except
for the singers who live close to the Alabama line and sing in all
respects much like their Alabama neighbors, the Mississippi Sacred
Harpers look down at the pages of their book and translate the
four note shapes into seven syllables as they sing!

The singing folk in Mississippi have evidently favored the music
in the Sacred Harp to that of William Walker's Christian Harmony, but Walker's seven-shape book was, at least several decades
ago, more popular for the teaching of singing schools. Preferring
the substance of one book and the system of the other, the Mississippi singers have been faced with a dilemma. The compromise,
gradually evolved, is to use the Sacred Harp book and its four
shapes with the Christian Harmony syllable names. This calls for
quick mental substitution, converting the fa sol la noteheads of the

first three steps of the scale to *do re mi* and the seventh-tone note-head *mi* to *si* (the *fa*, *sol*, and *la* for steps four, five, and six of the scale are of course common to both systems).

To practitioners of the four-syllable solmization, and perhaps to anyone else, this is a surprising accomplishment. But for the Mississippi singers, it is the only way they can render the songs by syllable. They have come to know the steps of the scale in terms of seven corresponding syllables, and they cannot abandon this system even though the note-heads of the book they sing from are, for them, insufficiently or incorrectly shaped. One singer, displaced from Mississippi to Georgia, explains that he can sight read from the *Sacred Harp* without much difficulty by translating in his mind the first *fa sol la* shapes into his concept of the tones *do re mi*. What he cannot do when he sings with the four-shape singers in Georgia is to think *do* and sing *fa*.

Thus the Sacred Harp's reliable help-to-sing, the *fa sol la mi* notation, has become a stumbling block to the Mississippi song-sters—especially if they go out of state to sing. And yet they would as soon relinquish all seven of their syllables as give up their song book. That this paradox exists at all—and that it is resolved so nonchalantly by the Mississippi singers—makes this surely one of the unlikeliest stories of the shape-note phenomena in America.

With seven shapes or four, the singing in any of the Sacred Harp areas is so lively and self-sufficient that no one misses piano, guitar, or organ—necessary fixtures for most singing groups. Some of the Sacred Harp old-timers recall that Whitt Denson, son of fasola patriarch S. M. Denson and a "new-book" writer as well as a Sacred Harp composer, would occasionally play the piano at singings. But only rarely have the singers in any area tolerated in-strumental accompaniment to their tunes. Along with the piano, the Sacred Harp singers have long forsworn the tuning fork, a staple for even a shape-note pioneer like "Singin' Billy" Walker. Probably in a few areas pitch pipes were once used in Sacred Harp singings, but they are never seen today. For these music funda-mentalists, taking the key from a pitching instrument probably smacks of mechanical control, of the "metallic" sound spoken of above, which the Sacred Harpers in all instances avoid. But there may be a more practical reason.

If rigorously applied to the key signatures as marked, a pitching device would often lift these tunes beyond the range of the average singer's voice. The large majority of the Sacred Harp tunes, as fixed on the page, call upon the tenor or treble parts to sing as high as F on the top line of the staff. In fact, most of the songs go as high as G and A—for either treble or tenor, and often for both. B or B flat above the staff is used in a few instances, and even the alto in several songs stretches up to an F or G. How high the keys in the Sacred Harp run may be illustrated by the old standard "Amazing Grace" ("New Britain"), which is transcribed in the key of G in the Southern Baptist hymnal but in the *Sacred Harp* is written in C, three steps higher! The Sacred Harp folk, it is true, savor the high tones by the tenor and treble, the "reach" for the notes by the voices.[20] Accordingly, "Amazing Grace" as written in their book is closer to the way they like to sing it than are the versions found in the average church hymnal. And in the case of many songs employing the top F and G of the staff, the singers as often as not "sing at" the tones as written. In practice, however, most of the songs with consistently high notes are sung in a key lower by a step or a half, and sometimes one and a half or two steps, to make the topmost notes accessible.

Raymond Hamrick quotes the late Marcus Cagle, one of the best of the twentieth-century shape-note composers, as saying that the Sacred Harp composers keyed the songs as they did to keep as many notes as they could within the range of the staves as they were writing and thus avoid leger lines—to bring, in other words, the highest and the lowest notes as close as possible within the top and bottom lines. And John G. McCurry in his 1855 *Social Harp* had prescribed that "before you commence writing your tenor, you must find the highest and lowest note, and if there is more than one octave in the tune, you must bring the tune as near within the stave as you can." Deciding on a particular key was therefore often a matter of convenience for transcribing and reading the music. In later editions of the *Sacred Harp,* dozens of songs have been rewritten in a lower key to accommodate the "pitcher" and the singers. But many other songs must still be reckoned with by the keyer of the music.

Nor is the problem of pitching the songs as simple as lowering the key a step every time, even if the keyer knew how to sound that key exactly to start with. In "Amazing Grace" the alto and bass parts can comfortably be lowered several steps, but in many other songs the bass runs almost as low proportionately as the treble runs high. In pitching such songs, the keyer must reach a desirable balance between these extremes, as affected by the capabilities of the class and the condition of their voices. The seasoned pitcher, for example, will set the music slightly lower in the opening session of the singing than he will later in the day when the voices have become more flexible. And toward the end of the singing the songs may need to be dropped down a bit if the voices have hoarsened. (In most cases, though, the singers forego this convenience.)

The pitching of the music, then, is variable—from area to area by different pitchers, or by the same pitcher at different points in the day. Certainly it is a much more complicated process than striking the tuning fork, but for those who acquire the art it becomes, with time, natural and instinctive. The keyers do not, as a rule, have "perfect pitch." What they do possess is a highly developed sense of relative pitch. The pitching methods vary with individuals, but in general they know, without much reckoning, what the key of a song is supposed to sound like—not as written, but as performed. Ultimately they rely on familiarity with the tune—and the adjustments that must be made if its range of tones is remarkable—rather than on the indicated key signature. One prominent keyer summed up the process by saying, "it's kind of like learning to fix an automobile—you've just got to have a knack for it."

Some keyers, for whatever key they are working toward, begin with a reference tone: a basic, low tone they can always "hear," sometimes the lowest note they can comfortably sing. Whether correctly or not, they have come to associate this sound with a particular note, and they can build a key on this foundation, work' ing their way up the scale. Other keyers use familiar songs as points of reference; keying a song in A minor, they think of "The Child of Grace" or "Calvary" or some other well-known song in that key whose sound they can somehow recall. And they may make mental adjustments, keying a song in D minor from their recollection of a song written in D major, like "Sharon," whose key note they can hear and which they can use to build the minor chord on. The opening tone for almost all the songs is either the first, the third, or the fifth tone of the key, any of which the keyer can summon with little difficulty. But a less experienced pitcher will occasionally be thrown off by the few songs which begin the melody with the seventh tone, creating a major triad for a song written in a minor key ("Never Turn Back" and "Can I Leave You" are examples), or one like "Saints Bound for Heaven" which, although written in B flat major, opens on a minor chord.

If the pitcher recognizes his key note as being faulty immediate' ly after sounding it, he can usually try again and adjust the pitch as desired. But once the song is begun, he may often find he is stuck with the key as it is, despite attempts to change it. That is, after a song has been sung through with the notes, the keyer—or the leader—may sometimes suggest that the pitch be revised. At this point the keyer will often sound his original key note, move a step up or down, sound the new triad, and then have to smile, along with the others, at the realization that the entire class has, with the beginning of the song, reverted to the original key.

At the black singings in South Alabama, the keyer of the music for each session is appointed ahead of time and given a special seat as well as financial reimbursement. Such accommodations are made in recognition of the degree to which the skill and flexibility of the pitcher make possible the success of the singing. At a mo' ment's notice the pitcher must locate the key for each song and sound the opening tones for the parts. He must be sure of the key and be able to impart this sureness to the others. But he must also have enough of a critical sense to know if adjustments should be made. In the recipe for a successful keyer, as Raymond Hamrick, keyer of the south Georgia Sacred Harpers, has said, "equal parts of humility and confidence must be blended."

Finally, some mention should be made of the musical worth of the typical site of Sacred Harp singings—the rustic church-house. This is a perfect setting not only because it is "down home" and the singers are comfortable in it but also because the acoustics are so pleasing. In an article on "The Performance of William Billings' Music," Richard Crawford and David P. McKay have noted that "Colonial churches, with their high ceilings and bare wooden walls, offered a resonance that magnified the sound of Billings' music in a way impossible to duplicate in most modern buildings. A fuging tune sung in its original surroundings must indeed have fit the composer's description of the genre as an 'ocean of harmony' and 'musical warfare.' "[21] This is a truth not lost on the Sacred Harp participants, who regularly perform the songs of Billings and his contemporaries in surroundings much akin to those of Billings's day. These singers know, in terms of sound effect, the relative worth of building interiors. When they discuss acoustics, they refer admiringly to the hard floor and heart-pine walls and ceilings of favorite sites and speak regretfully, if not disparagingly, of the carpeted floors and spiritless sound of other churches or buildings where a few sessions are held. It is fortunate, of course, that these acoustically splendid houses—old country churches all— are also the most accessible for the Sacred Harp gatherings. Given a choice, however, the singers would not exchange any dozen of the one-room structures they sing in for the finest halls in the land.

3

The Background and
Early History

The Sacred Harp was not born until the mid 1800s when B. F. White published his book of melodies and the rural southerners drew their ritualistic singing forms around it. Still, the Sacred Harp phenomenon is the product of a movement and a style whose beginnings go back much further: in particular to colonial America, where foreign influence merged with native soil to create our first American music. From one point of view, the musical arts in these early times were not impressive. Music, as much as any other aspect of the cultural life in this period, was closely connected with the church. And in some respects, the religious music of the Colonies experienced a "decline" similar to the one cited by spokesmen in England about the same time. Additionally, America, like any infant nation, exhibited a need in all phases of its life for a successful kind of order, for form and system. And form must either evolve with time or genius or it must be borrowed.

The people who settled this continent were, for the most part, dissenters of one sort or another. Hostile as they were to centralized authority—governmental, religious, whatever—they were wary of adopting, or falling into, any system associated with the past. But without something by which to judge and regulate itself, the nation could only dawdle in semichaos, a condition evident in its music no less than in its government. And such a condition could not of course remain in a country which would adopt "Progress" as its motto. As the wheels of cultural advancement were gradually set into motion, men arose to decry the "stagnant" musical situation and to propose other systems. And ultimately what they did not invent, they borrowed.

Psalm-singing had been the almost universal form of church song among those groups which had any at all. And critics of the time would have us believe that this was religious music at its lowest ebb. According to their list of indictments, instrumental ac-companiment was rare, and vocal discipline was almost nonexis-tent. Tune books were scarce. There was no harmony and little imposition of timing. For such critics, the music was uninteresting and appallingly slow. Against this background in the first third of the eighteenth century, the Reverend Thomas Symmes and other clergymen began to speak out for singing "by note" and for the institution of singing schools and singing teachers, which had flourished in the Old World. In 1720 in a document entitled *The Reasonableness of Regular Singing, or Singing by Note,* Symmes presented his elaborate diagnosis. "The Declining from, and get-ting beside the Rule," he concluded, "was *gradual* and *insensible. Singing-Schools* and *Singing-Books* being laid aside, there was no Way to learn; but only by hearing of *Tunes* Sung, or by taking the *Run of the Tune.*" But, he continued, "we are well inform'd, that in other countries, where *Singing-Schools* are kept up, Singing is continued in the Purity of it: Where they are not, it is degen-erated, as it is among us."

The demand for singing "by note" instead of "by rote" began to produce results. About the time of the publication of Symmes's treatise the first two tune books to be published in America (both in Boston) emerged, and both were significant innovations. John Tufts in a series of editions of his collection of songs, most of which took the name of *An Introduction to the Singing of Psalm Tunes,* initiated singing by note with the European scale *fa sol la fa sol la mi,* but with his own symbols (the first letter of each syllable) placed on the staff rather than the European regular notes. Thom-as Walter's 1721 *The Grounds and Rules of Musick Explained,* which introduced the European form of notes (diamond-shaped and square note-heads), soon overtook the other in popularity and was widely used for decades.

The *fa-sol-la* solmization had long been at home in the British Isles. Charles L. Etherington states that "since the seventeenth century, and perhaps even earlier, a *sol-fa* system had been in vogue among amateur musicians in England and had received some recognition from professionals. . . . Its use had been advocated by Campion and Playford in the early seventeenth century, and it was the method used in many instruction books two hundred years later."[1] Actually this *sol-fa*, as George Pullen Jackson says, was a truncated version of a much older form. By the time of Queen Elizabeth, Jackson relates, "the primeval *ut re mi fa sol la si* sequence and other manners of note singing had simmered down, among the masses in England, to the three syllables, *fa, sol,* and *la,* with a *mi* thrown in to serve in a comparatively rare melodic emergency. To fill out the seven notes of the octave these early Britishers sang, ascending, *fa sol la,* repeated them for the next three notes, and then added *mi* as their 'leading' tone or pointer to the coming *fa* which completed the octave."[2] Thus it is not surprising that the system so long and so widely approved in the old country would eventually be absorbed into New England.

To a nation musically ignorant the *sol-fa* note system of the new tune books offered a tremendous boost. Formerly, melodies would have been "lined out" by the preacher or deacon for the congregation to approximate; now songs with harmony could be presented visually and systematically. Furthermore, the new tune book, with the possibilities of musical proficiency it offered, was available to any citizen. As teacher and pupil both rose to the prospects of this musical discipline, singing began to be less a function of the church alone. With the emergence of the singing school, American music took on an increasingly secular quality.

The singing school materialized about the time that the first tune books appeared, but it experienced the peak of its popularity in New England during the last quarter of the eighteenth century.

The singing-school teacher, whose sole credentials were likely to be enthusiasm and a little self-instruction, usually moved from town to town, at each locality starting a subscription for his school, which he might announce in a local newspaper, as in this extract quoted by Irving Lowens: "Mr. Munson respectfully acquaints the *Gentlemen* and *Ladies* of the town of Salem that he opens a Singing-School *This Day,* at the Assembly-Room, where Parents and other Subscribers are desired to send their Children at 5 o'clock P.M., and young *Gentlemen & Ladies* to attend at seven in the Evening. N.B. Subscriptions are taken in at Mr. Samuel Field's in School-Street, and at the Printing-Office. Salem, September 14, 1773."[3]

The school normally lasted about two weeks, in which time the young were taught the basic rudiments of reading and performing music. Songs were rehearsed with the notes first, part by part, until they were mastered. Then the words were attempted. For these singing novices, every aspect of the musical system had to be externalized, and this policy extended from the rendering of the tune with solmization to the keeping of time, in up and down beats, with the hand. At the end of the school, the whole class gave a concert. The music was performed in three- or four-part harmony: tenor (melody), bass, treble, and sometimes counter (comparable to the modern alto). Men alone sang the bass and usually the tenor. The counter could be sung by either male or female voices. Doubling of voices in both the tenor and treble parts was common. And many singing-school students of the time, anticipating the sentiments of Sacred Harp singers today, probably agreed with William Billings in finding "such a conjunction of masculine and feminine voices . . . beyond expression, sweet and ravishing."

As Lowens has remarked, the "enormous popularity" of the singing school during the eighteenth century was "obviously due to more than a great love for music or for learning. Here was a rare chance for approved social intercourse between boys and girls. No doubt the youngsters welcomed the break in routine provided by the chance to learn to read music, but they also used the singing-school as a place where they could make new friends, exchange notes, flirt, walk home together after lessons, and, in general, enjoy themselves." For illustration, Lowens cites a letter written by a Yale undergraduate in 1782: "At present I have no Inclination for anything, for I am almost sick of the World & were it not for the Hopes of going to singing-meeting tonight & indulging myself a little in some of the carnal Delights of the Flesh, such as kissing, squeezing &c. &c. I should willingly leave it now, before 10 o'clock & exchange it for a better."

If the popularity of the singing schools derived in part from such secular "Delights," it also owed much to the special type of song which was the forte of singing-school participants and of the singing community at large—the "fuging tune." European masters of musical form had illustrated before the time of the "fuge" in America that fugal parts could be delicately and intricately inter-spersed to please the subtlest ear; yet this was neither the claim nor the purpose of the popular tunes of the singing-school days. Beyond the novelty of observing the theme assumed in turn by each of the parts, the fuging tune was—and is in its adaptation in the Sacred Harp today—music for the singer rather than the listener.

The fuging tune was brought to prominence largely through the efforts of William Billings (1746–1800), a composer and singing-school teacher from Boston and the chief figure in early American music. Billings was by trade a tanner, but his love of music super-seded all other interests. Mainly self-taught, Billings dismissed all established musical principles with a cavalier attitude typified by his statement "Nature is the best Dictator." While Billings him-self exalted Nature and originality above all, his style exerted a considerable influence on other composers of the time. At the height of his career, the compositions of this flamboyant singing master were widely popular.

Musicologists have disdained Billings's "gaucheries" and the lack of humility with which he approached his work, but they have generally conceded a strong if undisciplined vein of genius. Along

with a flair for dramatic and rhythmic effects and a gift for melodic line, Billings's outstanding characteristic was the infectious enthusiasm he brought to all his endeavors. His celebration of the
fuging song from the preface to his *Continental Harmony* is a
good illustration:

There is more variety in one piece of fuging music, than in twenty pieces of
plain song, for while the tones do most sweetly coincide and agree, the
words are seemingly engaged in a musical warfare; and . . . each part seems
determined by dint of harmony and strength of accent, to drown his com-
petitor in an ocean of harmony, and while each part is thus mutually striv-
ing for mastery, and sweetly contending for victory, the audience are most
luxuriously entertained, and exceedingly delighted; in the mean time, their
minds are surprizingly agitated, and extremely fluctuated; sometimes de-
claring in favour of one part, and sometimes another.—Now the solemn bass
demands their attention, now the manly tenor, now the lofty counter, now
the volatile treble, now here, now there, now here again.—O inchanting!
O ecstatic!

In a few years, such enthusiasm for the music of the upstart
Yankee composers and teachers—effectively elicited by Billings,
Justin Morgan, and Daniel Read—began to wane. Just as the long
development of vocal polyphony had gradually withered in England, the young America, ever sensitive to the critical tenets of the
Old World, began to put away the vigorous music it had so enjoyed. Traveling singing masters gave way to the "better music"
advocates, Lowell Mason and Thomas Hastings, who made of
church music in the mid-nineteenth century an enterprise in the
Great American Tradition. Advocates of a superior music insisted
on imported compositions and improved teaching methods. Organs began to be common in churches, thereby reducing the need
for the strong harmony and the dearly bought musical discipline
of the folk. By the time of Billings's death in 1800 the fuging tunes
were already losing ground in New England, especially in the
cities, where the singing classes and societies had never performed
the important community function they had provided for the scattered farm folk in the countryside. And overall, there is a striking

symbol in the fact that Billings—who in a sense represented the culmination of an era of music—was to die in poverty, his family unable to provide a tombstone for his grave.

In the East, it is true, the singing schools did not disappear altogether for decades, but more and more they were tucked away in smaller towns or rural areas. Little remained for the self-made singing master but to move on to less sophisticated areas: to the West, where the same progressive forces would soon overtake him, and to the rural South, where his teaching and his music would longer be welcome. In the cities many applauded this trend as a deliverance, for critical standards in the nation had risen sharply. Doubtless the singing-school movement in its diffusion had spawned a generation of teachers less capable than Billings and his kind; but with the apparent upgrading of "musical science" in the country, even legitimate exponents of the singing-school technique might have suffered the disdain of the Lowell Mason school.

Jackson has quoted, from the 1848 *Musician and Intelligencer* of Cincinnati, a Miss Augusta Brown, who attributed "the low estate of scientific music among us" to "the presence of common Yankee singing schools, so called." "We of course can have no allusion to the educated professors of vocal music, from New England," this critic wrote, "but to the genuine Yankee singing masters, who profess to make an accomplished amateur in one month, and a regular professor of music (not in seven years, but) in one quarter, and at the expense, to the initiated person, usually one dollar. Hundreds of country idlers, too lazy or too stupid for farmers or mechanics, 'go to singing school for a spell,' get diplomas from others scarcely better qualified than themselves, and then with their brethren, the far famed 'Yankee Peddlars,' itinerate to all parts of the land, to corrupt the taste and pervert the judgment of the unfortunate people who, for want of better, have to put up with them."[4]

Yet there were others who could regret the passing of an era in which music too had been democratic. While the singing-school teachers were still common in Cincinnati in 1848, Robert Stevenson has reported this lament of the editor of the *Boston Courier* in the same year in an area where the Yankee singing masters were already a lost breed: " 'The good old days of New England music have passed away, and the singing-masters who compose and teach it, are known only in history as an extinct race.' The good old tunes, Billings's *Majesty*, Read's *Sherburne*, Edson's *Lenox*, could once 'fill a meeting house quicker than the most eloquent preacher in the country,' but all their glory is vanished like Ichabod while instead pompous 'professors' now pummel the ears of their pupils with precepts that profane the sanctuary." [5]

It now appears that this unhappy editor was not alone in his sentiments. Judith T. Steinberg has reconstructed the story of the "Old Folks" concerts in New England and in the process has shown that there lingered in that area for half a century a "wide affection and respect among ordinary people" for the music of the singing schools. [6] The most popular of the singing groups and touring companies which entertained audiences with "ancient psalmody" was a group that performed from around 1856 until 1868 under the directorship of Robert Kemp, a shoe merchant from Wellfleet, Massachusetts. Kemp claimed to have given over six thousand concerts to a total audience of over five million. The "Old Folks," dressed in period costumes and aided by an oldfashioned pitch pipe, sang "hymn tunes" and "anthems and choruses," including the best known of the fuging tunes of Read, Billings, Swan, and Holden, as well as Billings's "Easter Anthem" and Harwood's "Dying Christian." As Steinburg has said, the widespread success of these Old Folks concerts offers impressive evidence that "the music of the Yankee tunesmiths did not simply die out in New England. Although superseded by other styles of church music, its roots were strong enough to withstand such relative neglect. Its revival was a grass-roots movement that reclaimed a harmonic style, not just certain particularly popular tunes." [7]

Predictably, Kemp and his singers got bad reviews from the

second-generation Mason boys, Lowell Mason, Jr., and Daniel Gregory Mason, who published the *New York Musical Review and Gazette,* and from others who shared their distaste for tunes so "coarse, rude, and uncultivated."[8] Even well into the twentieth century music critics could find little good to say about the era of the singing schools. Increasingly, however, this rhythmic music with its modal flavor has come to seem fresh and energetic, especially in contrast with the stuffy or banal religious music which was to take its place. Irving Lowens, in his comprehensive *Music and Musicians in Early America,* states the opinion that while "some indubitably poor tunes were current . . . an astonishingly large number seem to have been of greater intrinsic merit and expressiveness than most of those then being imported from Europe. If the tunes in the American idiom possessed no other virtue, they were certainly alive musically, unsophisticated and untrammeled by the 'laws of musical science' which reduced much of orthodox church song to a dead level of mediocrity. And they still remain very much alive today."[9]

Perhaps the music of the singing-school days that Lowens speaks of here is most alive today in the singing sessions of the Sacred Harp, where it is not so much a relic of the past as, even now, a music of the present. But before settling in the South, the singing-school movement introduced an innovation which has also remained a vital part of the Sacred Harp method and style: the "buckwheat" note system, the printing of music in shaped note-heads. By means of shape or "character" notation, the singing-school movement, already withdrawing to more rural areas and eventually to the South, showed a capacity for adaptability in the best sense of survival technique.

What the purveyors of the singing school needed, especially in less sophisticated areas, was a simpler process for learning to sing. They hit upon a method, anticipated by Tufts's syllable letters almost a century before, of giving each note-head one of four shapes so that its appropriate syllable could be realized immediately. The advantage of such a system, as Dorothy D. Horn has said, is that it "dispenses with the whole wearisome business of learning key signatures, thus removing one hurdle in the teaching of sight-singing. Obviously, if one knows the shape for the keynote, a signature is unnecessary." [10]

There has been some question about who authored the shape-note idea: Andrew Law, a New England singing-school master, or William Little and William Smith, sometime collaborators who together brought out *The Easy Instructor* in 1801. Apparently Little and Smith's system of notes antedates Law's first published system by as much as two years. While other notations arose to rival Little and Smith's and Law's, which varied only in a different assignment of the same shapes to the *fa sol la mi* syllables (the *fa* and *la* symbols reversed), the system that the two tune-book compilers derived became the accepted form of "patent notes" in the West and the South.

The geographical spread of new song books using the four-shape notation points the progress of the singing-school movement southward. From Pennsylvania into Virginia, Kentucky, and the Carolinas, following the movement of the immigrants into this country, came notable singing masters, like Andrew Law and Amzi and Lucious Chapin; and the work of these men gave impetus to the compiling of new tune books. The Shenandoah Valley of Virginia in particular was an area of much song publishing and musical activity. The Chapin brothers, authors of some of the most widely published melodies from this period including "Ninety-Third," "Twenty-Fourth" ("Primrose"), and "Vernon," taught singing schools there. From that area also came one of the most influential of all the southern song collections, Ananias Davisson's *Kentucky Harmony* (1815), as well as the 1820 *Supplement to the Kentucky Harmony*. Joseph Funk's *Choral Music* (1816), an oblong book of songs in German, was compiled and published in the vicinity of Harrisonburg, Virginia, as were some editions of Funk's later English volume, *Genuine Church Music* (1832). Virginian James P. Carrell brought out *Songs of Zion* (1820) and the *Virginia Harmony* (1831) there.

The push westward into the Missouri Territory gave Allen D. Carden opportunity to teach singing schools in that section from his popular *Missouri Harmony* (1820). And from Kentucky and Tennessee came a half dozen other tune books, including William Caldwell's *Union Harmony* (Maryville, Tennessee, 1837) and William Moore's *Columbian Harmony* (Wilson County, Tennessee, 1825). William Walker of Spartanburg, South Carolina, published the *Southern Harmony* in 1835, and from Georgia came the *Sacred Harp* and then William Hauser's *Hesperian Harp* (1848) and John G. McCurry's *Social Harp* (1855).

While many of the four-shape books lapsed after one appearance, others were revised and enlarged for subsequent publication. But obsolescence was inherent in the almost universal success of the four-shape notation. The logic of a system which used four names for seven notes was self-defeating against the threat of the inevitable system which would give a separate name to each note. The *do re mi* notation, imported from the continent to the East, won immediate favor over its country relation as a superior musical technique. With the general acceptance of the seven-shape notation, no new tune books in the four shapes appeared after 1855. Yet the *Sacred Harp,* one of the last and the most popular of these, lived on through numerous republications and continued to rival the most successful of the seven-shape tune books.

White and King and the Song Book

The October 23, 1844, edition of the *Columbus Enquirer* (Georgia) carried the following notice: "Just published, the Sacred Harp, containing a complete collection of Sacred Music, principally original and adapted to the refined taste of connoisseurs of the art, as well as to the instruction of learners. This work is edited by B. F. White & E. J. King: Two gentlemen extensively known as music teachers." The cover of this most durable of four-shape hymnals, published in Philadelphia and now available for the populace to "call and examine" at several localities around Columbus, identified itself as "A Collection of Psalm and Hymn Tunes, Odes, and Anthems; Selected from the Most Eminent Authors. Together with Nearly One Hundred Pieces Never Before Published. Suited to Most Metres, and Well Adapted to Churches of Every Denomination, Singing Schools, and Private Societies. With Plain Rules for Learners."

The book bore the name of E. J. King as coauthor with B. F. White, but the role of King, of whom almost nothing has been known until recently, has always been minimized. The 1866 edition of the *Christian Harmony,* crediting a song to King, states that he was "junior author of the 'Sacred Harp' " and that he died a few weeks after its 1844 publication. Although the names of both men had appeared after the short *nota bene* on the preface page, White's name alone is signed to the preface—a statement by "the Compiler," who, "having passed the meridian of his life, and entirely withdrawn from the business of teaching, is disposed to leave this work as a specimen of his taste." Because of his publishing experience, his work in song compilation, his personal direction of three revisions of the book, and his leadership in the singing movement, B. F. White is usually given most of the credit for the authorship of the work.

Records now show that E. J. King was Elisha J. King, the son of John and Elizabeth DuBose King and the grandson of Joel King, who had served in the Revolutionary army.[11] One of thirteen children, Elisha J. King was born about 1821 to an apparently well-to-do family of cotton planters in Wilkinson County, Georgia. Around 1828 the family moved to Talbot County near Talbotton, which King was later to honor by the tune entitled "Talbotton." The 1911 James edition of the *Sacred Harp* comments that King was reputed to be "an educated man" and quotes William Walker in the *Christian Harmony* as saying that King's death was "much lamented by his Christian brethren and musical friends." King's obituary in the *Christian Index* states that he had been a member of the Baptist Church for about six years and that he was "a pious and promising young man . . . [who] died in the full triumphs of faith. Several days previous to his death his conversation was upon religious subjects entirely."[12]

Joe S. James in his history of the Sacred Harp mentions that King, like other contributors to the *Sacred Harp,* had received musical instruction from Major White. He had already achieved some prominence of his own as a singing-school teacher, however, and there is no reason to qualify James's assessment of him as starting out with "bright prospects as a musician." Like White, King often rearranged or harmonized existing melodies and thereby prolonged the life of such tunes. The share of songs attributed to him in the first edition of the *Sacred Harp* is larger than that of any other composer, even that of White himself, and includes such indispensable entries as "The Child of Grace," "Bound for Canaan," and "Gospel Trumpet."

The Columbus paper has recorded that the *Sacred Harp* was, by October, 1844, "just published." For the King family, however, the autumn of that year was a bleak season. Elisha, then only twenty-three, died on August 31. Within the next fifteen days his father and a niece, the daughter of Henry and Mary King Snellings, were also dead. Robert Snellings, the husband of King's sister Elizabeth Louisa, died at about the same time. (Whether the family was taken by a contagious illness cannot today be determined.) When the estates of the three men were settled the following February, King's share in the *Sacred Harp,* one-half the copyright and seven hundred copies of the book, was sold (all but one hundred books) to Henry Snellings.

Even with the untimely death of E. J. King, the King family was still to figure prominently in the story of the Sacred Harp in its early years. Joel King (1809–1871), the eldest of the King children, was mentioned by James as also being a music teacher. In the appendix to the second edition of the *Sacred Harp* (1850), his name is listed first after B. F. White's as members of the committee appointed by the Southern Musical Convention to revise and enlarge the *Sacred Harp*. Also included in the eight-name list is E. L. King, whom James at the distance of nearly sixty years identified as "a close relative of E. J. King" and, at the time of the second edition, "a young man . . . a splendid director of music." He added that this E. L. King had "helped to write" the three songs (actually four) credited to him in the 1850 edition. Since John King apparently had no brothers, and thus no King nephews, there is little reason to suppose that the E. L. King of the second edition of the Sacred Harp was other than Elias L. King (1828– 1876), Joel and Elisha King's younger brother.

The details of E. J. King's life, for so long completely obscured, have still scarcely emerged. Nevertheless, the brief span of this man's presence left its impression on the *Sacred Harp* and on the field of American folk hymnody in general. His arrangements and compositions were reprinted in such tune books of the day as Walker's *Southern Harmony* (in its later editions) and *Christian Harmony,* William Hauser's *Hesperian Harp,* and John McCur-ry's *Social Harp*. And in bringing to the pages of the *Sacred Harp* songs such as "The Bower of Prayer," "Frozen Heart," "Dull Care," "Reverential Anthem," and "The Dying Christian," Eli-sha J. King gave the book much of its distinctive flavor, both musi-cal and textual.

It was not the promising young pupil, then, but the experienced teacher, now past "the meridian of his life," who would assume the direction of the *Sacred Harp* for the next thirty-five years. Like William Billings, Benjamin Franklin White had been a singing-school teacher and a prominent figure in his area. After moving to Harris County, Georgia, from South Carolina around 1840, he served as mayor of Hamilton, as clerk of the inferior court of the county, and as a major of the militia before the Civil War.[13] A versatile man, he was editor of a newspaper, the *Organ,* an outlet that gave him the opportunity to publish the songs he avidly composed and collected. He was also responsible for an-other institution designed to foster interest in the singing of sacred songs. This was the Southern Musical Convention, founded and

A 1919 Sacred Harp singing school at Highland School in Clay County, Alabama. Talmer McCain, the teacher, is fourth from the left in the front row. (Photo courtesy of Lessie Roberts.)

Terry Wootten leads a song at the 1977 Georgia State Convention at Nidrah Plantation near Leslie, Georgia.

Mrs. Ruth Denson Edwards directs at a singing in her honor held at Zion's Rest Primitive Baptist Church, Jasper, Alabama.

A special "lesson" is often reserved for members of the Sacred Harp's youngest generation of singers—like these young cousins from Ider, Alabama.

organized largely through his efforts and presided over by him for approximately two decades.

The bulk of information on the life of B. F. White was left by James in his history and by Jackson, who interviewed a few of White's remaining children and grandchildren. White was born the youngest of fourteen children to a sturdy South Carolina family in the first year of the nineteenth century. Both his father and his oldest brother, Robert Jr., who raised the young B. F. White from infancy, lived to be over a hundred years old. White himself died, as a result of injuries from a fall, at the then uncommon age of seventy-nine. As well as inheriting a measure of his family's longevity, this youngest son, as James says, "fell into line" after his father, a man "inclined to music." White's daughter, Mrs. Mattie America Clarke, told Jackson that her father had been a fifer at the age of twelve in the War of 1812.

But other than the traits his lineage had bequeathed him, Benjamin Franklin White, like the statesman and philosopher he was named for, was given few advantages outright. His achievements —social, political, and musical—grew out of his own industriousness. And in all, he made of his life, as he attempted to make of the songs he wrote, a pleasing strain, a harmonious whole. He imparted a love of music to his children, nine of whom (from the fourteen born to him) lived to adulthood and most of whom became singers, instrumentalists, or music teachers. White's neighbors and many acquaintances held him to be deeply religious, hard-working, kind, and generous to a fault. In sum, he was an ideal of his time and place: the complete, self-made man—citizen, soldier, teacher, father, and friend.

White had little formal education to prepare him for the production of a song book regarded, in his region, almost on a level with the Bible. His stint in "literary school," James reports, constituted a period of no more than three months. Further, "He took up the science of music without a preceptor." But White must not have looked upon this as a handicap. Like Billings, he believed that the best instructor was nature itself. James relates that "he would sit for hours at a time and look at the different freaks of nature, its system of regularity and harmony with which it did all its work, and would watch and listen to birds as they sang from the branches of the trees, and learned as much or more from these observations than he did from other men's works."

Whatever the source of his inspiration, White composed tunes, sometimes from fragments of melodies he had heard, that captured the affection of the singing public. He may have stood behind William Walker and L. P. Breedlove in the ability to write a fluid melodic line, but the best of his tunes take their place among the foremost songs of this era: songs such as "The Lone Pilgrim," one of the favorite religious ballads of the region; "Loving Jesus" (written with "Searcy"), an infectious, rhythmic interweaving of voices; and "The Morning Trumpet," White's version of a haunting camp-meeting song that Gilbert Chase has called "one of the glories of America's music"[14] (see Appendix B). White's particular genius was for transcribing folk motifs into the three-part idiom of the shape-note hymnal. But perhaps equally as important, he passed on his musical theory and style to a generation of young singers who then contributed songs of their own to the book, especially in its later publications.

From the first, the *Sacred Harp* was conceived and nourished in a community situation. According to James, between B. F. White's home and the street, "there was a beautiful grove of oak, hickory and other large trees, and in the yard was an old-fashioned well of pure water." Great crowds of people would gather there and "in this grove, veranda and house sing the songs long before they were published in book form." James relates that "all the tunes" composed by White and others were introduced in the *Organ* before they were published in the later song volume. A privately printed history of Harris County, Georgia, has revealed, however, that the newspaper did not begin publication until 1852, eight years after the *Sacred Harp* was first distributed.[15] Thus the tunes appearing in the first and second editions of the book could not have been first published in the *Organ*. The *Sacred Harp* does confirm, though, that some of the tunes dating from the third and fourth editions were first printed there. Further, James relays the report that the songs published in the four edi- tions of the *Sacred Harp* were chosen from a field of over three thousand compositions, and that prodigious figure, if anything close to the real one, certainly represents a community effort. At any rate, in James's words, White and "his friends would take the newspaper as the music was published and sing the songs as print- ed, and thus discover the defects and make all necessary changes before they were selected for the book." In this way, the *Organ* and the singings from the newspaper printings nurtured public interest and served as a sounding board for the melodies that would eventually emerge as additions to the later publications of the *Sacred Harp*.

In large part, the *Sacred Harp* drew material from earlier tune books which in turn had depended on other song volumes. White, for example, took a considerable number of songs from the popu- lar 1835 *Southern Harmony* by William Walker, including songs Walker himself had assimilated from other sources. Indeed, the *Sacred Harp* is a composite of the American and English sacred melodies which had been popular among the shape-note hymnals over a fifty-year period, including a representative sampling of most of the prominent American authors: William Billings, Dan- iel Read, Timothy Swan, Oliver Holden, Stephen Jenks, Jeremiah Ingalls, Ananias Davisson, James P. Carrell, and William Moore, all of whom had authored song collections of their own. Many of the best-known tunes of the old singing-school days are included in the Sacred Harp volume. In 1860 Robert Kemp published a compilation of tunes used in the Old Folks concerts of the 1850s, a select number of the standard melodies of New England a half century before. Of its forty-seven sacred entries, this collection contains over twenty songs and anthems that were appearing about this time in the various editions of the *Sacred Harp*.[16]

Still, White and King drew deeply from local soil. According

to Jackson, the four editions of the book through 1869 included
two hundred and seventeen songs by over seventy writers of the
Georgia and Alabama area.[17] The foremost contributors among
these local writers were White, King, Leonard P. Breedlove, Elder
Edmund Dumas, and the brothers John P. and the Reverend
H. S. Reese (also spelled Rees), all friends and fellow singers.
Most of the songs by these writers share a common characteristic.
They are not in the tradition of consciously artistic or, as Jackson
would say, "composed" music, but are instead obvious folk products. Unsophisticated but lively, many of the tunes are naturally
melodic and rhythmic in a way that reflects their previously oral
existence.

A story that has been passed down orally to the present-day
fasola singers from over a century ago illustrates the artless cir-
cumstances by which the Sacred Harp songs often took shape. It
concerns the tune "Weeping Pilgrim" by J. P. Reese, one of the
revisers of the 1859 and 1869 editions of the Sacred Harp and one
of the most significant contributors to the volume. The song is a
spiritual written in G major, its predominant 2/4 time broken in
the middle by a phrase of 3/4 time that accompanies the words "I
weep and I mourn and I move slowly on" (see Appendix B). This
3/4 section closes effectively on a plaintive deceptive cadence (V–
VI[6]), an unusual pattern in Sacred Harp composition. According
to the legend, Reese had gone down into a wooded pasture area,
there in the solitude to work out some notes to the tune he was
writing. As he was puzzling over a chord to resolve the middle
section of the song, the mournful lowing of a cow came to him
through the thicket. As Billings and White would have agreed,
Nature had spoken. And it was that tone, so the story goes, that
Reese sought to approximate in his song.

Other than B. F. White, the most influential figure in the ten-
ure of the shape-note system in the South was William Walker
of Spartanburg, South Carolina, White's brother-in-law. (White
and Walker married the sisters Thurza and Amy Golightly.) The
lives and works of the two writers are curiously paired. Walker

is credited with the *Southern Harmony* of 1835, the standard four-shape hymnal in the South before the *Sacred Harp*. According to James's history, which is told, admittedly, from the Sacred Harp point of view, White, then a resident of Spartanburg, was in collaboration on the hymnal with Walker, who was nine years his junior. An arrangement was made between White and Walker, James reports, "for Walker to go north and have the book published, there being no publishing houses in the South with a plant suitable to print the book." But, in James's words, "Walker took the manuscript, and he and his publishers changed the same without the knowledge or consent of Major White and brought it out under the name of Walker, giving Major White no credit whatever for its composition. Walker also entered into a combination with the publishers and in this way managed to deprive Major White of any interest in the Southern Harmony, although all the work, or most of it, was done by Major White." And "on account of this transaction and treatment," James writes, "the two men never spoke to each other again."

White's departure to Georgia after the incident furthered the breach, but the competing song collections of the two men have coexisted, if with some strife, in the same areas of the South up until the present. Shortly after the Civil War Walker realized the certain threat to the four-shape system by the seven-shape. To keep pace with the time he published his *Christian Harmony,* a hymnal with the Smith and Little four shapes and three shapes of his own invention. (The revision of this book now in use in Alabama, Georgia, and Mississippi is published in Jesse B. Aiken's seven-shape notation, a system first employed in Aiken's Philadelphia-based *Christian Minstrel* and eventually adopted by most southern seven-shape publications.) As the *Sacred Harp* is the sturdiest representative four-shape hymnal, the *Christian Harmony* long ago achieved supremacy over the other seven-shape tune books of its era.

Especially around the turn of the century, the rivalry between these kindred traditions in some parts was intense. Today many fasola adherents sing from both books. Surprisingly, they find little difficulty in using four shapes at one singing and seven at the next. While the *Sacred Harp* remains the central force in their musical lives, some of these singers have within the last decade or so taken on the *Christian Harmony* as a side interest. (The danger for the Sacred Harp, as noted in chapter 2, is that large doses of "modern harmony" might alter the ear of the singers and subtly change their preferences.[18])

The existence of such long-standing traditions as the Sacred Harp and the Christian Harmony was virtually unrecognized in historical studies of early southern life until George Pullen Jackson's discovery of them in the 1930s. Although a number of secular songs are known to have been popular among the southern forces in the Civil War, little if any mention of the Sacred Harp music has been made in such a context. Yet with the widespread popularity of the fasola tune books from Virginia to Texas, it would be inconceivable that the Sacred Harp and Southern Harmony songs did not constitute a considerable part of the musical activity of the southern soldiers, as well as of the people at large.

At least one source, a letter written by Sergeant-Major William Jefferson Mosely from Richmond, Virginia, to his mother in Macon, Georgia, in the fall of 1863, attests to the fact that the Sacred Harp was very much alive during the Civil War years: "There are some of the boys here," this young Confederate officer wrote, "that start playing cards and gambling as soon as they draw their money and in two days they haven't got a cent." "I have been in the war two years and I do not know one card from another," he assured his family, "but I do know my notes, and we have some of the best singings around the camp fire I have ever heard, since Troupe Edmonds and E. T. Pound used to teach singing school. . . . Ma, you and the girls get out the old Sacred Harp songbook, turn to the old song invocation on page 131, sing it, and think of me."[19] Undoubtedly, whether at the homestead or around the camp fires on strange hillsides, many people of the region in these troubled times, turned for sustenance to their song books, calling up rich melodies with words that spoke to them of the uncertainty of earthly happiness and the eventual triumph of God's justice.

> Will God forever cast us off,
> His wrath forever smoke
> Against the people of His love,
> His little chosen flock?
>
> No prophet speaks to calm our grief,
> But all in silence mourn;
> Nor know the hour of our relief,
> The hour of Thy return. ("Mear")

And when the war was ended, community singings began anew and singing-school teachers resumed the task of educating the children of each community in their "notes." Indeed youngsters eager to learn to sing from the book sought out their own instruc- tion. Earl Thurman, historian and for many years secretary of the Chattahoochee Convention, relates information told to him by W. B. (Bill) Matthews about how his father and uncle in their boyhood days after the close of the war gathered firewood for J. R. Turner in the Villa Rica community in Georgia. Then in his home at night, "by the brightly burning oak and hickory logs," Professor Turner, one of the stalwarts in the early history of the tradition, would teach the boys to sing out of the *Sacred Harp*. Like so many others whose training was no less informal or rustic, the Matthews brothers were reputed to be excellent singers.

By the time of B. F. White's death in 1879, the Sacred Harp was so well established that it had survived both the years without organized singing during the Civil War and the awkward after- math, when life in the South was in many cases drastically "recon- structed." The reason doubtless is that singing of this type had become a way of life in these southern regions. But Sacred Harp singing is community song, and it probably could not have sur- vived as such after these disruptive times had it not been effectively organized almost from the first. Besides singing societies and singing schools, several musical conventions, beginning with the original Southern Musical Convention of 1845, emerged before the war to propagate and perpetuate the singing of melodies from the Old Harp, and with the return of peace and order these conventions, which disbanded or held only token sessions during the war years, resumed with renewed interest the pattern that had already been set. The success of the Southern Musical Convention brought similar conventions into being in the next few decades throughout Georgia, Alabama, Mississippi, Texas, and bordering states, offering community organization in sparsely settled rural areas where, except for the church, people experienced little else in the way of organized institutions.

Earl Thurman in his history of the Chattahoochee Convention, one of the most historic of the Sacred Harp singing conventions, has re-created a picture of the lonely social life of the rural southerners and suggested the importance the burgeoning singing societies and conventions held for their memberships. "During that period," Thurman writes, these folk "lived in an atmosphere of what present-day dwellers would term almost complete isolation. In the rural areas there were no telephones, radios, or motor vehicles during the first fifty years of the Convention's life. Most of the rural post offices received mail only once a week and many of the people would have to travel several miles to receive their mail. There were no rural free delivery routes in that period." "Transportation," he continues, "was wholly by horse drawn vehicles and over roads that were, in many cases, little more than trails. Wagons were much more common than buggies and many used ox drawn vehicles or rode horseback. Many singers thought little of walking five or ten miles to a Sacred Harp singing." Thus isolated, "rural residents spent most of their days working on their farms with an occasional trip to the nearest town, visiting a few neighbors now and then and attending the community church service once each month. The monotony of this existence grew rather oppressive at times." It was into such a social vacuum that the early conventions spread the discipline and the enjoyment of community singing from Major B. F. White's tune book.

The Camp Meeting and Its Songs

The shape-note system represented the first modification of the fasola tradition in its shifting from the East to what was then the South and West. And eventually the creation of the conventions would provide the permanent community organization this type of singing had never, or rarely, enjoyed in New England. Another influence preceding that of the convention system was the camp-meeting revival. The era of the camp meeting, which began in Kentucky and Tennessee and quickly spread in all directions, dates from about 1800. The business of the revivals was the saving of lost souls, and this they set about with great fervor—with preaching, praying, shouting, and singing. In their inception the camp meetings may well have created the pattern for the "singin's" in which thousands in later years would throng to sing from the Sacred Harp book. As well as religious meetings, the revivals were great social gatherings—primarily nondenominational—and in this respect they prefigured the Sacred Harp gatherings.

The most concrete influence of the revival meetings on Sacred Harp singing came in the form of a special type of song created to the needs and the spirit of the camp meetings—the revival chorus or spiritual. In the early days of the revival movement, hymnals were not available for the large crowds that usually gathered. In fact at a typical meeting the only hymnbook on hand might have been the preacher's. And since many of the outdoor camp meetings were held at night, books would not always have been useful anyway. For this reason, and for others, the camp-meeting song had to be different from the hymns that had been used in church services. In "The Early Camp-Meeting Song Writers," an 1859 article in the *Methodist Quarterly Review*, B. St. James Fry writes that the singing at the earliest revivals often consisted of the lining out of a hymn by the preacher with the congregation joining in after every two lines. However, "it was soon felt," he adds, that the traditional church hymns "gave but imperfect expression to the ardent feelings of the worshipers. . . . Hymns, or 'spiritual songs,' as they were more frequently called, to the cultivated ear rude and bold in expression, rugged in meter, and imperfect in rhyme, often improvised in the preaching stand, were at once accepted as more suited." These spiritual songs were more "quickly committed to memory" and, more important, "they made vocal thrills of joy and groans for redemption, which else had been prisoned voiceless in the heart."[20]

Basically the revival spirituals and shouting songs, as Jackson surmises, were simplifications of the folk hymns, with which a majority of the folk were at least vaguely familiar. From an examination of the revival songs preserved in the *Sacred Harp,* the creation process of these becomes evident: expressive or well-remembered lines from the hymns were instituted for the verses, which the revivalists and those familiar with the hymns sang, and then a simple and recurrent chorus was improvised for everyone. It was the repetitive chorus that reflected the true spirit of the camp meeting, and the way the great crowds bore down on the familiar refrain doubtless stirred the conscience of many a bewildered reprobate. The choruses were evidently conceived spontaneously—"often improvised in the preaching stand"—and the single images upon which they always focused testify to the intensity and simplicity of the feeling which threw dogma aside to dwell on the prospect of heaven and the joyful camaraderie of Christians.

As the revivals grew widespread, the verse parts to the camp-meeting songs became so well known as to be interchanged with ease from song to song, and endless variation became possible, with the congregation sounding home the chorus after each additional verse. The verse of the typical song contained two lines (or four treated as two) of a general nature which Jackson characterizes thus: "It was the epigrammatical completeness and independence of each pair which led the singers to transplant them at will from song to song. Thus they became what have been called 'wandering' rhyme pairs, homeless distichs which had a way of turning up whenever conditions were right,—that is, whenever the vocal voltage was high enough and the rhythmic gait of the song under way fitted their pattern." [21]

Among the more famous of these verse pairs are the following, all from the *Sacred Harp*:

> Farewell, vain world, I'm going home;
> My Savior smiles and bids me come.

> When I can read my title clear,
> To mansions in the skies,
> I'll bid farewell to ev'ry fear,
> And wipe my weeping eyes.

> O when shall I see Jesus,
> And reign with Him above,
> And from the flowing fountain,
> Drink everlasting love?

> O who will come and go with me?
> I'm bound fair Canaan's land to see.

> On Jordan's stormy banks I stand,
> And cast a wistful eye
> To Canaan's fair and happy land,
> Where my possessions lie.

> Come, thou fount of ev'ry blessing,
> Tune my heart to sing thy grace;
> Streams of mercy, never ceasing,
> Call for songs of loudest praise.

> Jesus, my all, to heav'n is gone,
> He whom I fix my hopes upon.

With each of the verse pairs would then be added a chorus, like the one from the most famous of all the camp-meeting songs:

> I am bound for the promised land,

> I'm bound for the promised land,
> Oh, who will come and go with me,
> I am bound for the promised land.

Frequently the main line of the chorus would also be added as a tag after each of the verse lines, as in the Sacred Harp song "Traveling Pilgrim":

> Farewell, vain world, I'm going home,
> Where there's no more stormy clouds to rise.
> My Savior smiles and bids me come,
> Where there's no more stormy clouds to rise.
>
> To the land,
> To the land,
> To the land I am bound
> Where there's no more stormy clouds to rise.

Among the many such lines from the camp-meeting songs preserved in the *Sacred Harp* are these:

> On the other side of Jordan, Hallelujah
>
> I am bound to die in the army
>
> Till the warfare is over, hallelujah
>
> I am on my journey home
>
> And shall hear the trumpet sound in that
>   morning
>
> To play on the golden harp
>
> And we'll all shout together in that morning

Tune-book compilers from this period were soon interested in the popular revival songs, and by the time of the Civil War more than fifty revival song books had appeared, a few of them going through as many as twenty-five editions. Ananias Davisson's 1820 *Supplement to the Kentucky Harmony* was among the first of many southern tune books to include camp-meeting songs along with the standard repertoire of fuging tunes, anthems, and the older hymns. The most skillful of the tune-book editors were able to capture the spirited rhythm of the revival favorites and fit the songs with appropriate harmony.

By the time of the composition of the *Sacred Harp* in the 1840s, White and King could select from a field of songs generated by the camp meetings throughout the span of the movement, and they (and White's associates in subsequent editions) reproduced a good number of the revival melodies. In *Stray Leaves from the Portfolio of a Methodist Local Preacher* (1870), Lucius Bellinger, a revivalist of that era, lists memorable song refrains from the camp meetings he participated in from about 1825 to the Civil War. Checking this list off against the contents of the *Sacred Harp* reveals the importance of that volume as a repository of the revival songs. Among the several fragments of verses and refrains noted that appear in the *Sacred Harp* (slightly varied in a few cases) are "There is a happy land, far, far away," "Our bondage here will end by and bye," "Till the warfare is over," "Where now are the Hebrew children? / Away over in the promised land," and "We have but one more river to cross."[22]

Some of the revival choruses in the *Sacred Harp* were reproduced from earlier tune books, but many more of the songs of this type appearing in the book were adapted for three- and four-part harmony for the first time by White, King, J. P. Reese, and others who had likely heard some of these unwritten tunes from childhood on. The addition of these songs brought another dimension to the *Sacred Harp*. It also gave the book some of its most appealing melodies, some of its most affecting combinations of music and text.

4

The Revisions

Today modern modes of travel and communication have brought Sacred Harp singers and their singings closer together. In the past, the average singer was aware of a central tradition only through his own community and, vaguely, through area conventions, which brought representatives of neighboring communities together. Thus looking inward, the various areas which celebrated the old songs often developed different customs, as more or less faithful to the traditional way of doing things they admitted or refused progressive measures or the influences of their particular locale. Both the impetus for and the result of major divisions were the varying revisions of the original song book.

The common base of the tradition, the original volume and its subsequent revisions under White's leadership, was a source of uniformity within the Sacred Harp territories for many years. But the later individual revisions, reflecting the differing values of the revisers, established trends which distinguished them from their kindred. With the loss of communication the Sacred Harp people, like the men of Babel, divided into area groups and with time grew more distinct from each other. They still speak the same language—the basic core of songs can be found in all the books—but the accents are different.

None of the Sacred Harp singing groups still uses one of the original White editions. Instead four—and now three—principal revisions of the *Sacred Harp* have competed, since the death of B. F. White, for the affection of the folk. These are everywhere known as the White book, the James book, the Cooper book, and the Denson book. The James book, persisting in central and south Georgia until 1976, is now no longer used. The White book is restricted to the northwest corner of Georgia and the area around east Atlanta. The rest of the Sacred Harp territory is divided between the Denson and Cooper revisions. The Denson book claims the rest of Georgia, north and central Alabama, the southern tip of Tennessee, and north Mississippi. The Cooper-book area extends from west Florida to Texas, including southern Alabama and southern Mississippi. How these revisions emerged and what their implications are for the Sacred Harp tradition is the topic of this chapter.

The First Editions

While B. F. White was living, the Sacred Harp was revised and enlarged three times under the auspices of the Southern Musical Convention: in 1850, 1859, and 1869. The 1850 revision increased the breadth of the book from 263 to 366 pages; the 1859 revision grew to 429 pages and the 1869 to 477 pages. A few generalizations can be made about the changes in the Sacred Harp in these early editions as they anticipate the trends apparent in the later revisions. The 1844 edition, like all of the subsequent ones, was based in large part on the standard formula for tune books in the early nineteenth century: hymns, anthems, and fuging tunes. White and King employed a representative sampling of the songs included in almost every other tune book of the time: Billings's anthems; hymns by Chapin, Davisson, and Moore; and fuging tunes by Read, Morgan, and Shumway. But though the eighteenth-century four-part fuging tunes were in abundance in the Sacred Harp, White and King and their colleagues in the first editions— T. W. Carter, L. P. Breedlove, J. T. White, John Massengale, and others—did not, as a rule, compose in the fuging-tune style, nor did they grant the alto line recognition in their tunes. Rather, the inclination of these southern tunesmiths in the first few decades of the Sacred Harp was for the three-part folk hymn. Undoubtedly the Sacred Harp folk enjoyed as good "class music" the

fuging tunes that were published with the book in 1844. But in
the heyday of the revival spiritual the singers and writers were
probably more deeply attracted to the simpler spirituals and folk
hymns than to the songs written in the more florid fuging style.

In the 1859 book, however, Absalom Ogletree, Oliver Bradfield (founder of the Chattahoochee Convention), and H. S. Reese
each had a song written in four parts, and several of the new
songs in this edition showed experimentation in the fuging style.
There were a few fuging tunes by the Reese brothers (J. P. and
H. S.) and one by Ogletree. By 1869, there were roughly a dozen
new fuging tunes and an even larger percentage of songs in four-
part settings. In fact, the 1869 edition demonstrates the most significant change in the *Sacred Harp* under White's directorship. In
the 1850 and 1859 editions, the committee given the task of revising the book by the Southern Convention had simply added an
appendix of new music each time. But by 1869, the Sacred Harp
was a quarter of a century old and with each successive edition
getting larger and with new music continually being written, the
caretakers of the book apparently decided that it was time to
shake the book up a bit, to economize. Accordingly, they sorted
out dozens of older or what they deemed less successful songs, so
as to make room for others which they hoped would also "prove
favorite compositions." Just as significantly, the increasing emphasis on the composition of fuge tunes and other songs in four parts
revealed the gradually changing taste of "the singing public."

The four-part tunes, of course, had not taken over the book. Nor
did the writers seem to be adding or bypassing the alto line as a
matter of conviction. With the exception of White, whose position on most musical matters had long been fixed and who always
composed in three parts only, the contributors to the 1869 volume
were likely to write one song in four parts, another in three. Still,
the course for the future was already being set. A similar trend
could be observed in the increase of fuging tunes. The songs written in that style actually amounted to a small percentage of the
new compositions, yet the interest represented by even that slight

increase anticipated the popularity of the Sacred Harp fuging tune in the twentieth century.

With the 1859 edition, and much more with its 1869 successor, the fuging tune appeared to be taking on the prestige it had enjoyed in New England at the end of the eighteenth century. Similarly, the style of the Sacred Harp writers seemed to be evolving toward the four-part setting. But even though such a progression is in evidence, it can not be said that the 1869 edition is substantially different from the first one. The four original editions of the *Sacred Harp* are all of a piece. They share the steadying influence of B. F. White himself. At a time when the traditional tune book was being threatened by obsolescence, William Walker, author of the immensely popular *Southern Harmony*, reversed his position, disavowed the four-shape notation of his standard tune book, and brought out the new seven-shape *Christian Harmony*. B. F. White, on the other hand, kept close by the *Sacred Harp* and insured the integrity of the volume. Each of the four editions of the book during his lifetime bears the mark of his singular presence.

The New Sacred Harp

White's death in 1879 halted the work toward a fifth edition of the *Sacred Harp*, but a movement to modernize the old book began almost immediately. Ironically, the heralders of the new style within the tradition were some of White's own progeny. In 1884 two of White's sons, J. L. (James Landrum) and B. F., Jr. ("Frank"), brought out *The New Sacred Harp: A Collection of Hymn-Tunes, Anthems, and Popular Songs,* containing music composed in the gospel-song idiom and printed in seven shapes.

The era of gospel music began to emerge, like other features of the New South, with the close of the Civil War. From its earliest stages the gospel-hymn was propagated by a new institution which undermined the faith of the rural folk in the traditional modes of song. "Normal Music Schools" had arisen in the Northeast before the war, and a decade or so later they had established themselves in the South as well. These music schools were proposed as an im- provement upon the old singing-school process. Summoning experts in the field of protestant religious song, the normal schools provided courses in harmony, note-reading, church psalmody, piano, and organ to those who would then return to their rural constituencies for a singing school in the new "improved" techniques and music.

Instrumental accompaniment, now available throughout the South, also altered the music being written during this period. Other influences on the new music, as Jackson points out, were jazz and the popular secular music of the time, as evidenced in the syncopation and dotted eighth-note patterns, the repetitious chords and rhythm. It would seem that chromaticism and syncopation, so prevalent in the gospel songs, would have presented something of a stumbling block at first for the rural people in general, as they still do for the Sacred Harp following. But the gospel-hymns began to be accepted widely, and it would be difficult to overestimate their popularity in the South for almost a century.

The modernization of the White sons' *The New Sacred Harp* is shown by its incorporation of the alto part throughout and its in- clusion of a number of songs by the normal-school disciple A. J. Showalter, whose later contributions included the well-known "Leaning on the Everlasting Arms." The book also contained, in a greater percentage than in the *Sacred Harp* itself, many short hymn tunes. Between the new-technique songs and the earliest of the old type, the more typical songs of the *Sacred Harp*—the fug- ing tunes and revival spirituals—were slighted. The White sons' book evidently did not achieve a very wide or lasting following. For the present, no other information about its history has emerged, and Jackson does not even mention it.

Joe S. James's history of the Sacred Harp did relate information about J. L. White himself, undoubtedly the guiding force behind the book. Like his father, White was a popular figure, a composer, a singing-school teacher, and a leading spirit in the organization of musical conventions. "Several years ago," according to James's

1904 account, "he wrote all the tunes in the Sacred Harp into seven shape notes, but after doing so decided not to publish it, as he believed the Sacred Harp, as left by his father and the others who aided him, would be more beneficial in its present shape than to change its notation." The elder White had earlier confronted the seven-shape threat head-on. Pressured by the infiltrations of the *Christian Harmony* and other seven-shape books into Sacred Harp territories, he had announced with finality in his 1869 "Preface,"

To those who are tenacious and scrupulous as to the different terms by which musical sounds should be expressed, allow us to say that we have carefully and earnestly studied the subject for forty-seven years, during which period we have been especially vigilant in seeking musical terms more appropriate to the purpose than the four names used in this book; but candor compels us to acknowledge that our search has been unavailing. The scheme which our prolonged and laborious examination has inclined us to prefer to all others has had the sanction of the musical world for more than four hundred years; and we scarcely think that we can do better than abide by the advice—"Ask for the old paths, and walk therein."

Perhaps the younger White was at last persuaded by his father's sentiments. At any rate, though he had toyed with mixing seven shapes and Sacred Harp tunes in his *New Sacred Harp,* he chose not to strip the old book itself of its traditional vestment and dress it up in the fashionable seven-shape style.

The Cooper Revisions

The first really significant revision of the *Sacred Harp* came out in 1902 under the supervision of W. M. Cooper of Dothan, Alabama. The Sacred Harp had long before drifted into south Alabama, as into other southern states, but it is notable that the impetus for a new revision would arise in an area beyond the sphere where the tradition was strongest and most historic. It had been over thirty years since the *Sacred Harp* had last been revised, and a new edition was clearly essential if the tradition was to survive. Certainly the subsequent editions of the Cooper revision in 1907 and 1909 testify to the new interest which the book stimu-lated. But it must appear regrettable that the first revision after White's death did not emerge under the auspices of those who had been taught by the founder of the tradition. Those who considered themselves to have received the mantle White had passed down— though they admitted a revision was needed—could never sanction such an interloper.

The Cooper revision won wholesale acceptance in the newer western areas of the tradition, but it was never adopted in the territories where the original editions had flourished. Still, though the uniformity of the movement was now gone, the Cooper book was beneficial, both for what it represented in the way of suste-nance in the newer areas and for the controversy—often bene-ficial—it inspired in the older areas. The Georgia and north Alabama singers needed just such a jar to prod them into the sub-sequent action that would rescue their own failing tradition.

Prefacing the new Cooper edition was a statement of loyalty to "the old paths" by the reviser. "For more than fifty years," Cooper wrote, "the Sacred Harp has been justly regarded as a veritable treasury of song, and its grand old melodies have been sung over and over so many times by the generations who loved them, that the book itself has come to seem almost like a sacred thing." "One would hesitate, therefore," he added, "before attempting to alter such a book to add or take away from its pages." Cooper did make changes, however, some superficial, others more substantial. First of all, he transposed a good many of the songs into a lower key, probably closer to the key they might be sung in. He also substituted descriptive or first-line titles for many of the old tune names ("Life Is the Time to Serve the Lord" for "Wells," "The Road to Life and Death" for "Windham"). But even though he had sworn loy-alty to the original book as it stood, Cooper did alter the character of his revision through the addition of a number of new gospel songs, as well as "Rock of Ages" and "There's a Great Day Com-ing." Finally, the Cooper revision was given over to one more substantive change—one to which all subsequent revisions would likewise be compelled—the all-out installation of the alto part.

In universalizing the alto part, the Sacred Harp made its first and only *major* concession to modernism in the book itself. The alto or a corresponding fourth part was in actuality nothing new. The English madrigals had often admitted five or six separate parts. And in the early New England times, it was common to see tunes printed in four parts: tenor, bass, treble, and alto or counter. In early America, however, as noted in chapter 3, many systems vied for acceptance. Accordingly, the fourth part was not yet stationary in its position. Some of the tunes placed the fourth part in the eventual alto position—below both the treble and the melody. Others carried a part above the melody, and sometimes above the treble. In the *Sacred Harp* this type is represented by "New Jerusalem," a song by the well-known composer Jeremiah Ingalls, in which the alto part rides consistently above both tenor and treble parts. A third variation put the fourth part in the old alto clef rather than the bass or treble. This treatment of the fourth part, as in the song "Greenwich," occurred frequently in most editions. (As the Cooper book had done, the 1971 edition of the Denson revision changed the alto clef in these songs to the standard G clef.)

William Billings was one of several early writers whose works appear in the *Sacred Harp* volume with original alto parts. But White and most of the other immediate contributors to the *Sacred Harp* constructed their songs in only three parts. Probably the singing masters who migrated southward to instruct these rural tunesmiths taught the standard method of composition in three parts. At any rate White and the others approved the alto to the extent of admitting to their volume a considerable minority of tunes with the fourth part.

The principal modernization that the alto part represents is of course that of harmony. Otherwise the alto only provided a convenient alternate part corresponding to the bass for those women with low voices. But with respect to harmonization, as critics sometimes mention regretfully, the addition of the alto took some of the austerity out of the Sacred Harp sound. The original spare harmony, without the relief of the convenient third on which the alto usually centers, gave the music a tension that seemed to accord with other elements of the music as well as the texts. The added third in many cases serves to sweeten the effect, to pad the har-mony.

In regard to the harmonic developments of medieval musicians, Manfred Bukofzer has said, "Especially in 4-voice music, it was inevitable that they should eventually come round to the third, if they wished to avoid the continual doubling of one tone."[1] The same inevitability revealed itself in the four-part music of the Sacred Harp. This is not to say that wherever there was an open fifth in the Sacred Harp, the alto part plugged the interval; the fourths and open fifths still abound. But the new part did push the sparser harmony built on these intervals into a minority.

And if purists regret the introduction of the alto, it must be ad-mitted that the modernizing step was an inevitable and vital com-promise, a move for survival. Already losing ground to the new music and new shape notes of the *Christian Harmony* and gospel-music folk, the Sacred Harp could not let these upstarts have the monopoly on the increasingly popular fourth part as well. Too, there were surely singers in the ranks of the Sacred Harp who had become fond of the alto in those tunes which already employed it. The singers whose range was limited to a lower register probably pushed for the universal use of a low part. With pressures from without and within, the caretakers of the Sacred Harp tradition could hardly have taken another alternative.

It is inconceivable that such a move was achieved without some struggle. Jackson, however, does not mention any controversy over the alto part, and the singers themselves can offer few clues. Two of the Sacred Harp patriarchs, T. B. McGraw and H. N. McGraw (both now deceased), close friends of the Denson brothers and re-visers themselves of the later Denson edition, could not remember any opposition in their area to the early alto additions. Interviewed in the late 1960s, they recalled instead a general puzzlement on the part of everyone as to why White had not included the alto part in the first place. But such astigmatism often afflicts hindsight. Only one source, and an unlikely one at first, reveals a hint of opposition. Carl Carmer's *Stars Fell on Alabama* (1934), a series of imaginatively written sketches of Alabama places, customs, and folk life, includes a description of a Sacred Harp singing in the northern part of the state. Carmer does not particularize the date or the location of the singing any further than the "Sand Mountain" area, a traditional stronghold of the Sacred Harp in the twentieth century. In the author's firsthand account of the singing session, with a crowd he estimates at "surely more than two thousand people," this bit of dialogue is recorded:

> "Trebles on the left. Basses on the rght. Tenors in the center."
> "What about altos?" I whispered to Knox.
> "Don't mention the word," he said. "The real Sacred Harpers think it's a newfangled and wicked affectation. They've been having a big fight with the Christian Harmony folks about it." [2]

Carmer's description of the singers' book shows it to be the James edition of 1911. Although the James book had included altos with most of its songs, these Sand Mountain singers had apparently chosen to ignore them. How long certain Sacred Harp groups held the alto part in low esteem is not known. Certainly the altos have now long enjoyed recognition in the Sand Mountain singings as elsewhere. The blanket propaganda of subsequent revisions must have sealed the issue for good.

The Cooper book was copyrighted again during W. M. Cooper's lifetime in 1907 and 1909, and further editions were brought out in 1927, 1950, and 1960. Most of these editions added new music, both traditional-style Sacred Harp songs and tunes written in the gospel-song style. Picked up along the way were "Sweet By and By" and "There Is a Fountain Filled with Blood," as well as a W. M. Cooper imitation of "O Why Not Tonight," titled "Be Saved To-Night." The 1950 additions, "Guiding Spirit" and "Jesus Saves," were apparent attempts to slip in some lively songs

from rival books. The two tunes can be recognized as barely dis-
guised versions of Paine Denson's "Manchester" from the first
Denson revision and John McCurry's popular "Raymond" of the
1855 *Social Harp* and the 1911 James and 1935 Denson books.
New texts were given to both of these songs as if to remove the
obvious similarity.

The James Revision

The major rival of the Cooper book in the older territories was the
James revision, the "*Original Sacred Harp*," arriving almost a decade after the other. The James book was the heir to the major
Sacred Harp following which White's original edition created and
which the Denson Revisions of later years would eventually in-
herit. The revision committee, appointed in 1906 by the United
Sacred Harp Musical Association, consisted of twenty-three outstanding singers and writers of the time, with Joe S. James as the
chairman.

The James revision coincided with and helped to promote a re-
awakening of interest in the Sacred Harp in the Georgia and eastern Alabama districts. The minutes of the Chattahoochee
Convention session of 1902 quoted enthusiastic letters from a recently formed but already substantial convention in Douglasville,
Georgia, and from the new Panther Creek Sacred Harp Singing
Society, which reported to the convention "good attendance and
growing interest." We think the Old Harp best of all the singing
books we know," they volunteered, "and hope to soon see it back
into general use again."[3]

But while such groups looked to the future with optimism, they
realistically admitted that a new revision was essential. In their
report to the Chattahoochee Convention, a committee from the
new Douglasville Convention hailed "with profound gratification
and sincere pleasure the unprecedented interest being manifested
in the growing sentiment and the popular favor of the Sacred

Harp in our section," but also took this opportunity to call the "attention of the owners of the rights of the Sacred Harp to a much-needed revision." Further, they announced, a "committee of five from our convention was appointed to confer with the own- ers of the rights of the Sacred Harp . . . and we suggest in this connection that your convention appoint a similar committee." The report was signed by four officers of the convention, including J. S. James. Four years later the most comprehensive of the singing conventions, the United Association, of which James was then president, started the groundwork for a new edition, and in 1911 the *"Original Sacred Harp"* was brought before the public.

Earl Thurman, historian of the Chattahoochee Convention, maintained that the introduction of the book produced "the great- est revival of singing in the history of Sacred Harp singing." "The effect was remarkable and one not easily described," he wrote. "All through the Sacred Harp territory the word was being car- ried that something grand was being done for the beloved book— something that would put new blood flowing in the life stream of Sacred Harp singing." With this revival, he added, "singers at- tended annual singings in greater number than ever in the history of the book."

Since the success of the Cooper edition may have provided much of the motivation for the James revision, the Cooper follow- ing was naturally resentful of its competition. In a pattern long associated with American music and the sacred song books, a dis- pute over publication rights arose. Cooper took legal recourse to verify his claim for exclusive rights to the title and songs of the *Sacred Harp*. Further, he claimed that the new alto parts to most of the songs in the James Revision were copied from the alto lines he had written. Indeed, many of the altos in the James book do appear to have been based on the altos in the other book. Given the rigid harmonic practices of the Sacred Harp, however, and with each of the other three parts already established in chordal arrangement, there would have been little room for individual dif- ferences in the composition of the alto parts—even if the James revisionists had worked altogether independently of Cooper's book. In any event, the court attempt failed, and the James edition was freed to spread its influence.

With 609 songs, the James revision was the lengthiest volume of the Sacred Harp ever compiled. It was also the largest in size, measuring ten and one-fourth inches by eight inches. Except for the supplying of the altos and the addition of extra verses to some of the songs and notations of historical or biographical information to most of them, the 1869 edition was transferred almost intact into the larger volume. Seventy-one songs were added, but most of these were tunes that had been included in the earlier editions and later discarded. A significant trend reflected in the book was a shift of interest "westward" to Alabama. Jackson noted that "Alabamians living at that time composed twenty-eight of the newly added tunes and living Georgians composed but six." T. J. Denson, the eventual organizer of the Sacred Harp Publishing Company, was listed on the revision committee, and S. M. Denson, "the most active individual on their committee," was credited with the 327 new alto parts.[4]

If the James revision was conceived as a replacement for the other new editions, which these revisers must have considered spurious, it was wrought as an answer to the seven-shape movement as well. In the preface, the editors obviously had in mind the proponents of the gospel-song style as they declared that the Sacred Harp songs therein were "as far from secular, operatic, rag-time and jig melodies as it is possible. To this end, the music composed and compiled is in four shaped notes, and written on four staffs in dispersed harmony—some call it old harmony. In these compositions there are but few of the twisted rills and frills of the unnatural snaking of the voice, in unbounded proportions, which have in the last decade so demoralized and disturbed the church music of the present age, in this section, but in other sections to an alarming extent. We do not think a note of warning in this respect is out of place." It is of course ironic that the revisers would disdain "secular . . . and jig melodies" and even "rills and frills . . . of the

voice"; but what struck the Sacred Harp traditionalists as objec-
tionable in the increasingly popular music was a *new* kind of secu-
larity, an "unnatural" music in that it had departed from the
traditional sounds, even from the "old harmony," which had been
esteemed for so long.

These very revisionists were responsible for another publication
that came out two years earlier. The 1909 *Union Harp and History of Songs,* according to its preface, was compiled by a group
of revisers who were almost to a man the ones credited for revising the James book. The volume was commissioned, the preface
states, by the 1907 meeting of the United Sacred Harp Musical
Association, of which James was still the president. Though the
volume contained many of the traditional songs, it had also opened
its pages to such a random list of the standard evangelical hymns
of the time as "Leaning on the Everlasting Arms," "Oh Why Not
To-Night," "Sweet By and By," "Work for the Night Is Coming," "Home Over There," and "Nothing But the Blood." Even
a song attributed to S. M. and T. J. Denson and J. S. James—"The
Great Roll-Call" (carried over into the James revision also)—
mimicked the echoing phrases so characteristic of the gospel hymns.

If the editors felt compelled to include the gospel-hymn types
in their collection, a paragraph in the introductory section indicates that this was but a compromise move to appease modernizing forces which demanded not only new tunes in new styles but
also a remaking of the old ones. The editors state here that, though
they had corrected necessary errors in the old songs, they had
stayed

near the old land marks of the standard hymns and tunes, which have so
successfully stood in the past, and will in the future stand all adverse criticism. Whatever corrections have been made, they are believed to be abso-
lutely necessary to meet the severe criticism of the modern harmonists, and
which will in no way interfere with the old ideas, harmony, melody and
general plans. They have stood as they are for years, and pleased the music-
loving people. We prefer not to make the fatal mistake, made by some of
our musical brethren, in radically changing these standard tunes to make

them conform to what they are pleased to call modern harmony. In nearly every case the alterations, in place of benefiting the tunes, have greatly impaired the melody of them, and to a considerable extent, destroyed the sacredness of the song. Such errors we have tried to avoid.

Perhaps the reason the same revisers were at work on two such different volumes at the same time was that they were trying to please the modernists within the ranks by publishing a supplement to the *Sacred Harp*. This book would contain the new kind of music, so that there would be no need to reduce the old *Sacred Harp* to the new indignities. Whatever the motivation, the *Union Harp* makes it clear that the leaders to whom the *Sacred Harp* was entrusted came dangerously near the brink of a complete modernization. The volume turns up occasionally now in some book collector's hands, but few clues remain to what kind of use it enjoyed.

The J. L. White Revisions

Another revision, also a product of 1909, must have been abandoned soon after its publication. Copies of the revision have only recently surfaced, and its disclosure in this study is apparently the first since the time of its original appearance. This is the Fifth Edition of the *Sacred Harp,* brought out by J. L. White in Atlanta.[5] The revision committee for the new book offered the following explanation on the introductory pages: "A Committee was appointed by the United Sacred Harp Musical Association to confer with the White heirs, looking to a revision of the HARP, but their plans having failed to materialize and mature, and having given said Committee Two YEARS to formulate same, and the Chairman of said Committee having released all claims thereto; and believing it justice to the singing public that a revision be made as speedily as practicable, the Compiler, through the aid of Southeast Alabama friends and others have formulated plans and have revised the book."

Acknowledging "the almost universal demand" for such a pub-

lication, the son of B. F. White stated in the preface that his goal
was to revise the *Sacred Harp* "in such a way as not to destroy
the identity of our honored father's work." First, he said, the body
of the book would remain unchanged "where practical." But at
the same time that he promised to "preserve and maintain the old
harmonies" he also advised that the work would correct "many
errors in harmony." Further, the book would include new songs
which would "conform to the modern rules and laws governing
harmony and composition." And in a strong judgment of the old
Sacred Harp, White expressed hope that this revision would "supply a long felt need for a higher class of religious music . . . and
supplant an element of so-called music, placing in its stead . . . a
high class of vocal collections." His own set of rudiments, which
he called "a plain and simple theory" and which were aimed, like
the new music, at supplanting old values, White recommended—
not to the old-fashioned "singing school"—but to the "Singing
School Department."

By composition and format, this fifth edition is the oddest of all
the Sacred Harp collections. In the first section of the book White
reproduced nearly three hundred pages of the earlier *Sacred Harp*
editions, including his father's rudiments. Then, renumbering from
"one" at the end of the pages from the original books, White produced his own rudiments and a unit of songs totaling close to two
hundred pages, including approximately sixty-five tunes already
appearing in the first section but now shorn of the free-style "dispersed harmony" which the Sacred Harp followers had always
found so appealing. Altos were added to these songs and the treble and bass parts were remade into close harmony.[6] Several other
Sacred Harp songs not in the first unit were also included in the
second section and many of these were similarly doctored. Wedged
in like props between the remade tunes were Lowell Mason hymns,
several gospel entries, and the now ever-present "Rock of Ages,"
"Just As I Am," and "Happy Day."

Different in approach as they were, the two versions of the
Sacred Harp tunes were yoked together in one book like the Old

and New Testaments: the new intended to perfect the promise of the old, and therefore to replace it, under the enlightenment of "modern harmony." In a note at the end of his own rudiments, White suggested that in putting forth these musical theories, he had "reference only to music written by musical scholars." "It is a matter of much regret," he continued, "that a large amount of the music of the present day is written by persons who may have some indefinite ideas about melody—but who know very little concerning Harmony, and positively nothing at all of Form." White was apparently conceding that many of the traditional Sacred Harp writers had a way with melody. But what he wanted to demonstrate to them and to their adherents by his before-and-after format was that they could plainly profit by some lessons in harmony, above all in what he loosely classified as "Form." It was White's watered down reinterpretations, however, that suffered by comparison—at least in the opinion of the body of people who were interested in a new edition of the *Sacred Harp*.

In all cases White left the melodies substantially as they were, though he could not resist occasionally pruning or at least rearranging the passing or neighboring tones. Most of the violence was done to the bass and treble parts. The range of the bass remained much the same, but White removed from the bass line any pretensions to counter-melody. And with the treble, the voice part most obviously characteristic of the Sacred Harp "dispersed harmony," White systematically clipped off the high notes in many of the songs, reducing the treble range for the most part to intervals hovering around the melody line.

For the early Sacred Harp writers, of course, it was an ideal that every part to the degree possible be melodic and yet altogether "make harmony." But White took away the freedom and much of the appeal of these individual parts, forcing treble, bass, and alto to serve as handmaids to the single melody line. How essentially White changed the character of the songs can be seen by noting the "before" and "after" versions of the bass part in "Heavenly

Armor" and the treble part in "Ninety-Third Psalm" (see Figures 1 and 2).

In William Walker's "Heavenly Armor" the rolling bass line is a melody itself, quite as lovely as the tenor. And yet it moves hand-in-hand, harmonically and rhythmically, with the other parts. In White's revised version, the bass is stiff and lame. And overall what is missed in the song is the richly textured effect achieved when all the parts move together but with some melodic integrity of their own. (It might be added that although White did not change the melody of "Heavenly Armor," he did provide an alternate note at the end of the first phrase so that, if the singer chose, he might return to the key note, rather than the fifth, and thus avoid the old Mixolydian cadence. Whether he had awareness of the modes or not, White, with just enough background in contemporary music theory, would have known that this cadence was not the proper ending for a song written in what he considered to be the major mode.) As with the bass in "Heavenly Armor," the original treble line of Chapin's "Ninety-Third Psalm" (erroneously attributed to Ingalls in the James and Denson revisions) can hold its own as a tune. The rise and fall of notes is nothing less than melodic. And yet this counter-melody does not spoil the melodic flow in the tenor line and in a way even augments it. White's revised treble, instead of distinguishing the tenor, actually impoverishes it, making the tune seem no more than ordinary.

White's fifth edition and the *Union Harp* were published in the same year, but in compiling their own volume the *Union Harp* editors were undoubtedly aware of White's approach to his revision, and in fact some of the same men may have worked on both volumes at the same time. Whether or not the *Union Harp* editors had White in mind when they wrote it, the passage from their preface quoted above sums up the failure of White's 1909 revision. The editors spoke of a "fatal mistake" made by some of the "musical brethren" in revising the standard tunes "to make them conform to . . . modern harmony." Such alterations, instead

HEAVENLY ARMOR

From J. L. White's "Fifth Edition"

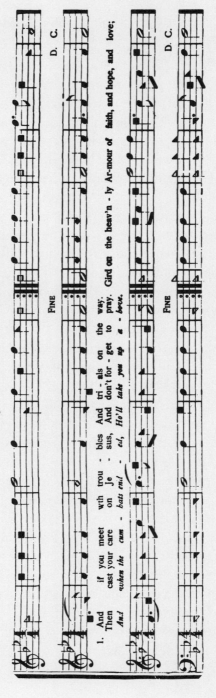

1. And if you meet wth trou - bles And tri - als on the way.
Then cast your care on Je - sus, And don't for - get to pray. Gird on the heav'n - ly Ar-mour of faith, and hope, and love;
And when the cum - bats end - ed, He'll take you up a - bove.

From the standard editions

NINETY-THIRD PSALM

From J. L. White's "Fifth Edition"

From the standard editions

of improving the tunes, had "greatly impaired the melody of them," if not "destroyed the sacredness" of the songs. Similarly, though from a very different perspective, Alan Lomax, in the text accompanying his 1959 recording of a Sacred Harp singing for the *Southern Journey* series, explained that the unconventional harmonies heard in many of the Sacred Harp songs resulted from "the blessed ignorance of some of the early composers who had more feelings for folk music than knowledge of the 'rules of harmony' and . . . the powerful character of some of the old tunes, themselves, which demanded a really fresh treatment."

What White failed to see, then, was that many of these tunes, like Ananias Davisson's brooding "Idumea" (see Figure 3), were most at home in the context of the open, unrestrained harmony with which they were first conceived. Davisson's melody, which had been sung throughout the South for almost a hundred years when White reworked it, is one of the most haunting in the shape-note collections. Both the *Sacred Harp* and the *Southern Harmony* had carried, along with the melody and the bass, a treble line which, though it was not Davisson's original line, as Rachel Augusta Brett Harley points out, was at least "similar in contour" as it was in spirit.[7] In his revision, White did not bother the melody and left the bass part essentially the same, but in restricting and regularizing the treble and the added alto part he tamed the stormy beauty of the setting and ruined the song.

In fairness to J. L. White and his experimental edition, it must be granted that the musical theories operating on the Sacred Harp of the time were in flux. Before the traditionalists and the modern harmonists were finally committed to their separate ways, they struggled among themselves, and the result was a compromised music. Torn between "the good old way" and the demands of progress, the Sacred Harp of the time was in a frustrated state. J. L. White's fifth edition with its two mismated units is, above all, the evidence of that frustration.

Another possibility to explain the character of the revision is that White wanted to issue a new edition of the book to satisfy

IDUMEA

From J. L. White's "Fifth Edition"

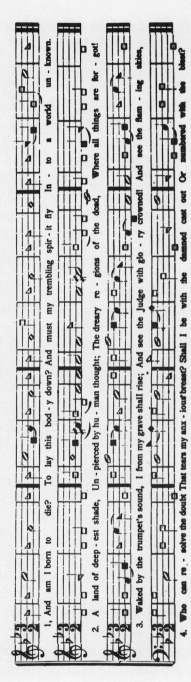

From the standard editions

the old Sacred Harp following and at the same time so renovate the *Sacred Harp* as to make it acceptable to some of the southern churches, thus accomplishing his father's longtime goal. Certainly White suggested this as a concern in his preface, stating his efforts to place "within reach of all, a high class of vocal collections suit-able for all Church and Religious worship." As it turned out, of course, the *Sacred Harp* was still not welcomed by the churches, and the revision did anything but please the singers.

As with the *Union Harp,* the credited revisers of White's fifth edition included such figures as S. M. Denson, T. J. Denson, and M. F. McWhorter: members of the revision committee of the United Sacred Harp Musical Association. But a statement in the introduction to the 1911 James revision suggests that the affixing of many of these names was unwarranted. "Several attempts have been made within the last two or three years to revise the Sacred Harp by others," this introduction says, in what would have to be a reference to the White book, "but the work was done in such a way this committee could not endorse and accept the same, al-though their names are attached to some of these books as endors-ing them. This, however, is without authority by the members of the committee." The book was not accepted, at any rate, by the United Association. That it was not well received in general is evidenced by J. L. White's immediate preparation of another and less radical revision in 1911.

Furthermore, notations in the ledgers of the Cleburne County Sacred Harp Convention of Cleburne County, Alabama, and the Mulberry River Sacred Harp Convention, centered around Jeffer-son County, Alabama, reveal the increasingly adamant attitude of the singers against such attempts to erode their musical tradition. Both of these conventions, two of the few with records extant from the time, met in session in August and September of 1910 and passed resolutions condemning White's 1909 book. The Mul-berry River Convention sent a copy of its resolution to White, notifying him that the convention members "hereby oppose the last revision of the Sacred Harp, favor the old as it stands." The

Cleburne County Convention unanimously agreed "not to use nor recommend using" the revision, "owing to the fact that the harmony and music are arranged different to that of the old Sacred Harp," and requested that their resolution be read "in open session" of the United Convention. To this, the Cleburne County organization added a statement urging the revision committee of the United Association "to proceed to publish a book that will . . . meet the approval of the Sacred Harp singers," and recommended that such a book be presented "as it now is with the errors corrected and the new appendices at the back and the music added be of the Sacred Harmony and arranged as in the Old Book." Similarly, the Mulberry River Convention advised, "If any revision—put an addition at back as formerly with any new changes necessary without destroying the Identity of any of the songs therein. All the new compositions to be composed by old Sacred Harp singers only." In thus requesting that future songs be "of the Sacred Harmony and arranged as in the Old Book" or that they be composed "by old Sacred Harp singers only," the Alabama singers were speaking as directly as they knew how for nothing less than an *exact* continuation of the traditional styles.

In 1911, after his setback with the fifth edition of the *Sacred Harp,* J. L. White attempted once more a compromise between the traditional styles set forth by the early fasola patriarchs and his personal yen to publish in the new musical forms: the "Fourth Edition, with Supplement." The revision was printed from the original plates of an 1870 edition, another one of those unexplainable editions which happened in the case of not only the *Sacred Harp* but many other shape-note song books both in New England and in the South.

This 1870 edition, coming one year after the last "standard" B. F. White edition, was exactly like the 1869 edition with the exception of the title page. The 1869 edition, like each of its predecessors, was directed by White and a few other prominent musicians and sponsored by the Southern Musical Convention. Yet the preface to the 1870 edition was signed by White alone, with no mention of a supporting convention, and was copyrighted by him and D. P. White, one of his sons. Until his death in 1879, B. F. White had planned to join again later with the leaders of the Southern Musical Convention on preparations for still another edition, so there is no evidence of a rift between White and the others. What exactly the edition does represent it is too late to determine. Jackson was evidently not aware of its existence for a number of years, for he does not refer to it until 1944 in *The Story of the Sacred Harp*. A copy of the book had probably only then turned up—a mysterious, long-lost relation to the family of standard editions.

White's 1911 revision, then, used the plates of the 1870 printing, but with a supplement of many of the hymns and gospel songs appearing in his fifth edition. White also included at the back of the book his rudiments from the 1909 work, so that the body of music within this revised fourth edition is enclosed by two sets of rudiments, B. F. White's at the beginning and the younger White's at the end. Significantly, though, White did not bring into the seventy-three-page supplement the reharmonized versions of the old Sacred Harp songs which had so antagonized most of his singing public. And instead of the ambitious 1909 preface extolling the "modern laws and rules governing harmony and composition," White introduced the new fourth edition with a statement as modest in tone as it is in length: "There being such a universal demand for the old fourth edition and it being my wish to perpetuate the music as written by my father and the dear brethren associated with him, I herewith submit for your approval the fourth edition, with supplement. The Singing School Department on the last twenty-six pages I recommend to all teachers and students of music."

In this revision White credited as advisors thirty men from Georgia, Alabama, and Florida, including Absalom Ogletree and H. S. Reese, compatriots of his father. (The names of the Denson brothers, listed under the revision committee for the fifth edition, are missing this time.) White's book was once popular in northern

Georgia, in areas of eastern Tennessee and northern Alabama, and in northern Mississippi, where it was used by both white and black singers. When it was no longer available in Mississippi, the singers there converted to the Denson book, which also gradually won out in all areas of north Alabama. The active use of the White book is today restricted to north Georgia.

The Densons and the Denson Revisions

Although the Denson revision was the last revision to emerge, it is more traditional than the other two now in use. The reason for this is probably that the first revisers were experimenting with new forms whose implications and effects they could not always foresee, whereas the editors of the Denson book were aware that definite schisms had emerged. They were attuned to the strong feelings of the singers who repudiated the modernizing trends, and for the most part they turned back to the old modes of singing and composing.

The Densons were natural choices to take up the stewardship of the Sacred Harp movement, for they were well grounded in its music and tradition. The first edition of the *Sacred Harp* had included a two-page "Christmas Anthem" by James M. Denson, originally of Walton County, Georgia. The 1911 James book stated in the information below the piece that Denson had composed a number of songs which he intended to publish in a song book of his own, but that he died before doing so. Denson was an important figure in the early Sacred Harp organization (he had served as vice-president of the Southern Musical Association during its second year of existence), but he could hardly have known that the Denson name, through a younger generation, would become synonymous with Sacred Harp music among the singers. Two of his nephews, S. M. and T. J. Denson, affixing their name to the book they committed their lives to serving, became "the deans of the Sacred Harp" in the twentieth century.

Seaborn McDaniel and Thomas Jackson Denson were born in 1854 and 1863 respectively, the younger of the four sons of the Reverend Levi Phillip Denson, a Methodist minister, and, like his brother James, a man of musical inclination. (The oldest of Reverend Denson's sons, William, was away with the Confederate forces when the youngest was born. When his father wrote to tell him of the news and granted him the privilege of naming his brother, William honored Thomas Jackson Denson with the name of his commander, the famous "Stonewall" Jackson.) Educated in London, Denson preached his first sermon, his descendants report, "in John Wesley's church." Eventually he settled in Cleburne County, Alabama, and founded a church of his own, known as Denson's Chapel. When prospectors followed a rich vein of gold down across North Carolina and Georgia into Alabama in the 1830s and 1840s, Cleburne County gave rise to booming towns of colorful name like Arbacoochee and Chulafinnee. Arbacoochee, where Thomas and Seaborn were born, had become by the middle 1840s a town of several thousand, complete with saloons and a racing track. There after the main gold surge had passed, the two brothers, Mrs. Ruth Denson Edwards relates, spent part of their youth searching for gold nuggets in the mines. They soon turned to music, however, and more substantial rewards. In 1874 Seaborn taught his first singing school, and records show that at the age of thirteen Tom Denson led the assembly in B. F. White's long and complicated "Red Sea Anthem" at that year's session of the Chattahoochee Convention.

The two brothers married sisters from another family of Sacred Harp singers, the Burdettes. Seaborn married Sidney Burdette, and Tom married the younger sister, Amanda. After his first wife's death in 1910, Tom then married Lola Mahalia Akers. The brothers and their families resided in several Alabama communities, notably in Winston County, still referred to as the "free state of Winston" because it detached itself from the Confederacy during the Civil War. (The county's relatively poor farmers did not own slaves and preferred to cling to the Union.) After long and productive lives of teaching, singing, and composing in the music they loved, the Denson brothers died within a year of each other, Tom in 1935 and Seaborn in 1936.

The Denson brothers were known foremost as singing-school teachers. They so thoroughly covered the Sacred Harp territories and their teaching methods were so successful that it is almost impossible to find a singer in the Denson revision area who does not in some way trace his Sacred Harp instruction and background to the two Densons. As Jackson notes, Seaborn Denson taught his first singing school when the Sacred Harp was just thirty years old and B. F. White was still active in its propagation.[8] With singing schools in Georgia, Alabama, and Mississippi, Seaborn Denson, by Jackson's estimation, taught between eight and twelve thousand young rural songsters their notes.[9] T. J. Denson also began teaching at an early age and continued until his death in 1935. In singing schools from Georgia to Texas, he was credited with teaching more Sacred Harp singers than was any other man. Children and grandchildren of the two brothers continued the teaching tradition.

The work of the Denson brothers and their descendants is a principal reason why the Sacred Harp has for years now been strong in Winston, Walker, Cullman, and Cleburne counties in Alabama, where they lived and did most of their teaching. As a testimonial to the impact of the lives of the two brothers, a granite monument to their memory was placed on the courthouse square in Double Springs, Alabama, in 1944, the centennial of the Sacred Harp, "by the loving hands of their families, pupils of their singing schools, and legions of singers and friends."

The Denson brothers, it will be recalled, were leaders in the publication of the James edition in 1911. Thomas Denson was on the revision committee, and S. M., the author of the alto parts, was music editor. This experience, and their field work in the many areas of the tradition, primed them for the work on the edition which was to bear their name. In 1933 Thomas Denson organized the Sacred Harp Publishing Company, of which his sons

Howard and Paine were to be president and secretary, respective-ly, and purchased all legal rights to the *Sacred Harp* from the James family. The committee formed to work on a new volume consisted of twelve men, including the Densons. Both of the older Denson brothers died before the revision was completetd in 1936, however, and Paine Denson took over the major editorial work. The revision was subsidized by Lonnie P. Odem, one of the re-visers.

In some respects the Denson revision took up where the James book left off. In the preface the new revision made claim to being "the true successor of the James Revision of 1911," a position also evidenced in the title: "*Original Sacred Harp*" (*Denson Revi-sion*). But there were differences. The James volume had attempted to include most of the songs from each of the B. F. White editions, thereby justifying the title word "original." The Denson revisers, on the other hand, trimmed the volume down again, taking out 176 of the less popular tunes "in order to reduce the size of the book and give space for music by present-day writers." Forty-one new pieces were added. "The most radical change," the preface admitted, "has been the re-writing of the rudiments and the addi-tion of a Chapter on Harmony and Composition." This rewriting, by Paine Denson, brought the rudiments closer in line with con-ventional music theory. But the songs themselves, even the new twentieth-century products, relinquished none of the traditional style or technique.

Three editions under the sponsorship of the Sacred Harp Pub-lishing Company have followed the initial Denson revision. The first was produced in 1960 with the help of a music committee composed of A. M. Cagle, H. N. McGraw, T. B. McGraw, J. El-mer Kitchens, Hugh McGraw, and Ruth Denson Edwards (daugh-ter of T. J. Denson). This new "Denson Revision" added 117 pages and 103 songs: 91 newly composed pieces by 39 contem-porary authors and 12 songs from other sources, chiefly the 1911 James book. For various reasons—mainly the poor quality of bind-ing material and paper and the large number of printing mistakes

—this edition was not felt to be satisfactory, and in a few years plans for a new printing were undertaken. When the board of directors found that the old plates would not do for a reprinting, they authorized, in 1966, a new edition under the supervision of the same music committee. Copyrighted in 1967, this edition deleted twenty-two songs from the former one (two of these were among the songs restored from the James book) and added a dozen tunes, including a few more songs from the James book. The volume now contained 573 pages—the introduction and rudiments, and 547 pages of songs.

When the supply of books was again depleted, the company decided that still further alteration should be made, and once again a new edition rather than a reprinting was settled upon. This 1971 edition was prepared by a committee consisting of Hugh McGraw (chairman), J. Elmer Kitchens, Ruth Denson Edwards, Walter A. Parker, Palmer Godsey, and Foy Frederick. A few more technical errors were corrected, and an introduction and a short, up-to-date history by Ruth Denson Edwards were supplied. The alto line was added to twelve songs. Raymond Hamrick of Macon, Georgia, composed one of the alto parts and Hugh McGraw, the others. Also the few alto parts still written in the old alto clef were transposed to the G clef. Finally, an index of first lines was included. Serving as consultants on this newest edition were two devoted friends of the Sacred Harp, Dr. William J. Reynolds, Secretary of the Church Music Department of the Sunday School Board of the Southern Baptist Convention, and Dr. Emory S. Bucke, book editor for the United Methodist Publishing House. Five thousand copies had been printed for both the 1960 and 1967 editions, and approximately 5,600 were printed for the 1971 edition. When the stock of this latest edition was exhausted in 1976, five thousand more copies were ordered.

As well as issuing editions of the Sacred Harp hymnal, the Sacred Harp Publishing Company has produced in the last fifteen years six record albums. Each recording offers about fifteen songs, with solmization as well as words, except on the longer anthems. The songs on the albums and the singers who perform them are all selected by the board of directors of the company; in the independ' ent spirit so characteristic of the tradition, each of the fifteen di' rectors is allowed to choose one song and four singers. This means that, with the directors, approximately seventy'five voices are brought together in the studio where the recordings are made. Normally about four thousand albums are produced. When these are sold, a new recording is planned, the directors decide on the songs to be performed, and the singers—from Georgia and Ala' bama, and occasionally some from as far away as Texas—are noti' fied when to meet for the taping.

The recordings make possible a select group of singers, with a balance of parts regulated by the studio equipment. In deference to those attempting to learn to sing by the records, the tempos are slowed a bit. The recordings are excellent technically, and they are probably a valuable means of exhibiting or teaching the Sacred Harp tunes and singing style. The only complaint that could be made is that under studio'control conditions some of the spirit evaporates. One misses the natural accompaniment of Sacred Harp singing—the sound of feet patting on the wooden floors—or the feeling of abandon the singers project when singing for themselves alone and not the microphone. But it is enough to say that the record albums have been warmly received by the Sacred Harp following.

Today, it would seem, the Sacred Harp Publishing Company is more tightly and efficiently run than it was during the period fol' lowing the initial Denson revision in 1935. At the present, the stock in the company is distributed among approximately two hundred persons or estates. The stockholders meet every two years and elect fifteen directors, and the directors in turn appoint the managing officers. Thus far the publishing company sounds much like any other corporation, yet it differs from most in two obvious respects. First of all, the stockholders do not share in the profits of the company's ventures, except in the broadest sense. Second, the Sacred Harp Publishing Company is probably the only corpora tion in the world whose directors sing at their meetings.

For these people, publishing books is not an end, but a means of improving and preserving their song. And the song, with prayer, they use to open and close their meetings is the evidence in gen eral, and the reminder to them in particular, that this is so. The stockholders do not invest their money with the expectation of reaping profits; rather they buy stock as an act of service in the perpetuation of their tradition. From the capital pooled by the sale of stocks, the company is able to print more copies of the songbook or make a new recording. And whatever profit the records create becomes a fund for a new edition of the book, and vice versa. The company allows the directors a small commission on the books and records they sell as a convenient and efficient way of distributing these materials and as a means of reimbursing the directors for their services in general. (They receive no salary and are not otherwise paid for their travel expenses in attending meetings.)

A word should be said about Hugh McGraw, the executive sec retary of the Sacred Harp Publishing Company. In ordinary life a businessman from Bremen, Georgia, McGraw has become per haps the chief promoter and good will agent of Sacred Harp music. Now in his late forties, McGraw somehow passed his early life on the periphery of this tradition without being fully exposed to it. Then in 1953 he walked into his first Sacred Harp singing and immediately "felt a shiver" at the sound he heard. When the class sang the plangent fuging tune "Alabama," he knew he had come home: "I thought that was the prettiest thing I'd ever heard." That night he called "Uncle Bud" McGraw, his second cousin and a well-known singing-school teacher, and asked to be taught to sing that music. With the help of his mentor, Hugh McGraw took up a study of the song book very likely unparalleled in thorough ness and intensity.

Having schooled himself in the theory and style of the Sacred Harp tunes, McGraw composed several songs for the 1960 edi tion of the book, one of which, "Living Hope," has become a steady favorite at singings in the Denson-book area. Probably the foremost teacher in the Sacred Harp today, McGraw regularly holds singing schools in Alabama and Georgia. He has taken groups of singers to perform in Israel, in Washington, D.C., for the Festival of American Folklife, and in Montreal for the Man and His World Exposition. And he is as comfortable holding a session for college students, regional ministers of music, or members of the College Music Society as he is with third or fourth graders in a rural Georgia singing school.

McGraw's business leadership has been a major force in keeping the Sacred Harp Publishing Company secure and has insured its ability to furnish the singers with books and records. (The Denson revision of the Sacred Harp book, even up through its handsome 1971 edition, has never sold for more than five dollars. By way of explanation, it might be noted that the Sacred Harp folk have managed to get by without the notorious "middle man.") He seems to move easily among the sometimes conflicting desires of his constituency, and his personal ambassadorship for the Denson book has won sympathetic interest from singers in the other segments. A father and young grandfather and the manager of a clothing manufacturing plant, Hugh McGraw is preeminently a singer of the Sacred Harp, and the present and immediate future of the tradition depend obviously on his continued energies and service.

The Colored Sacred Harp

In 1934 an unusual entry appeared in the line of variant Sacred Harp publications: *The Colored Sacred Harp,* a slim paperback collection of seventy-seven songs compiled by J. Jackson (Judge Jackson, 1883–1958) of Ozark, Alabama. At that time a strong fasola tradition existed among the black singers in the southeastern corner of Alabama and the northwestern part of Florida.

The Alabama and Florida State Union Sacred Harp Singing Convention had been meeting since 1924, but Sacred Harp singing must have been popular among the blacks in this section for much longer than that. John W. Work in his 1941 article "Plantation Meistersinger" related that the 1938 convening of the Henry County Convention (of Alabama, a black convention) was the fifty-eighth meeting of that body.[10] Into the twentieth century the singing in these conventions was based on the Cooper revision of the *Sacred Harp,* the same book the white singers in that area used. Earlier than that, these singers, like all other Sacred Harp groups, must have depended on one of the later B. F. White editions.

The story of Judge Jackson and the publication of his book was told by Joe Dan Boyd in a 1970 article, "Judge Jackson: Black Giant of White Spirituals." Jackson was a self-educated man who had progressed from "field hand to farm owner and businessman in Dale County, Alabama." Around the turn of the century he heard his first fasola song, and at least by 1904 he had composed shape-note tunes of his own. Boyd speculates that Jackson's early works were "influenced directly by the 1902 revision of the *Sacred Harp* by William M. Cooper . . . with whom Jackson was acquainted to the extent their differing colors allowed."[11]

By the late 1920s Jackson had published broadside copies of a few songs, and within a few years a song volume for black Sacred Harp singers compiled by Jackson was authorized by the Dale County Colored Musical Institute and the composition committee of the Alabama-Florida Union State Convention. In the depression years of the thirties the publication of the *Colored Sacred Harp* had to be subsidized by Jackson himself and his "associate author," Bishop J. B. Walker. A Chicago firm printed one thousand copies of the book and shipped them by freight to Ozark, Alabama, where, Boyd writes, "Judge Jackson and his young son Japheth picked them up in a mule-drawn farm wagon."[12]

The *Colored Sacred Harp* represented an attempt to offer compositions by black Sacred Harpers in the same style and format as

those in the regular book. Jackson compiled the book, wrote eigh-
teen of the songs, and wrote or revised parts of others. Contribu-
tor of the second largest number of songs (fourteen) was the
Reverend H. Webster Woods, a Methodist preacher who had
been taught his rudiments by Jackson. Nine of the compositions,
Boyd relates, were by members of Jackson's family. The opening
pages of the collection included a "Report of the Committee," an
introductory statement by a committee "appointed by the Dale
County Colored Musical Institute and the Alabama and Florida
Union State Convention." Also on these opening pages, along
with a picture of the author and of the associate author, is a general request: "We ask your co-operation both White and Colored to help us place this book in every home. That we may learn
thousands of people especially the youth how to praise God in
singing."

Work noted that some of the songs in the book "made use of
many well-known old hymns,"[13] and George Pullen Jackson reported that many were variants of the original Sacred Harp melodies. If it is not fair to say that a majority of the tunes in the
Colored Sacred Harp were versions of the older songs, it is obvious that some of them are built on phrasal units that occur in songs
from the regular volume. (This can also be said, to a lesser degree,
of some of the twentieth-century songs in any of the Sacred Harp
books.) But other tunes bear little resemblance to the songs in the
standard books. Many of them present troublesome rhythmic patterns and syncopations not found in the regular volume. For the
most part, the writers of these tunes seem to have had little concept of phrasing. Although misbarring is evident in many of the
standard Sacred Harp melodies, it is usually in a consistent fashion (i.e., a 3/4 song barred as 4/4). In this collection, the misbarring is rife and unpredictable.

The most memorable song in the collection is "Florida Storm,"
credited to Jackson (see Figure 4). When Boyd and Jackson's
survivors went through the author's memorabilia, they found an
old broadside sheet headlined "subject: The Florida Storm" and

FLORIDA STORM

J. JACKSON, 1928

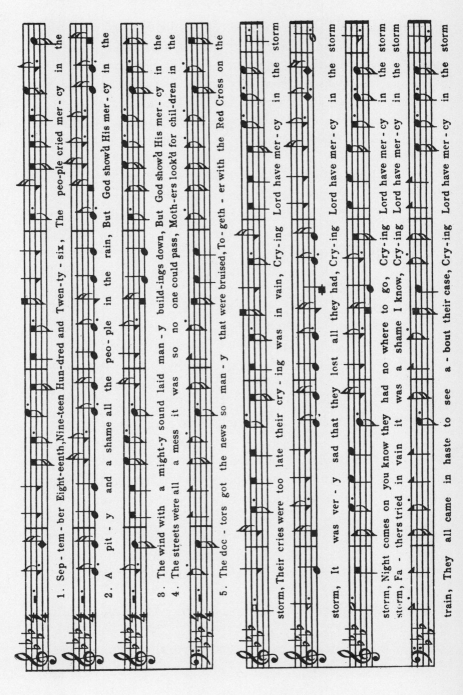

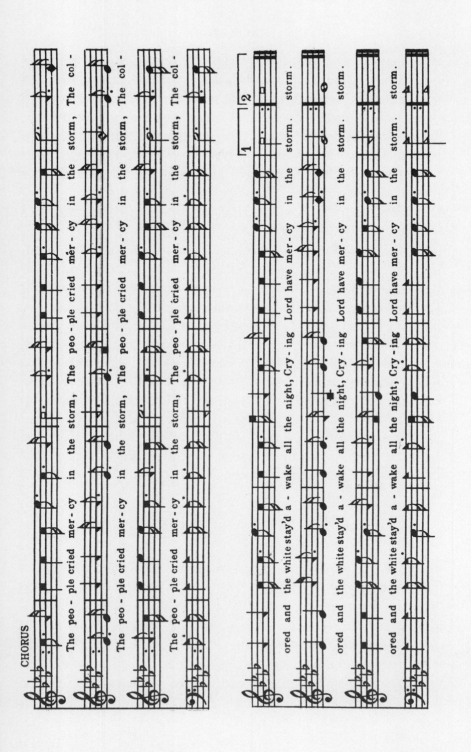

CHORUS

The peo - ple cried mer - cy in the storm, The peo - ple cried mer - cy in the storm, The col -

ored and the white stay'd a - wake all the night, Cry - ing Lord have mer - cy in the storm. storm.

attributed to "Frank Spencer, PhD."[14] The sheet contained, with-out music, the text from which Jackson had evidently selected the words for his song. Whether Jackson merely drafted a tune al-ready accompanying the text is unknown. The syncopation in Jackson's printed tune, however, is unnecessarily difficult, and the barring awkward. Jackson must have known or conceived a more natural fitting of words to music but was unable to transcribe this into notes. At any rate, the singers in performing the song rebar the music as they sing, altering the syncopated patterns and straightening out the melodic line.

In 1973, with the help of federal and state grants, a new hard-cover printing of the *Colored Sacred Harp* appeared including an added short sketch of the life of Judge Jackson and his work. Still, the future of Jackson's compilation seems doubtful. It has not gained a foothold in the other areas where blacks have sung Sacred Harp music—Mississippi and Texas—and may not have been in-troduced there. Although it has sometimes been used for radio and local television programs in the south Alabama area, the *Colored Sacred Harp* has never supplanted the Cooper book for the black singers there and is not usually represented in their conventions. A few songs such as the unique "Florida Storm" have caught the fancy of the singers, but otherwise they prefer the standard body of tunes available in the Cooper book.

The Significance of the Revisions

In *White Spirituals* Jackson told the story of an annual Southern Harmony singing in Benton, Kentucky, which was, as far as he was able to determine, the last of its kind anywhere. The final printing of the four-shape *Southern Harmony* of 1835 was in 1854, a few years before its author, William Walker, was to di-vert his enthusiasm to the seven-shape *Christian Harmony*. The lack of subsequent reprintings of the once widely popular volume —Walker claimed shortly after the Civil War to have sold

600,000 copies of the old book—had left only this meager representation at a small Kentucky town where a number of elderly
singers gathered each year. The Benton singers, with effort, had
so far been able to preserve their singing. The organizers of the
singing, chiefly settlers who brought the books with them from
North Carolina, were able to summon only twelve copies for
their sessions beginning in 1884. But through the years, the singers had acquired books from adjoining counties, bringing the total
up to thirty.

The Benton singing, in contradistinction to the rest of the
Southeast where the book was once almost universally a favorite,
had only thus barely survived the drought which came with no
republishings. The direct relationship between the living singing
tradition and the occasional replenishing of the store of song volumes is thus dramatized in the almost total disappearance of a
once-vital tradition. In 1939 and again in 1966 facsimile editions
of the Southern Harmony volume were made generally availa-
able. But while the new books may have prolonged the life of the
Benton singings, they evidently have not resurrected any of the
other groups.

The *Sacred Harp* emerged from the same general tradition as
the *Southern Harmony*. If one accepts James's account, then
White was at least coauthor of both volumes. The appeal and
character of the two books, at any rate, were basically the same.
And just as in the case of the Southern Harmony, the life of the
Sacred Harp was inseparably bound to the supply of books on
which the tradition fed. In his essay on the Sacred Harp, Donald
Davidson reconstructed a situation suggestive of the sort of bind
that could come over the singing from a scarcity of books: "As
ten o'clock came near, Brother Oakes began to get worried. There
was a shortage of books. In the past they had depended on old
man H——, who regularly appeared with an armful of 'sacred
harps,' some to lend, some to sell. He was not at the Unadilla
singing last Sunday, a voice said. He must be sick then, said another, for he was never known to miss a singing. Brother Oakes

went through the crowd and returned. There were nine books, he said. That would do to begin with—everybody come in!"[15]

Like the *Southern Harmony*, the *Sacred Harp* was fortunate to have a dynamic compiler and author who would initiate and supervise several editions. A significant difference in the life of the traditions, however, was that the *Sacred Harp*, unlike the *Southern Harmony*, was to be given another publishing (a revision actually) not long after the Civil War, when cultural life in the entire South had to restructure itself. The Southern Harmony, with no new books to sustain the tradition, could not survive the blight of the war. The eventual exhaustion of song books, together with the occasional disruption by war times, continued to sap the strength of the Sacred Harp from time to time as well. And on the other hand the singing expanded and regained territory it had lost when times of peace returned and when, every few decades, a new edition or reprinting of the song volume stimulated a declining tradition.

Between 1844 and 1870, the period of the original editions of the *Sacred Harp*, James records that the *Sacred Harp* was "almost the only song book used in the teaching of singing schools outside of the cities," presumably in Georgia and the immediate southern area. But after 1870 the *Sacred Harp* "began to wane and it was not so extensively taught in the singing schools as before." Probably the intrusion of the seven-shape and round-note books and the modernizations of the influential Southern Musical Convention were responsible for the decline of the song book in those years, though the abandonment of a fifth edition in 1879 resulting from B. F. White's death can not be overlooked as a factor. By 1904, in any case, James could write of the *Sacred Harp* that "within the last six or eight years it has revived again and is coming into general use." While this late revival was not connected with any new edition, the publications of the Cooper editions beginning in 1902 and the James edition and J. L. White edition of 1911 further revitalized the Sacred Harp movement.

Some of the older singers remember at least two distinct lapses of the movement since that time. The period roughly between 1925 and 1935—notably the Depression years—was a time of dwindling interest in many of the areas. Then something of a rebirth occurred with the publication of the Denson revision, which seemed to give a new spirit to the singers in the central territory. A second lapse was during World War II, when cars instead of buggies had become the chief mode of transportation for the singers. The gasoline rations prompted by the war curtailed the opportunity to travel to singings and thus enfeebled a number of the annual sessions. Since that time the 1950 and 1960 editions of the Cooper book and the 1960, 1967, and 1971 editions of the Denson revision have provided interest and sustenance for the singings and have insured a ready stock of song books for new converts.

Almost all the revisions of the *Sacred Harp* have added new music to the core of tunes carried over by each of them. Many of the editions have claimed songs from other editions. The 1911 James book picked up tunes left out of the 1869 *Sacred Harp*. The 1960 and 1967 Denson books retrieved melodies from the James revision overlooked by the earlier Denson book. A 1964 reprinting of the James book added two songs from the Denson volume and one each from the Cooper and White books. It has always been thus with American music. No other art form in this country has been so regarded as common property. From the first, the songbook compiler borrowed his neighbors' tunes, mixed them with his own, and offered the combined product to the public as "a Collection of Tunes, Odes, and Anthems" by "the most eminent authors," as well as numerous pieces "never before published." Whenever possible he brought out other editions, representing each one as "new," "enlarged," and "much improved" and describing his work as "Now well adapted" to all needs: "singing schools, choirs, social and private singing societies."

Throughout the history of the Sacred Harp, the urge to improve or renew the storehouse of songs has been vital. And where this urge is lacking or where it remains unfulfilled the song tradition dies. The many and recent revisions of the Denson and Cooper books indicate the continuing strength of the Sacred Harp. And the exchange of tunes between the James and Denson folk was a healthy sign for that tradition, signaling the inevitable merging of the two. In fact, as far apart as the varying revisions have carried the Sacred Harp followers, there are evidences that they may yet again belong to one band. When it was apparent that the James book would not go through another printing, the Denson revisionists had already accommodated the James singers by making room for some of their choicest tunes in the Denson book. In addition, in the late 1960s several singing schools were conducted with the Denson book in a south Georgia district where the James book had hitherto been used exclusively.

Inroads have also been made into the Cooper territory. In Florida, where the Cooper book reigns, one weekend convention holds a night session from the Denson book. Also at many Alabama Cooper-book sessions, singers who are fond of some of the Denson-book tunes assemble after lunch before the singing officially reopens and harmonize on favorite songs from the other book. In fact, a few Denson books are brought to the singings for this purpose. And those singers who have hurried off from the dinner tables in order to savor this forbidden fruit sing away for fifteen or twenty minutes. Then, as the others begin to filter in, some old-timer finally gets enough and opens his blue-back Cooper book. "All right, now let's have some *real* singin'."

This loosening of attitudes has been in part the result of a few singers from the Cooper book areas who have become hooked on the Denson singings and now travel considerable distances from south Alabama, Florida, and Texas to attend sessions in the Denson province of north Alabama and Georgia. In this case the singing style, the way the music is rendered, is as much a factor as the book itself. Many of the Cooper book singers would never concede that the Denson singings are of a better quality than their own, but some of their number do so without hesitation. One Florida singer declares that he had never heard Sacred Harp singing "in its purity" until he attended a Denson-book convention in the

Birmingham, Alabama, courthouse in the 1940s. He has proved a frequent visitor ever since. Another Florida devotee, curious about the Denson singings, first drove up for a session in north-west Georgia in the late 1960s. The music he heard from that churchful of singers moved him so deeply that he now stays close enough by to get to a singing in north Alabama or Georgia each weekend throughout the summer months. "I just sat there all day with tears in my eyes," he says now about that first visit. "I'd heard Sacred Harp singing all my life. But I'd never heard any-thing like that."

The Denson- and Cooper-book songs and singing styles are still far enough apart (the singing from the Cooper book by the seg-ment of black singers draws the spread even further) to prevent a merging of the two in the immediate future. But some visiting and exchange goes on between all the different groups—more today than ever before. If this trend continues, a single broad-minded revision might again tie all of these singing adherents together as they have not been since the days of B. F. White and his sturdy, community-approved editions.

5

The Conventions

In August of 1898 the J. B. Blair family of Winston County, Alabama, packed a covered wagon with provisions and set out for Carroll County, Georgia, two hundred miles across state. The object of their three-day trek was the annual session of the Chattahoochee Sacred Harp Singing Convention of western Georgia. Probably they spent the first nights with friends along the way and during the four days of the great singing assembly stayed, as was customary, with some family near the Flat Rock church where the sessions were held. Each day at about eight or nine o'clock they assembled with other Sacred Harp enthusiasts, perhaps a thousand in all, and sang until about four in the afternoon, taking an extended recess only at noon when dinner would be spread on the grassy hillocks under the shade of trees.

The Blair family, whose journey is recounted by Earl Thurman in his history of the Chattahoochee Convention, is representative of the many Sacred Harp adherents who have traveled to the Chattahoochee singing, a musical institution dating from before the Civil War and continuing into the present. Today, as in the 1890s, Sacred Harp singing consists of a network of local singings and conventions, like the Chattahoochee, occurring on annual dates throughout the year. Conventions, as distinguished from other singings, draw singers from several communities or from broader areas to an annual singing assembly, usually lasting for more than one day. The conventions as the central agencies of the movement have been responsible for propagating the singing and for instituting and distributing the revisions and republications of the song book. In addition they have provided vital communication among the singers within the various territories.

With its political overtones, "convention" might seem an unlikely word choice for the singing assemblies; it summons a picture of delegations, resolutions, and debate. Yet, though little
besides the name has remained from former times, the singing
"convention" once had exactly these characteristics. A review of
the times may help to explain why.

The Sacred Harp conventions were instituted in an era when
singing was a fundamental part of community life in much of the
South. For evidence, witness the reaction of British song collector
Cecil J. Sharp in the early twentieth century to what he called an
"ideal state of society" in the Southern Appalachian region, where
the characteristics of that earlier era had been in part sustained:
"I found myself for the first time in my life in a community in
which singing was as common and almost as universal a practice
as speaking."[1]

In the areas where the Sacred Harp thrived, how and what one
sang were matters of interest and concern to the whole community. Organized singing was religion, recreation, and esthetic pur-
suit all combined. As such an important part of the cultural life,
the vocal arts flourished in a variety of forms. Even leading exponents of the Sacred Harp movement enjoyed other kinds of music,
often singing and composing in other forms. Before the Sacred
Harp tradition had solidified, the members of the earliest conventions saw their music in its broader context—as part of a very general tradition of sacred song. "Sacred Harp" was not what they
were engaged in; that was only the name of the book they were
using at the time. Accordingly, there was no reference to the
Sacred Harp in the official titles of the original conventions. Rather
these were called, for example, the Southern Musical Association,
the Chattahoochee Musical Convention. The statement of purpose of the Chattahoochee Convention used the phrase "to renovate, improve, and systematize *our Southern music*" (Italics
added). Initially the Sacred Harp book was merely a means to
this end. It was not until a decade or so later, with the tradition
taking root, that the Sacred Harp became an end in itself.

These folk took Major B. F. White's book and contributed songs to it or, by consistently avoiding certain tunes, shared in the culling process. In essence, then, they did "renovate" and "improve," and they also "systematized," producing over the years a network of activity and an efficient and satisfying method of composing, publishing, and performing the best of their collective talent. They made the book and its system their own, and in the exchange, the *Sacred Harp* claimed them. Gradually over the first couple of decades, the singers came to feel that the *Sacred Harp* was not just a book, but a special institution deserving of an existence beyond the changing fads which have always characterized the musical tastes of the nation. If this music was to endure—and increasingly they felt that it should—then the purity of the strain had to be safeguarded. Other books and styles should not be permitted to crowd the *Sacred Harp* in its own house.

Beyond providing the enjoyment of a large singing, the aim of the conventions came to be, not just "the improvement of music," but the management and preservation of the community's interest in the Sacred Harp. In the later conventions, the policy toward the Sacred Harp and variant kinds of music was usually set in the constitution or bylaws, as in the following from the 1875 constitution of the Warrior River Convention of North Alabama: "We have adopted the Sacred Harp and will use no other book in our convention."

Most of the conventions announced that they held no other official allegiances. In phrasing that varied little from place to place, virtually all of the associations declared that, as a body, they had "no partiality for the different opinions which now affect the public" nor "any sympathy for any of the religious creeds that divide public sentiment." But on the matter of the song book to be used—at least from the conventions formed as late as the 1870's—there was no hedging.

Concerned as it was with different and sometimes differing localities within an area, the convention was planned and regulated as democratically as possible. These rural songsters were only a generation removed, in spirit if not in actuality, from the liberating Declaration and the founding of the American way of life, with emphasis on the principle of democracy. Inevitably, in creating a local governing institution, they wanted to build on the same principle. Illustrating the democratic nature of the singing gatherings, even into the twentieth century, Andrew Lytle gave this description of a convention he had observed: "There is a grand meeting at the county seat once a year, and here the neighborhoods sing against each other and in unison under one general leader, who always remembers to turn the meeting over to each district leader for one song. This is a privilege jealously looked after; and if anyone is by chance overlooked, he will rise and make himself known."[2]

The rules and bylaws of the conventions were written to insure a democratic method. Of primary concern was the matter of representation. Article 2 of the constitution of the Warrior River Convention exemplifies a typical policy: "This convention, when organized, shall consist of teachers, leaders, and delegates from different schools and organized Sacred Harp Societies in our bounds, who, on producing letters from their respective schools and societies certifying their appointment, shall be entitled to seats." The formal membership was often restricted, as shown in Article 9 of the same constitution: "Each teacher shall be allowed five delegates from each school and society, instructed by him to represent it in the convention."

Beyond these organizational policies, strict rules were imposed as to conduct. In the Southern Musical Convention, a leader was not allowed "to vary in rendering music from the way it was written." The Warrior River Convention even made this stipulation: "No person shall speak more than twice on the same subject without leave from the President, and no person shall be interrupted while speaking unless he departs from the subject and uses words of personal reflection." Joe S. James reveals that, in the case of the

Southern Music Convention at least, such strictures were faith-
fully carried out: "On several occasions, charges were brought
against members, and oftentimes they were expelled." But while
the constitution and bylaws of the conventions speak of "order
and decorum," with provisions in case "any member shall so de-
mean himself as to bring reproach upon the cause," the immediate
concerns of the singing body were not always so lofty. Problems
of a peskier nature often confounded the membership—as when,
for example, over a period of some twenty years dating from
1867, the constituents of the Chattahoochee Convention made
annual resolutions to curb the abuses of tobacco addicts among
their number: "[Resolved] that it is indecent to spit amber on
the church floor, and that we will refrain from same." By 1888,
the date of the last reference to the tobacco problem, the assembly
had at last adopted a get-tough policy; this time to the resolution
was added a fine for violation: "under penalty of ten cents."

The conventions, each one over a particular area, were auton-
omous, like so many musical states. They treated each other with
neighborly respect, often corresponding on matters of general interest. A typical attitude was expressed by the Mulberry River
Convention in its policy statement: "This Convention shall correspond with any sister convention who will correspond with us."

The power of the conventions in propagating and regulating
the singing movement in the South was great. They had the power
of life and death over song books and singing styles. With a single
nod from the delegates they could banish a song book and bring
another into being. The Southern Musical Convention, according
to James's history of the movement, assumed the role of authority
over all the teaching of the Sacred Harp in its area: "At each of
the sessions," James reports, "a committee was composed of the
best teachers, and when they proved proficient in the profession,
a certificate was given them, or license, which contained the official signatures of the officers of the convention, and when a teacher exhibited this license, no further question was made about his
qualification to teach vocal music." He adds that the licenses or

certificates were never given unless the candidates had fully proven their worthiness, with the result that "the country had in all parts men who were well versed in music for their teachers."

References in the minutes of the Chattahoochee Convention indicate that convention's similar interest in insuring the quality of singing. While the activities of each session were given over largely to singing, it was also customary for individuals to address the assembly on matters of musical interest or offer instruction as to correct methods of singing and leading. The record says, for instance, that the Chattahoochee, in its 1893 session at Powell's Chapel Church, "called for correspondence and rec'd from Salem, Ala. J N Hutchenson a graduate in Sacred music . . . he being requested to address the convention on Saturday at two o'clock P.M." Further in the minutes the secretary noted, "Prof. J. N. Hutchenson addressed the convention on vocal music and was well listened to and it had a good effect." In 1868 at the fourth postwar session of the reconvened Chattahoochee, the secretary recorded that "the Convention was well entertained by a lecture from the chair on intonation."

One of the most intriguing phrases to be found anywhere in the convention's ledger refers to remarks made at the same session by J. P. Reese, the song composer and singing-school teacher who in musical correspondence to the *Barnesville Gazette* wrote under the pen name of "Rubin." "Many calls being made for Reubin," the minutes read, "he made one of his telling efforts on *crank and heel rising time*" (italics added). The phrase is such a lively vehicle for an analogy that it begs to be explained. But the knowledge of whatever advice "Rubin" had to offer on the topic of "crank and heel rising" tempo has, like the echoes of the songs heard that day, long since disappeared. What may be gleaned from these references, though, is some idea of the vigor with which the conventioneers pursued their music and of the good spirit with which they received instruction.

The conventions were usually responsible for the overseeing of and the correlation between the regular singings within their ter-

ritories. At some point these directing bodies began to print pamphlets of the minutes of their sessions. For some time, large singings
and conventions had often "spread the minutes" of their meetings
—as the terminology used to go—in the area newspapers. This
amounted to an account of who directed the sessions, what songs
were used, and where the body resolved to meet the following
year, if the location of the singing was subject to change. The separate pamphlet of minutes not only recorded the goings-on of each
convention, but also included a directory of the singings sponsored
by that convention for the coming year. Such pamphlets proved
to be a handy and reliable reminder of when and where to go for
a day or more of singing. And in time practically all the conventions adopted the practice, a few of the smaller district conventions eventually merging their publications with those of larger
bodies.

There are many separate publications of minutes today, but the
most comprehensive is the one produced each year by the Denson
revision folk. This compilation is the work of no central organization other than a general secretary, for several years now Mr.
W. A. Parker of Birmingham, to whom the secretaries of most of
the singings in this region of the Sacred Harp send (along with a
small fee for printing costs and labor) the minutes of their singings. The network behind this publication was probably left over
from one of the big conventions, but the subsequent merging of
sister conventions has now obscured whatever skeletal organization was originally there. The publication, called the *Directory
and Minutes of Annual Sacred Harp Singings,* covers most of the
Denson-book singings in Alabama and Georgia and several sessions in Florida, Tennessee, and Mississippi. It is thus a major
source of uniformity within the Denson-revision branch and has
doubtless been a factor in the gradual proselytism of the other
groups.

At the front of this publication is a list of all the singings for
the coming year, divided by months, with occasional directions to
rural localities. (The 1976–1977 publication listed approximately

370 singings.) The body of the *Directory and Minutes* is made up of the minutes of all the singings in the central area from the previous year. The page or two on each singing gives the names of the officers of the convention and the order of the day's activities, with a list of all the leaders and the songs led by each. Beyond its possible interest for the historian, such information is immediately helpful to the singers, since each entry of minutes indicates something of the attendance and the territorial spread of the participants at all the singings. In the days before the printing of the minutes, singings were announced by word of mouth, and singers were perhaps aware of the exact data concerning few annual gatherings outside their own area. Now a singer in Texas can confidently strike out for a singing in Georgia with not only an idea of where the singing is to be found ("2½ miles East of Ephesus School on Ephesus and Roosterville Road" for the singing at Hopewell Church on the third Sunday in June) but also a notion of how large and strong the session should be.

The *Directory and Minutes* aids communication in still another way. Every two or three years, as begun in 1967, the publication includes an alphabetized list of the singers and their addresses, forwarded by the secretaries of the various singings. The list of course is not complete—a segment of society more difficult to index can hardly be imagined—but it strives to be. And each subsequent edition has been more complete than its predecessors.

The Southern, the Chattahoochee, and the United

The two great conventions of the nineteenth century were the two last mentioned, the Southern Musical Association, founded in 1845, and the Chattahoochee Convention, organized in 1852. The Southern Musical Convention, in the years between its founding and 1867, met in nine different counties in western and central Georgia, within a hundred-mile radius of Hamilton, Georgia, the original home of the *Sacred Harp*. The Chattahoochee, by the time of James's account in 1904, had met in six neighboring counties in the Chattahoochee River valley in the western section of Georgia.

In its day the Southern Musical Convention was, in James's words, "the greatest organization of vocal musicians that ever met in Georgia." Similarly, the Chattahoochee remained for decades the largest gathering of singing enthusiasts in its area. Both conventions had suffered during the Civil War years; but while fasola singing in the southern region had generally diminished after the war, the Sacred Harp people in Georgia returned to the great conventions in droves. The 1866 meeting of the Chattahoochee Convention was, by James's account, "the largest singing convention held in all the country." The assembly convened at Pleasant Hill Church in Paulding County, Georgia, on a Thursday and dispersed the following Monday. Singers came from several states. The Sunday crowd, James reports, was an immense one—estimated at eight thousand people. As if to substantiate the estimate, James adds, "there were three wells close by, from which the water to furnish the crowd was drawn. Before one o'clock they were drawn dry, and it was almost impossible to get water."

In the next year an event at the prestigious Southern Convention set in motion a series of happenings which caused the Sacred Harp to be diverted at last from the territory in which it had been conceived. At the 1867 session, as the James account has it, "Professor" E. T. Pound of Barnesville (the author of several tune books) and others pressed for the use of additional song books of round and seven shapes in the convention. The new policy was adopted, and Pound was elected president. The traditionalists gradually withdrew from such heresy and began to merge into the ranks of the Chattahoochee Convention. And eventually the Sacred Harp withered in the very territory from which thousands of its books had issued to the extremities of the Deep South.

Granted, Pound and those with him did not abandon their interest in the Sacred Harp tradition, since they are mentioned as participants of the Chattahoochee Convention for many years.

Nor did the Southern Musical Convention at once relinquish the *Sacred Harp*, for it was to sponsor two subsequent attempts at revision of the volume under White's supervision. Still, as James implies, the Southern Convention in its diversification undermined the basic tradition which had previously centered on the single volume and thus eventually saw that tradition crumble. The demise of the original song volume in the central area did not, though, foreshadow a weakening of the tradition in the Chattahoochee region, where the Chattahoochee Convention remained strong as the largest convention in the state. As illustration of the popularity of this convention, James cites the 1902 session at Indian Creek Church with an estimated attendance of five thousand persons.

Of all the conventions, the Chattahoochee has maintained the most complete records including a membership list dating from 1852 to current times; it also had a historian in Earl Thurman, who in the 1950s traced the story of the convention from its beginnings and assembled sketches of the important members through the convention's first one hundred years. To Thurman, the Chattahoochee Convention was not "simply a musical association. The songs of the Sacred Harp have become an *ideal* in the singing life of the multitudes who owe allegiance to the Chattahoochee." The dedication and participation of the dozens of figures whose stories Thurman recounts do indeed demonstrate the importance of the convention in their lives. Thurman writes of J. R. Turner, who spread the influence of the convention by teaching singing schools in Alabama and Georgia for more than forty years; of Van Hembree, "a faithful soldier in a great cause" and a member of the convention for fifty-six years; of I. M. Shell, whose attendance figured strongly from 1852 to 1904. He records the contributions of Absalom Ogletree, a predominant force in the Chattahoochee for almost sixty years; of Anne Carter, whose membership spanned a period of more than three-quarters of a century; and finally of J. S. James, whose name was added to the convention list in 1866, half a century before his revision of the *Sacred Harp* would revitalize the tradition and the convention which supported it.

By 1921, according to Jackson, the Chattahoochee Convention had lost its primacy to the United Sacred Harp Musical Association, but it has continued up through the present. In August 1952 the convention held a centennial celebration at the courthouse in Carrollton, Georgia. Jackson himself addressed the singers on the occasion, congratulating them on the staying power of their convention through its first hundred years and challenging them to sustain their unique tradition.

By the turn of the century the sphere of the Sacred Harp influence in Georgia had moved perceptibly from the central part of the state to the Atlanta area. (In his history of the movement, James gives a list of "Leaders in the Sacred Harp" by counties, and the counties that he notes are all around Atlanta and to the West.) One result of centralizing the Sacred Harp influence in Atlanta was the founding of the United Sacred Harp Musical Association with headquarters in that city. Until 1928 J. S. James was president of the association which, according to Jackson, sought to "become the central organization of all local conventions, singings, teachers, and leaders that use the Sacred Harp."[3] After perusing the minutes of the association between 1914 and 1924, Jackson could find that such centralizing efforts had been only "partially successful." At a given session, he found that while several delegates were present from Georgia, only a few were in attendance from Alabama and Florida.

The Atlanta convention, however, was powerful in its own right as a drawing point for singers in the Georgia area. About a thousand singers attended each year during this period, according to Jackson, who attended the convention at the municipal auditorium in 1929, when the current mayor was "an enthusiastic Sacred Harp singer and leader." The United Association never managed to draw the Sacred Harp extremities under its jurisdiction, however, and at some point in the succeeding decades it gave up its seat in Atlanta to rotate around the various areas still strong in the tradition. Since this change in policy, the convention has been held at some community in either Alabama, Georgia, or Ten-

residents established the Hillabee Singing Convention, and by the same date the Ryan's Creek Sacred Harp Singing Convention of Walker County was created. The Clear Creek Mountain Home Singing Association of Winston County was organized in 1874; in the next year, the Warrior River Convention, toward the Sand Mountain area; and in the following year, the Coffee County Sacred Harp Singing Convention.

In the next decade conventions in the southern part of the state emerged in steady succession: the South Alabama Sacred Harp Musical Convention in 1883, the Houston County Sacred Harp Singing Convention in 1885, the Central Sacred Harp Singing Convention in 1888, and the Covington County Sacred Harp Convention in 1889. In the 1890s another Georgia emigrant, Greer Ward of Cobb County, moved to north Alabama and initiated the Albertville Sacred Harp Convention. In 1896 the Bear Creek Sacred Harp Memorial Singings of Winston County and the Rock Creek Mountain Home Sacred Harp Convention of neighboring Cullman County were formed. And there were more, both at the end of the nineteenth century and well into the twentieth.

At least two major conventions were formed in Alabama in the early 1900s: the Alabama State Sacred Harp Musical Association, founded some time around the turn of the century, and the B. F. White Sacred Harp Musical Society of Alabama, organized in 1915. Both conventions met in Birmingham (in July and August respectively) for three-day sessions. They apparently drew from different constituencies. Though their delegates assembled from roughly the same territories, the local singings represented in the conventions, according to Jackson, were usually distinct, one community being represented in the Alabama State Convention and a neighboring one in the B. F. White Convention.[5]

The Alabama State Convention may have been the best known of all the conventions. A number of historical reference works touching briefly on the Sacred Harp phenomenon mention it. Francis Butler Simkins refers to it in his 1953 *History of the South* as the highlight of the singing year: "The summer's activities came to a climax with a singing convention in Jefferson County Courthouse, Birmingham, followed by a basket picnic in Woodrow Wilson Park."[6] The convention was evidently well attended; Simkins states that the association had several thousand members, and Jackson reported that the singers in the 1931 session "packed the Ben Hur hall in Birmingham for three days running."[7]

In the ensuing years these two conventions lost ground steadily. In 1941 the two groups merged as the Alabama State Sacred Harp Convention, in what Earl Thurman called "the most important consolidation of organized bodies in the history of the Sacred Harp song book." Nevertheless the combined convention, now meeting like the United at a different community each year, is no better attended than a number of local conventions. The catalyst may well have been the increasing indifference of the Birmingham citizenry. Only one singing is held today in the city that was once the center of the Sacred Harp movement in Alabama, and, tucked away in a small church at the edge of the Birmingham area, it receives no publicity outside of the channels the singers themselves maintain.

The small towns and rural areas, however, have not yet given up their musical associations. Seven of the eight Alabama conventions founded over a hundred years ago are still holding sessions, and more than thirty others of more recent date meet at locations throughout the state each year.

The Conventions Today

With the years, the Sacred Harp conventions have reflected the changes of the singing phenomenon. Today the Sacred Harp has outlived the threat of the seven-shape books and the cries of the modern harmonists within its ranks. Accordingly, there is no need for delegates or the discussion and resolution of issues. The only pertinent issues at this point are not debatable. With some excep-

tions, the conventions have become altogether what they were intended to be originally, big singing assemblies. And if they have
done away with the formal mechanisms of democracy—the delegations, resolutions, and parliamentary whatnot—they have nevertheless retained the essence.

Exceptions to the increasingly informal methods of the conventions can be seen in the south Alabama black conventions from
the Cooper book, whose sessions give special emphasis to committee and delegate reports, printed programs, and the selling of
badges. The delegate systems may help to foster unity and communication in such instances, but the real motivation appears to
be merely an affection for form or the pull of tradition itself.

Representative of the democratic spirit of the present conventions is the change from the past in regard to "leading" policy.
Today most of the singers who wish to participate are summoned,
one at a time, by an arranging committee to lead the group in a
couple of songs until the time or the leaders run out. In an earlier
era only a few selected leaders directed the singing (for as long as
thirty minutes each). Typical of this early policy, the 1905 con-
stitutional rules of the Mulberry River Convention set up an arranging committee "to determine leaders and how long they will
lead." As an indication that being permitted to lead the group was
a high privilege in those days, the ledger of that convention contains this odd (and oddly spelled) stricture: "The leaders that are
not present at twelve o:clk. Saturday, unless providentialy hin-
dred shall not be aloud to lead." The new informality, however,
was making itself known by 1927 when an "amended clause"
was added to the bottom of the page: "To permit leaders to lead
who may arrive at any time during the session."

It is possible that the singing schools under the capable Densons had produced a generation of singers who were adept at leading. The 1936 entry in the Mulberry River Convention ledger
contains this statement: "On account of an abundance of leaders
the time was cut down to four songs." But Mr. W. A. Parker,
the general secretary for the Sacred Harp *Directory and Minutes*

and an articulate spokesman for the movement, sees the change in a different light. Mr. Parker maintains that in earlier days the leaders were indeed leaders: that is, individuals skilled and forceful in directing the group. Now, according to Mr. Parker, anyone can "lead" with the help of the "front bench leaders"—the premier singers on the front row who key the songs and often set or enliven the tempo with hand motions or a subtle patting of the foot under the bench.

The singers may have simply swapped the real leaders from the floor to the front bench as Mr. Parker suggests, but the present method of rotating leaders is indeed a felicitous one as Jackson, Davidson, and others have noted. Each singer can in this way have his favorite songs sung and at the tempo he desires (if he can wrest it from the foot-patting "front benchers," the old-timers would say). Also, to the extent that in leading each singer becomes not just a collaborator in the overall effect but an individual performer, the policy of having everyone share in directing the group insures a mastery of the singing techniques among the participants.

Many small singings are still closely linked with the rural communities in which they occur, but the removal of big conventions from the cities to rural churches has reflected an inevitable loss of contact between the urban areas and the old-time singing. Probably the singing is more congruous in natural surroundings anyway, for the movement from its roots up has been a folk tradition. But in earlier times many cities and townships in the South were composed of only first- or second-generation urban dwellers, and few would have thought it strange for the country folk to bring their singing to town for an annual song festival. That was what the township was in early days: the center of interests for the citizens in an area, the common meeting ground of the folk. With the growth of sophistication in the South, however, the Sacred Harp survived only in deeper rural areas, and in the cities it lacked a sponsor among the influential citizens.

The conventions, then, once had community ties which have

now largely disappeared. The smaller, one-day singings, meeting usually in rural areas exclusively, were often bound up with the interests of the community also. Like the conventions, but to a lesser extent, these rural institutions have gradually lost importance. The annual singing at Providence Baptist Church near Tallapoosa, Georgia, on the fourth Sunday in May is an example of an activity that was once a highlight for the people in that area. One former resident of the community who returns annually for the event commented that this singing "used to feed the whole community. The mill hands would come, eat, and leave. My mother used to cook for three days for that singing—Friday, Saturday, and Sunday. We'd bring the food in a trunk." Today a few interested citizens in the area return for the occasion, as well as a few families whose forebears were once involved, but the singing is no longer the community function that it once was.

Some of the singings coincide with the old Southern custom of decoration day, in which families return each year to bring flowers to the graves of their parents, grandparents, and other relatives. And one kind of singing that has more often retained its ties with the community in which it was conceived is that which annually memorializes individuals or families. In this case, relatives and friends converge each year for a singing (provided largely by the singers in the locality) which serves both as a memorial and a homecoming. In this way the roots of Sacred Harp singing spread much deeper into the community than might otherwise be apparent. One such singing is the annual Chafin, Harbison, and Hollis Singing and Reunion held at New Prospect Church near Bremen, Alabama, on the third Sunday in July. At some point in the history of these century-old sessions, the singing became linked with the three families, whose descendants along with the singers and others from the community now return each year for a reunion.

One of the distinguishing features of the conventions in most of the areas is the traditional "memorial lesson." This is a period set aside, usually on Sunday just before the dinner hour, to memorialize the singers or "lovers of Sacred Harp music" from

the area who have died during the past year. This part of the
session is a sober contrast to the spirited quality of the singing,
which by midday has been at its peak. A committee appointed to
the task compiles a list of the deceased to be read at the appropriate time. Two or three singers, selected by the families of the
deceased or appointed by the singing officers, lead a commemora-
tive "lesson" and often eulogize their friends or comment on the
implications of the mortality of the singers—the mortality, by
extension, of Sacred Harp singing as well.

Such a lesson was given by Mrs. Ruth Denson Edwards at the
1972 session of the Holly Springs Memorial Singing at Holly
Springs Church between Bremen and Carrollton, Georgia. Although Mrs. Edwards is considerably past the biblical allotment
of years the Sacred Harp people often sing about, she and her
octogenarian cousin, and his wife, have driven two hundred miles
from their homes in Alabama for this session. Once close to losing
both her hearing and her sight and surviving multiple operations
in the fight to regain them, Mrs. Edwards seems indomitable. The
years have not stooped her frame. And half a century of teaching
elementary-grade children has made her a master of simple rhet-
oric. As she speaks, the audience, of all ages, is entirely in her
grasp. Mrs. Edwards's memorial lesson is reconstructed here by a
listener who found her bearing and the conviction of her spontaneously worded address unforgettable:

When I was a little girl, I didn't *like* the memorial lesson. (She speaks
now for several of the young who are uncomfortable with this part of the
service.) I thought it was *sad*, and I wanted to get out of the church.
But my Daddy said to me, "Babe, there'll come a time when you'll think
that's the sweetest lesson of all." And that time has come. (Her voice
softens to a whisper.) That time has come.

All of you under the sound of my voice (her eyes span the crowd) . . .
will be touched by death, if you haven't already. Death has touched *me*
many times. The Death Angel has claimed two of my brothers and three
of my sisters. I'm the last of my family of the Denson-Burdettes, and Bob
there (pointing to her cousin) is the last of the Denson-Burdettes of *his*
family (of nine children).

For all of us—for all plants, all animals, for *all* forms of life—there's a cycle. . . . We're only born to die. We go through four stages. After we're born, we grow, we bear fruit (she waves her hands) . . . we age, and then we die.

When I was in college, I had to write a term paper in psychology. And any of you who've ever had to do that know that it's *hard* (the listeners stir, faces smile). And one of the things I read . . . was about the way people react to *death*. You know, any of you who have lost some-body . . . when you talk about it, you'll talk all the way around it, with-out ever saying it. We say, "when he passed away" or "when he left us." We won't say the noun "death," because death is a *condition*.

But the word "death" means *going home*. Death is a door . . . to . . . what is it? . . . "Joy" (quoting the Isaac Watts text now), "And yet we dread to enter there." But the idea of death doesn't bother me like it used to . . . (and now speaking of Sacred Harp singers) If there is a heaven—and there *is*—we know they're *there*.

The names of the deceased are mentioned again, with Mrs. Edwards commenting on those she knew. Mr. Lee Wells, a much-beloved, aged singer from Alabama is remembered especially: "He was a smooth and a graceful leader. Just before he died, he sat up on the Davenette and sang three songs—just as smooth and clear as he ever sang. He couldn't talk, but the Lord gave him voice to sing, and then he died."

She remarks again that death is a "going home," and reinforces her point: Mr. Wells, near death, could sing. She calls out the song she will lead, "Fleeting Days." Under her sure direction, the class sings with an effect that is not mournful, but measured and strong, with a full volume of sound:

> Our life is ever on the wing,
> And death is ever nigh;
> The moment when our lives begin
> We all begin to die.

At times the leader of the lesson will waive the singing of the syllables as a superficiality, all of the emphasis being directed in-stead to the import of the words from songs chosen especially for the occasion. In other instances, the notes may be used, as the leader deems it fitting to sing in memory of the deceased just as they had sung together in former times.

The memorial time is of course emotionally stirring of its own accord; but the singers are here vividly reminded of the death of many of their number, faithful in the tradition, for whom there appear to be no replacements. Painfully concerned as the singers are for the continuance of the singing even beyond their own knowledge of it, the list which is read at this time—often ten to twenty names in any given area—is like a bell that tolls the end of the singing itself. "We are passing away," they often sing, and they feel this truly.

It is also customary in many rural areas to have Sacred Harp singing at funerals. Here the singers around the community gather to sing before or during the funeral rites. Much like the volunteer firemen of another era, the singers in a locality are apt to regard this as civic duty, and they try, whenever possible, to help to "make a class." The preparations for such singing services are likely to be hurried and disorganized, and it is often difficult to summon an adequate number of singers from the community at short notice. As a result, the balance of parts and the quality of the singing are rarely up to par. If the singing in an area is weak, the faults will be magnified at such a time. Donald Davidson para-phrased a south Georgia singer's observation on the problem in this way: "Not so many folks could sing by the old way as there used to be. At a burying now, it was sometimes hard to find any-body to set a tune."[8]

Usually the singing on such occasions is rendered without the syllables. But to the uninitiated, this kind of singing, even without the notes, may appear strange, and the poorer quality of the sing-ing in general at these times probably does much to widen the breach of sympathy with Sacred Harp singing for those in the community but outside the tradition. For many others, these sounds, and the spirit they bring, help to render the occasion sacred; for them, the singing is as proper and natural as the cus-tomary scriptural reading and the words of the minister.

As with the decoration-day singings and the use of Sacred Harp songs at funerals, the conventions of the Sacred Harp have faded further into the background of ordinary life in the region. The Chattahoochee Musical Convention, the Mulberry River Convention, the Bear Creek, and the Warrior River conventions—these were once the focal points of the community's interest. Today they are noticed scarcely if at all by the majority of the citizens in the areas where they are held. But the Sacred Harp followers have their own channels of activity and communication, and for them the still-hearty conventions are the social highlights of the year. All of the singing associations are self-supporting—the officers simply pass a hat around—and a few of them carry enough money over each session to provide motel accommodations for visiting singers on the Saturday night between the two singing days. Singers around Newnan, Georgia, still remember a couple of elderly newlyweds who availed themselves of the hospitality of the United Convention when it met there one year. This just-married bride and groom drove into town for the singing and, cheerily sung to both days, enjoyed their honeymoon at the convention's expense.

In sum, the conventions bring the singing folk together from many localities and therefore offer a healthy communication, as well as the fellowship which is so important to the continued strength of the tradition. Most of all, they offer Sacred Harp singing at its best. This is what is meant when at a smaller, local session, with the singing going especially well, the class singing with unity and enthusiasm and volume, someone suddenly says—and the others nod in agreement—"Sounds just like a convention!"

6
The Outlook

At the present, the Sacred Harp appeals to a variety of interests for scholars and laymen alike. Newcomers are everywhere found in the midst of the Sacred Harp gatherings. They come to appraise, to marvel, and to learn; but perhaps above all, most of them come to enjoy. Some observers discover a storehouse of old music, strange harmonies, behavioral rituals. The interest for some is in the startling success of an unsophisticated system of sight reading by an unsophisticated people; for others, looking more generally, it is in the discovery of a "viable institution" by which generations pass on cultural values and a specialized knowledge with little to-do. Some undoubtedly come to indulge in a kind of cultural nostalgia, to form a link with a pleasing past. Some are attracted by the community demonstration of love and goodwill, the enjoyment of company and good food, or by a recreation that challenges and fulfills. Some come to bathe themselves in religious fundamentalism, the simple and fervent spirituality they sense all around. And finally there is the appeal of the deep and rollicking music itself, bearing the participants along in melody and rhythm by waves of sound.

Altogether the Sacred Harp tradition offers an amazing diversity of interests, and its longevity invites admiration. With the consolidation of so many practices from different eras, the Sacred Harp has reflected the way of the South—to some degree the way of early America and of the Old World. It has kept alive forms and customs that have disappeared elsewhere and, in many cases, have long since been forgotten. But what of the future? As the singing wavers between the strength that regenerates and the weakness that kills, singers and observers have to wonder if it will last. The past offers the first clues toward any partial answer.

It is an axiom often demonstrated that competition from with-out tends to produce unity within a group so threatened or chal-lenged. And this principle probably explains in some measure the uniform dedication of Sacred Harp adherents. Scorned for decades by the more progressive "seven-shapers," "round-heads," and "new-book" folk, Sacred Harp singers developed in defense an almost tribal sense of loyalty and responsibility to the movement. Yet more is involved than a periodic grouping of forces to halt the invasions of modernity. Variants of the fasola phenomenon have come and gone throughout the South at different times, but in contrast to most of the other movements, the long tradition of the Sacred Harp has significantly been recognized *as a tradition* by its participants. When W. M. Cooper said of the *Sacred Harp* in the preface to his 1902 edition that "the book has come to seem almost like a sacred thing," he was expressing what has been an elemental truth to a great number of people.

That this would be true is of course partially due to favorable cultural conditions, which allowed the tradition to form as it needed to, slowly and gradually. The steady stream, running un-obstructed through the years, left a deep imprint on an impression-able ground. And today the Sacred Harp people are well aware that they are part of a "phenomenon"; they need no cultural scholars from afar to tell them that theirs is a different cut from the prevailing way of life. As Jackson explained, "When one singer calls another one 'brother' or 'sister' and the older ones 'uncle' or 'aunt' it has a real and deep significance. It means that Sacred Harp singers feel themselves as belonging to one great family or clan. This feeling is without doubt deepened by the consciousness that they stand alone in their undertaking—keep-ing the old songs resounding in a world which has either gone over to lighter, more 'entertaining,' and frivolous types of song or has given up *all* community singing."[1]

Of many incidents which could be related, the "singing funeral" of T. J. Denson illustrates perhaps most vividly the unity of the Sacred Harp following and the intensity of their devotion. "Professor" Tom Denson, the well-beloved singing teacher and writer, died of a heart attack on Saturday, September 14, 1935, as he was readying himself to go to a singing. His funeral was held the next day at Fairview Cemetery in Double Springs, Winston County, Alabama, less than a week after the assassination of Huey Long. Imposing headlines in all the southern newspapers had told of Long's death, and for days thousands of awed citizens had filed past the funeral bier. In contrast, T. J. Denson died quietly and was buried in a matter of hours. Yet almost miraculously a great crowd of Sacred Harp singers, many from surrounding states, had arrived in Double Springs before the Sunday morning papers in the immediate area carried news of Denson's death. The news had been broadcast by radio stations in several key cities in the region and, from there, was passed on by word of mouth.

Many of the mourning singers had driven all night to arrive at the church in the hilly country of north Alabama in time for the funeral. By noon the line of cars seemed to those present to stretch almost infinitely on both sides of the road by the church, the modest building serving only as the focal point for such a crowd. Many floral wreaths were banked against the outside of the church, and the casket, with the family close by, was set in the open air. The singers, one of the family recalls, were spread out over three acres of land. The funeral was essentially a great singing in Denson's memory. One singer from Atlanta summed up the service by saying simply, "they read scripture and prayed, and then gave it to the singers." For two hours, in song after song, the large crowd of singers paid a stirring and appropriate tribute to the character and teaching of the Sacred Harp patriarch.

With the generations, the most notable and best-loved singing teachers and leaders like Uncle Tom Denson have passed into legend, and a century's rich history of song and friendship hallows the singing sessions and the book they celebrate. It is a tradition which, through story and memory, keeps the past near: stories of how Tom Denson would warn at the beginning of his singing schools, "If some of you don't like this music . . . all I've got to say to you is you'd better get out. If you stay here it's going to get a-hold of you and you *can't* get away," and of how "Uncle Shade" Barnett of Georgia would rap on the floor when a leader varied too much from what seemed the proper method of directing. The parents or grandparents of these present-day singers have relayed memories of B. F. White, "the embodiment of music"; of E. T. Pound and J. R. Turner in the heyday of the conventions; of J. N. Hutchenson of Salem, Alabama, "one of the most graceful singers that ever stood before a class"; of J. P. Reese, all of whose ten children were still living into the 1900's, occasioning J. S. James to speculate that "Providence has watched with special care over the offspring of this good and gifted man"; of James himself and his abiding affection for the shape-note singing he inherited; and of Absalom Ogletree, that venerable figure who stood at the center of Sacred Harp activity for three-quarters of a century, from the organization of the first convention in 1845 to well into the twentieth century.

James, for example, has left this reverent remembrance of Ogletree leading the difficult anthem "Claremont" at the Chatta-hoochee Convention in 1866 when James himself was but "a strip of a boy": "[He] did so without looking in the book, either to sing the words or the notes, and he repeated the entire five pages of this long tune with perfect ease and with great satisfaction to the large concourse of people present and credit to himself, and while he was singing the words of the same his eyes flashed and his countenance changed several times and accented the words as he spoke them. Any one at a reasonable distance could hear him speak the words distinctly, and we have heard many people speak of the elegant and impressive manner with which he rendered this piece of music."

Another testimonial to the strength and sufficiency of the Sacred Harp is that, while the majority of singings through the years have been held in churches or in other public buildings, private edifices were in a few instances constructed to house Sacred Harp singing. Odem's Chapel near St. Joseph, Tennessee, and Wilson's Chapel out of Carrollton, Georgia, are two of these. Odem's Chapel was built by Lonnie Odem, who also helped finance the 1936 Denson edition. One session a year is now scheduled at this location. With the decline of the singing in the area, the chapel does not echo to the Sacred Harp sound as strongly as it once did.

Wilson's Chapel in Carroll County, Georgia, has played a more important role. It has been the meeting place of the Chatta-hoochee Convention much of the time since 1938. When not petitioned for elsewhere, the Chattahoochee automatically returns to Wilson's Chapel. And in 1973 and 1975, with the Chattahoochee holding its sessions in another community, spokesmen for the Wilson family requested and were granted the right to host the sessions of the United Convention for those years. The chapel was erected by Matthew Wilson in the 1930s, Wilson himself doing all of the labor, even making the benches. Today both Wilson and his wife are buried in the yard nearby. (The building has been kept up by the Wilson family since Wilson's death in 1940 and was brick veneered in the 1960s.) Just off a narrow dirt road in a wooded setting, the chapel is little different from the one-room country churches in which the singers seem most at home. But no pulpit is in evidence—only benches, arranged in the pattern for group singing set almost two centuries ago. Long tables stand in the trees at back, ready to be laden with food when the crowds come again to sing.

There may one day be no activity at all in the chapels built for Sacred Harp singing. But even if the Sacred Harp ceases to exist, it will have brought up through the late twentieth century, to a generation which at least has begun to give it a deserving recognition, a vestige of culture from the past. And it may offer to a future generation, as Irving Lowens suggests, qualities which should be emulated. "Our folk-hymnody," Lowens has written, "is, of course, significant as a written record of the exact state of

the American singing tradition in the first half of the 19th century, but completely aside from its historical interest, it is a body
of music of great individuality, genuine merit, and melodic charm.
It is possibly the most valuable musical heritage that has come
down to us from early American times."[2] Lowens feels, as a number of other scholars do, that this "obsolete" music offers much
that is worthy of being incorporated into our present culture: "It
is my belief that the music that grew from the singing-school tradition has pertinence and significance in today's world and promise for tomorrow's. It is no mere historical curiosity, no mere
recovered treasure-trove of a musical antiquarian. It is rather a
new source from which our congregational song may perhaps draw
inspiration, strength, and vigor."[3]

But what of the singing tradition that surrounds the songs? As
the movement falters in the hands of the folk, should it be sheltered by the academic community? Certainly the singers, always
hopeful of a resurgence of interest, are from time to time heartened
by reports that their music is being taught in a few schools and
colleges. But a folklorist like Donald Davidson could be skeptical
about such experiments. Davidson questioned "whether we dare
risk the cherishing of folk song by the schools as a planned and
definite part of the school program itself." "The schools have been
so guilty of diluting and vulgarizing what they attempt to convey," he wrote, "that I am almost ready to say that they should
not be trusted with this precious heritage. I am tempted to declare
that I would rather risk leaving the preservation of folk song to
the old, anonymous, accidental process, even under perilous modern conditions, than to give it a place in a curricular or activities
program administered by the certificated products of our higher
educational institutions."[4]

It is probably true that the Sacred Harp, as a composite of folk
ways, could not exist in such a clinical situation. The Sacred Harp
songs may be transplanted, but the tradition itself can not be. It is
not at last the body of printed songs in the book that constitutes
the Sacred Harp, but rather the whole ritualized tradition that

envelopes the music, transforming it into a living enactment of the past. And this can not be simulated. Nor can the tradition stand apart from an appreciation of the religious nature of the songs and the inspiration for praise found therein. For the all-day Sacred Harp singing has always been, as well as social gathering and musical activity, a form of worship peculiar to those who engage in it.

There is a delight in and a feeling for this music that can not be transferred either. At a Sacred Harp session when the singing has reached a certain level—when the singers respond wholly to the music—it is almost as if they are only receptacles, vessels for some-thing age-old which lives again through them. As the old songs well up through and around them, the singers submit to the effects of the music with a kind of awe. Carl Carmer recognized this quality in the singing he observed in the 1930s: "In the front row a slim brown-eyed girl in an orange dress was throwing her head from side to side in the rhythm. Her black hair had fallen from a knot at the back of her neck, and flew about her face. She was gasping for breath. The silence that followed was restless. No one spoke, but there was much turning of pages—as if they were avoiding looking at each other. Relentlessly the perfesser drove them into the next song." When the singers adjourned for lunch, in this account, "the men and women who crowded out of the door were not the grim taciturn lot who had entered it. A note almost of hysteria sounded in their laughter. They seemed to be glad of escape—still a little fearful." And when they returned, Carmer records, "the restless feeling, the suppressed excitement returned."[5] It is the nature of this response, finally, that has fused the singers to the tradition through the years, and it is this quality also that can not accompany the songs in an academic situation.

Is this then the last generation that will sustain the old ways? It is the older people who make up the largest proportion at most singings, and the predominant number of aged singers was a fea-ture Jackson noted and despaired of forty years ago. But not all of the singers see this as a problem. Mr. L. L. Welborn holds that

the attendance at the singings has always leaned proportionately
to the older folk. He feels, as a number of the singers do from
personal experience, that the young people in the tradition have
often not responded to it until later in life. As Mr. Welborn remarks, "They came back to it as they grew older—they could see
the beauty, feel the power in it." Moving testimony in this regard
comes from another one of the Sacred Harp stalwarts, a man who,
like his father before him, has assumed the major responsibility for
shoring up the tradition in his entire area. This genial, respected
singer follows the singing far and wide and generously gives to the
fostering of the music he loves. But it was not always so. At the
close of one all-day gathering, he told of how he was once unsym-
pathetic to his father's devotion to the same cause. "I had to take
my daddy to singings all the time," he reflected, ". . . all over the
country. And I got so tired of it. I was glad when he died that I
wouldn't have to take him to those singings any more. But he laid
it on me. And to get peace of mind, I had to start singing those
old songs too."

It is not uncommon to see, here and there, enthusiastic sixty-
year-old beginners at the singing schools of today, persons who
once knew this singing at a distance and perhaps even put in a
session or two under a shape-note singing master, but never until
now pursued the discipline. It is as if the seeds that were once
planted in the minds of these late-comers have lain dormant all
these years; now warmed by some imperceptible influence, they
come alive and grow. And potential singers, long thought lost,
return to this tradition with a convert's zeal, reinvigorating the
others.

Perhaps, then, the rural children today who have attended the
singing schools and have not been heard from subsequently, will
with age return to the singing as their ancestors have done. Perhaps reverence for tradition and a nostalgia for the sounds that
are ingrained in the subconsciousness will draw them back, so that
thirty or forty years from now they will be not only singing the
old melodies but also turning over their children and grandchildren

to one of their number for instruction in the antique set of singing "rudiments."

Much of the strength of the Sacred Harp in the past has been a result of the singers' determination to pass on their beloved heritage to their descendants. J. A. Ayers, a retired bricklayer of Bowdon, Georgia, whose bass voice is almost legendary, recalled that his father bribed him to go to singing school with the promise, for the trip, of the father's best horse and buggy. And the late Elizabeth McCain Driver of Bremen, Georgia, told of how her mother, Mrs. B. T. Huggins of Carroll County, used to sing the Sacred Harp songs to the children as she churned milk: "She would sit there churning and sing and sing. She was so afraid she wouldn't raise a single singer." One of the marvels of family participation has been the McGraw clan of west Georgia. Today this family finds pride in the fact that almost all of the children, grandchildren, and great-grandchildren of the present generation can sing. Buford McGraw of Mount Zion, Georgia, himself a father and grandfather of singers, is quick to say, "We McGraws drown 'em if they don't sing." But behind the teasing facade of that explanation lies a remarkable family rapport in which the dedication and loving spirit of the elders inspire conformity among the youngsters.

More remarkable still is the Wootten family from around Ider, Alabama. Seven brothers and sisters, who still live within twenty miles of one another, inherited a love of this music from their father and mother. They were also blessed with good and strong voices. From childhood up, they sang together and with other relatives. The music of the Sacred Harp was and is a part of their daily lives. Their children, and in turn *their* children, have continued to prefer this music over any other kind. When the Wootten family gets together—with as many as thirty singers at one time—they form the core of perhaps the strongest community of Sacred Harp singers in the land. And with the youngest generation eagerly taking on the discipline of the singing school, the promise of the future is renewed.

Yet despite the perseverance of the singers and the strong family influence, the number of those who can sing this four-shape music is dwindling. As Jackson observed on the one-hundredth year of the Sacred Harp in 1944, "The Sacred Harp *may* persist another century. But it will be a wonder if it does."[6] The provincial southern areas, the final sanctuaries of this song tradition, are fast shrinking, and the old way of life, still preserved in many rural areas up through this time, seems doomed to eventual upheaval. Television and automobiles have undermined the young people's interest in a diversion which once, with the Saturday night hoedown, was about the only community recreation many rural folk knew.

But if modernism is winning the struggle with the fasola clan, it has also allowed them some consolation. Apparently doomed forty years ago, the Sacred Harp has caught a second wind, and it seems to have done this in part by using the very tools of that modernism that threatens it. While the singers today are far less numerous than those of an earlier era, many of the singings are just as vigorous, and the list of yearly sessions in some communities is growing rather than decreasing. Modern automobiles are enabling the singers from a wide area to converge in a matter of hours for a singing, while this same event would once have attracted the folk in the immediate area only. Recording equipment also has been a boon, allowing the Sacred Harpers to hear fasola singing at any time they wish. The Sacred Harp Publishing Company has produced six record albums. The last of these, a bicentennial record of early Sacred Harp music, was recorded in Birmingham, Alabama, where some two hundred singers met to participate in the open session. Several other records have been in general use as well. One distributor of the albums reported that singers in her area who had never owned a record player purchased one for these records alone. And at singings in any vicinity one or more tape recorders are usually in evidence.

For as long as they can remember, the Sacred Harp adherents have been hearing that their singing is a dying art. And, to be sure, the life of the tradition is a continuing concern for them. Still, in the middle of a class at one of the big sessions it is difficult to be pessimistic. At the courthouse singing in Cullman, Alabama, in July 1972 a Mr. Smith, over ninety years old, was called before the group to lead at the height of that day's session. After leading a song without the aid of a book, Mr. Smith recounted that he had been hearing for decades that "this old music is a-dyin'." With the gusto of a man half his years, he stirred the crowd by shaking his fist and proclaiming, "It ain't even *sick* yet!" Since the time that George Pullen Jackson first called attention to the existence of the fasola movement, Sacred Harp singers have appeared at folk festivals and similar programs over the country. Groups who sing the shape-note melodies have been brought to perform for banquets, church services, and radio programs. Today, Sacred Harp books and records are mailed all over the United States and to foreign countries. Interest from outside the movement is at an all-time high.

Members of folklore societies, colleges, and seminaries across the country are initiating Sacred Harp songfests. And in New England particularly the Sacred Harp seems on the brink of a renaissance—with regularly scheduled singings held in an area encompassing Boston, Philadelphia, New York, and parts of Vermont and Connecticut. In October 1976 fifty traditional singers from Georgia and Alabama chartered a bus to Middletown, Connecticut, for a singing hosted by Wesleyan University. Sacred Harp enthusiasts from several New England states also attended the rousing session, which provided a healthy and exciting cultural exchange. The 1977 reprise of this event set for Montpelier, Vermont, generated plans for a similar bus tour, with reservations filled six months in advance by southern fasola-ers anxious to share their music and watch it take hold. A group of singing fans in Boston has requested the following year's session of this now annual "New England Sacred Harp Singing Convention."

And yet the flush of new success may in a way be illusory. It could be said that the flower is being cultivated and the roots themselves neglected. It does little for the strength of the tradition to give the Sacred Harp broad exposure if the young at home are not being drawn into the movement. The fact that students at Harvard or Berkeley find this music engaging will not help much if the boys and girls in Haleyville, Alabama, or Tallapoosa, Georgia, are not interested in learning to sing it. In addition, the ease with which the singers can now attend the large conventions may spell the end for many of the small community singings. W. A. Parker, the general secretary for the *Directory and Min-utes*, sounded a warning in this regard in his open letter to "the Sacred Harp family" which prefaced the 1968–1969 minutes pub-lication. He noted the tendency of many to "leave or pass up community singings in order to attend a 'big' singing miles away." There can be no objections to attending the best singings, he granted, "and yet I believe the life of the Sacred Harp cause lies in the development of more community singings." For Mr. Parker and others in the tradition, it is not at the folk festival or through the record player but in the community setting alone that the Sacred Harp either lives or dies. And thus the singing schools and the traditional community singings of the rural South take on a greater significance than ever before.

Whether it falters or is somehow sustained, the Sacred Harp has been and is a proud and distinctive American institution. For vigor in group participation, for joy in song and community rap-port, it would seem to have no parallel in American life. Perhaps more than any other descriptive passage, Donald Davidson's essay on the Sacred Harp catches the essence of the exceptional appeal of this folk tradition:

Brother Oakes was a good leader. He tolerated no dragging. He swept all along—singers and crowd alike—with the strong trumpet of his voice carrying the air and the bulk of his great body that put out a commanding arm to wave us into the deep rhythm of the antique spiritual music. He knew words and tune by heart. He could fa-sol-la the tune with hardly a glance at the book. The songs of *The Sacred Harp* were a life that he lived, burningly and familiarly. Chosen by him, the songs went beckoning into the woods and fetched the people in. And they came in, leaving no bench unfilled, clustering at the doors and beyond.[7]

It is not Davidson's graceful prose alone that commends this portrait so to the imagination. It is the glimpse which it allows of a deep and genuine pleasure that has all but escaped contemporary society.

The future of the Sacred Harp is not assured, and in some areas the prospects already appear dim. But Sacred Harp singers are counting on the endurance of their tradition, are hoping that other generations will take up these songs and make of themselves communities of singers. And in the meantime they sing on, making their "joyful noise."

Appendix A
Traditional Sacred Harp Singings
Dates and Locations

The following is a list, doubtless the only one ever made, of Sacred Harp singings from all the revisions of the *Sacred Harp* song book. An effort was made to include all traditional singings (excepting those by folklore societies, college groups, or others beyond the scope of this study), but there are probably additional sessions whose existence is not known outside of the immediate area where they occur. Twenty-three separate pamphlets of minutes of Sacred Harp singing (several of these with very limited circulation) were consulted in formulating this list. Many other sessions not elsewhere recorded were related by Sacred Harp singers who for years had attended these or had heard them announced at singings.

The scene of Sacred Harp singing is a fluctuating one. Some sessions included here will probably have ceased to exist as soon as this list is published, and new ones will have been created. But the great majority of the singings have been occurring annually for years and can be expected to continue. Additionally, the list should help to show the spread and persistence of this tradition. Ten or more sessions occur simultaneously in the various states on half the Sundays in the year, and on at least six dates there are fifteen or more singings held. Some of the singings move from one location to another, as they are called for by interested communities or churches, and are marked in the list accordingly. Locations for the other sessions, when known, are given.

Most singings are scheduled and calculated with the Sundays of the month as the base. Thus a singing will be scheduled for the first Sunday of the month, the Wednesday night after the second Sunday, the Saturday before the third Sunday. Most two-day conventions are set according to the Sunday date instead of the Saturday date. If, for example, the first Sunday in June occurs on June 1, then the Saturday session of the Holly Springs Singing of the Denson revision group (set for the first Sunday in June and Saturday before) will occur on May 31.

The singings are divided here into sections according to the five overall groups of the Sacred Harp: Denson-book singings by white singers, Denson-book singings by black singers, Cooper-book singings by white singers, Cooper-book singings by black singers, and White-book singings. Within each section, entries are divided into annual sessions and other (monthly or irregular) sessions and then arranged chronologically.

Denson-Book Singings (White Singers)

Annual Sessions

January

NEW YEAR'S DAY   Pisgah Baptist Church, Highway 77, 1 mile north of Sipsey, Alabama.

1ST SUN.   Original Dutch Treat Singing, moves.

Dutch Treat Singing, Shady Grove Church, 3 miles north of Double Springs, Alabama.

Mount High Church, 7 miles west of Warrior, Alabama.

SAT.   Birthday Singing, Boldo Community, 6 miles east of Jasper, Ala.

2ND SUN.   Uncle John Kerr Memorial, Community Building, Cross Roads, north of Fruithurst, Alabama.

County Line Church, 10 miles west of Warrior, Alabama.

3RD SUN.   Odom Memorial Baptist Church, 3 miles south of Parrish, Ala.

Mount Moriah Baptist Church, 4 miles southeast of Fyffe, Ala.

SAT.   First Baptist Church, 806 Government Street, Mobile, Ala.

4TH SUN.   Barton's Chapel, 3 miles from Lynn's Park, Alabama.

February

1ST SUN.   Recreation Center, Jacksonville, Alabama.

Mount Hope Church, 4 miles northeast of Sipsey, Alabama.

2ND SUN.   Macedonia Baptist Church, Highway 195, on Farm-to-Market Road, near Haleyville and Needmore, Alabama.

Liberty Hill Baptist Church, Highway 75, then west on 26, 5 miles north of Oneonta, Alabama.

Zion Rest Primitive Baptist Church, Highway 69, Jasper, Ala.

3RD SUN.   East Side School, Highway 120, 5 miles east of Marietta, Ga.

Hopewell Primitive Baptist Church, 6 miles e. of Oneonta, Ala.

Sardis Primitive Baptist Church, Highway 78, just south of Lynn's Park, Alabama.

4TH SUN.   Rocky Mount Church, 1 mile south of Daviston, Alabama.

Mount Carmel Primitive Baptist Church, old 78 Highway, 2 miles north on Wolf Creek Road, Eden, Alabama.

March

1ST SUN.   Ephesus School Auditorium, Ephesus, Georgia.

Mount Olive Primitive Baptist Church, Highway 157, Cullman, Alabama.

New Flatwoods Church, Highway 11, 3 miles south of Nauvoo, Alabama.

Salem Church, 5 miles southwest of Gordo, Alabama.

2ND SUN.   Choccolocco Primitive Baptist Church, North Noble Street, near intersection with Highway 43, Anniston, Alabama.

Elvister Church, north of Highway 121 to Trafford, east of Warrior, Alabama.

Stewart Chapel, Highway 15, 1 mile north of courthouse, Houston, Mississippi.

FRI. NGT.   Stephenson and Wall Memorial, Pleasant Grove Primitive Baptist Church, Boldo Community, 6 miles northeast of Jasper, Alabama, on Highway 69.

3RD SUN.   Antioch Methodist Church, Highway 49, Heflin, Alabama.

Mount Pleasant Church, 9 miles east of Boaz, Alabama, and 2 miles south of Crossville, Alabama.

Pleasant Hill Primitive Baptist Church, Highway 363, 5 miles northwest of Fulton, Mississippi.

Union Hill Missionary Baptist Church, 2 miles west of Townley, Alabama.

Rocky Mount Church, 1 mile south of Daviston, Alabama.

SAT. & 4TH SUN.   Georgia State Convention, moves.

4TH SUN.   Bethlehem Church, Highway 35, 1 mile s.w. of Gallant, Ala.

Butler Memorial, Good Hope Primitive Baptist Church, Westside Community, 10 miles southeast of Lawrenceburg, Tenn.

Harmony Baptist Church, Highway 195, 8 miles north of Jasper, Alabama.

April

1ST SAT. AFTER EASTER   Harpeth Presbyterian Church, Hillsboro Road, Highway 43 between Franklin and Nashville, Tennessee.

1ST SUN.   Edwardsville Missionary Baptist Church, Highway 78, 6 miles east of Heflin, Alabama.

Old Enon Church, north of Lynn, Alabama.

Pleasant Hope Primitive Baptist Church, Highway 75, Snead Cross Roads, Alabama.

Pleasant Ridge Church, Highway 159, 11 miles northwest of Gordo, Alabama.

Providence Primitive Baptist Church, Highway 8, near Hayden, Alabama.

Providence Church, Ashland, Alabama.

Bethel Church, Bruce, Mississippi.

Mount Pisgah Church, Chambers County, Alabama.

2ND SUN. Antioch Baptist Church, west of Highway 75, 8 miles north of Ider, Alabama (DeKalb County).

Old County Line Church, 9 miles west of Warrior, Alabama.

Beech Grove, 2 miles s.e. of Haleyville, Ala., off Highway 5.

Second Creek Church, Highway 101, 6 miles southeast of Loretto, Tennessee.

State Line Church, 2 miles off Highway 78, Ga.-Ala. line.

Fellowship Church, Alexander City, Alabama.

Oak Grove Primitive Baptist Church, 12 miles north of Roswell at Birmingham, Georgia.

3RD SUN. Concord Primitive Baptist Church, Highway 113, 3 miles north of Carrollton, Georgia.

Old Union Baptist Church, Highway 107, 8 miles southwest of Winfield, Alabama.

Liberty Church, 7 miles south of Gordo, Alabama.

Pine Grove Church, east of Highway 11, 4 miles south of Collinsville, Alabama.

Livingston Chapel, Highway 22, 2 miles w. of Crane Hill, Ala.

Old Harmony, Highway 46, 8 miles south of Heflin, Alabama.

Rocky Mount Primitive Baptist Church, Highway 69, 3 miles east of Arab, Alabama.

Shiloh-Delta Church, Lineville, Alabama.

Ephesus Church, Fairfax, Alabama.

Old Valley Grove Church, 5 miles west of Ocilla, Georgia.

Enon Primitive Baptist Church, near Houston, Mississippi.

4TH SUN. Friendship Church, 2 miles off Highway 195, 8 miles southeast of Haleyville, Alabama.

Mount Moriah Primitive Baptist Church, Highway 75, 5 miles south of Snead Cross Roads, Alabama.

Providence Baptist Church, Highway 35, 8 miles northeast of Cullman, Alabama.

Antioch Primitive Baptist Church, s. of Carrollton, Georgia, at Banning, Georgia, off Newnan Highway.

Liberty Primitive Baptist Church, Childersburg, Alabama.

May

1ST SUN. Hopewell Primitive Baptist Church, Vance Road, 1 mile west of West Blockton, Alabama.

Oneonta Courthouse, Oneonta, Alabama.

Bethel Church, near Dime, Alabama.

Shady Grove Church, Keeton Cemetery, Highway 11, Nauvoo to Carbon Hill, Alabama.

Antioch Missionary Baptist Church, Ashbridge, Alabama.

Old Shady Grove Baptist Church, off Highway 71, near Dutton, Alabama.

Mount Zion Church, Ashland, Alabama.

Pea Ridge School House, Pea Ridge, 6 miles west of Hammondville, Alabama.

Poplar Springs Baptist Church, Calhoun County, Mississippi.

2ND SUN. Cross Roads Baptist Church, Highway 78, 3 miles east of Heflin, Alabama.

Mount Moriah Baptist Church, Calhoun County, Mississippi.

Mount Olive Primitive Baptist Church, Highway 183, Perry County, west of Maplesville, Alabama.

Old Flatwoods Primitive Baptist Church, 3 miles south of Nauvoo, Alabama.

SAT. Mattox Memorial, Harmony Church, 4 miles north of Lawrenceburg, Tennessee.

SAT. & 3RD SUN. Rocky Mount Church, 1 mile south of Daviston, Ala.

3RD SUN. New Canaan Church, near Empire, Alabama.

Poplar Springs Missionary Baptist Church, 4 miles north of Tallapoosa, Georgia, on Highway 100.

Zion Hill Primitive Baptist Church, near Snead Cross Roads, Alabama.

Concord Baptist Church, Calhoun County, Mississippi.

Cane Creek Church, 3 miles e. of Heflin, Ala. on Highway 78.

Lomax Primitive Baptist Church, Chilton County, Alabama.

SAT. Ashville Courthouse, Ashville, Alabama.

4TH SUN. Pleasant Grove Primitive Baptist Church, Highway 69, 5 miles northeast of Jasper, Alabama, at Boldo community.

Bethlehem Church, Heard Avenue South, Macon, Georgia.

Darien Church, Wadley, Alabama.

Gum Pond Church, 18 miles northeast of Cullman, Alabama, in Morgan County.

Providence Baptist Church, 3 miles s.w. of Tallapoosa, Ga.

Pilgrim Rest Church, 10 miles west of Carrollton, Alabama.

Doss Memorial, Sardis Church, 3 miles west of Highway 31 at Morris, Alabama.

Sullins School House, Highway 69, 8 miles n. of Hamilton, Ala.

June

SAT. Shady Grove Church, Wilburn, Alabama.

SAT. & 1ST SUN. Holly Springs Primitive Baptist Church, Highway 27, 2 miles south of Bremen, Georgia.

1ST SUN. Bethel Church, 8 miles south of Caledonia, Mississippi, in Lamar County, Alabama.

Liberty Church, 2 miles n. of Henagar, Ala. off Highway 40.

Ephesus Church, New Site, Alabama.

Fellowship Church, Highway 278, 8 miles w. of Cullman, Ala.

Union Primitive Baptist Church, off Highway 140, 5 miles east of Roswell, Georgia.

Pine Tucky Church, 5 miles south of Double Springs, Alabama.

Sherman Baptist Church, Calhoun County, Mississippi.

Shiloh United Primitive Baptist Church, Highway 11, 5 miles southwest of Attalla, Alabama.

SAT. & 2ND SUN. Hopewell Primitive Baptist Church, 6 miles east of Oneonta, Alabama.

2ND SUN. Mount Grove Baptist Church, Randolph County, Alabama.

Fellowship Church, Alexander City, Alabama.

Alpharetta Municipal Auditorium, Alpharetta, Georgia.

Pilgrim's Rest Church, DeKalb County, Alabama.

Harmony Church, near Empire, Alabama.

Johnson School House, Highway 44, 7 miles southwest of Carbon Hill, Alabama.

Mount Vernon Primitive Baptist Church, 13 miles northeast of Cullman, Alabama, on Highway 69.

Riverside Primitive Baptist Church, Highway 78, 2 miles west of Tallapoosa, Georgia.

Oak Springs Church, Calhoun County, Mississippi.

Mount Olive Baptist Church, 20th Street, Rome, Georgia.

New Hope Primitive Baptist Church, 1 mile east of Villa Rica, Georgia, on Highway 78.

SAT.   Addington Chapel, Bremen, Alabama.

3RD SUN.   Cross Roads Church, off Highway 5, 4 miles east of Wood-stock, Georgia.

Valley Grove, near Goldville, Alabama.

St. Michael Church, 4 miles north of Fruithurst, Alabama.

Hopewell Primitive Baptist Church, 2 miles east of school at Ephesus, Georgia.

King School House, Highway 278, 3 miles n.w. of Lynn, Ala.

Little Vine Church, near Empire, Alabama.

Carey Springs Church, Pontotoc County, Mississippi.

Pleasant Valley Church, 4 miles south of Gallant, Alabama.

Macedonia Church, 4 miles south of Section, Alabama.

SAT. & 4TH SUN.   Shady Grove Church, Highway 195, 4 miles north of Double Springs, Alabama.

4TH SUN.   Indian Creek Baptist Church, Highway 100, 4 miles north of Bowdon, Georgia.

New Hope Primitive Baptist Church, 12 miles northeast of Jasper, Alabama.

Andrews School, 1 mile off Thomaston-Yatesville Highway, Georgia.

DeLong Memorial, Ebenezer Primitive Baptist Church, Spaulding Drive, Fulton County, Georgia.

Mount Lebanon Church, 8 miles northwest of Fayette, Ala.

New Harmony Church, 5 miles south of Joppa, Alabama.

New Hope Church, Highway 278, 5 miles south of Jones Chapel in Cullman County, Alabama.

Bethany Church, Mountain community, Clay County, Ala.

July

JULY 3   Gauley Free Will Baptist Church, Calhoun County, Miss.

JULY 4   Liberty Baptist Church, near Helicon, Alabama.

Camp Branch Methodist Church, Shelby County, Alabama.

Mount Zion Church, Ashland, Alabama.

Shady Grove Church, Highway 195, n. of Double Springs, Ala.

Mount Herman Primitive Baptist Church, Calhoun County, Mississippi.

SAT. & 1ST SUN. Henagar Union Convention, Liberty Church, off Highway 40, 2 miles north of Henagar, Alabama.

1ST SUN. Bethlehem United Baptist Church, Highway 35, 1 mile southwest of Gallant, Alabama.

(EXCEPT ON JULY 3 OR 4) Antioch Primitive Baptist Church, Oxford, Mississippi.

Cross Roads Baptist Church, 9 miles north of Tallapoosa, Georgia, off Highway 100.

Pleasant Hill Church, 1 mile s.w. of Warner Robbins, Ga.

New Flatwoods Baptist Church, south of Highway 11 and 3 miles south of Nauvoo, Alabama.

Cold Springs Baptist Church, 17 miles southwest of Cullman, Alabama, at Wilburn.

FRI. NGT. Mount Vernon Church, Highway 4, near Curry High School, Jasper, Alabama.

SAT. & 2ND SUN. Cullman County Convention, Cullman Courthouse, Cullman, Alabama.

2ND SUN. El Bethel, Caledonia, Mississippi.

Providence Church, Calhoun County, Mississippi.

Mount Zion Church, Highway 159, 18 miles n. of Gordo, Ala.

Pleasant Grove Primitive Baptist Church, 5 miles west of Buchanan, Georgia.

3RD FRI. NGT. Picnic Sing, off Highway 100, between Bowdon and Tallapoosa, Georgia.

SAT. & 3RD SUN. Hillabee Convention, Rocky Mount Church, 1 mile south of Daviston, Alabama.

Walker County Convention, T. R. Simmons School, Jasper, Alabama.

3RD SUN. Mount Oak Church, 5 miles northeast of Arab, Alabama.

Mount Carmel Church, 5 miles east of Millport, Alabama.

Big Creek Church, Highway 120, 5 miles e. of Alpharetta, Ga.

Mount Zion Church, DeKalb County, near Fyffe, Alabama.

Mount Paran Church, 7 miles north of Fruithurst, Alabama.

Chafin, Harbison and Hollis Singing, New Prospect Church, 3 miles east of Bremen, Alabama.

Subligna Baptist Church, 5 miles south of Summerville, Ga.

SAT. & 4TH SUN. Cotaco Convention, Alabama, moves.

Alabama State Convention, Alabama, moves.

Mount Zion Methodist Church, west of Carrollton at Mount Zion, Georgia.

4TH SUN.   Macedonia Homecoming and Singing, Macedonia Church, Ashland, Alabama.

Courthouse, Hamilton, Alabama.

Dorsey Creek Church, Highway 69, 15 miles southwest of Cullman, Alabama.

Chickasaw County Convention, Mississippi, moves.

August

SAT.   Webster County Convention, Mississippi, moves.

SAT. & 1ST SUN.   Chattahoochee Convention, Georgia, moves.

FRI., SAT., & 1ST SUN.   Warrior River Convention, Alabama, moves.

1ST SUN.   Calvert Memorial, Johnson Grove Methodist Church, Bremen, Alabama.

Fayette County, Brewer State Junior College, Fayette, Ala.

FRI., SAT., & 2ND SUN   Calhoun County Convention, Mississippi, moves.

SAT. & 2ND SUN.   Tennessee River Convention, Second Creek Church, Highway 101, 6 miles southeast of Loretto, Tennessee.

North Alabama Convention, moves.

Lamar and Pickens County Convention, Zion Church, Highway 159, 8 miles north of Gordo, Alabama.

2ND SUN.   New Harmony Baptist Church, Highway 43, 2 miles southwest of Phil Campbell, Alabama.

Tallapoosa Convention, School Auditorium, Tallapoosa, Ga.

Rocky Mount Primitive Baptist Church, Highway 69, 3 miles east of Arab, Alabama.

Georges Chapel, Chickasaw County, Mississippi.

WED.   Elmore Center, 3 miles south of Gordo, Alabama.

FRI., SAT., & 3RD SUN.   Cleburne County Convention, Alabama, moves.

SAT. & 3RD SUN.   Boiling Springs Convention, Alabama, moves.

Rock Creek Mountain Home Convention, Alabama, moves.

3RD SUN.   Cedar Creek Church, Cordele-Albany Highway, 9 miles southwest of Cordele, Georgia.

Odem's Chapel, Highway 43, 2 miles n. of St. Joseph, Tenn.

Concord Primitive Baptist Church, County Road 14, Winfield, Alabama.

SAT. & 4TH SUN.   Bear Creek Convention, Shady Grove Church, Highway 195, 3 miles north of Double Springs, Alabama.

Calhoun County Convention, Alabama, moves.

Tallapoosa County Convention, Rocky Mount Primitive Baptist Church, 1 mile south of Daviston, Alabama.

Ryan's Creek Convention, Alabama, moves.

Lookout Mountain Convention, Pine Grove Church, east of Highway 11 and 4 miles south of Collinsville, Alabama.

Mississippi State Convention, moves in Mississippi. Cooper book also used.

4TH SUN.   Cherry Tree Convention, James Creek Primitive Baptist Church, 4 miles south of Highway 78 on state-line road, Itawamba County, Mississippi.

Mount Carmel Church, Highway 80, 7 miles west of Roberta, Georgia.

September

LABOR DAY Myers and Davis Memorial, Corinth Church, Wilburn, Ala.

Shady Grove Church, 2 miles east of Florence, Alabama, on Lee Highway.

Shoal Creek Church, 10 miles north of Heflin, Alabama.

SAT. & 1ST SUN.   Mulberry River Convention, Alabama, moves.

Clear Creek Convention (east), Alabama, moves.

1ST SUN.   Clear Creek Convention (west), Alabama, moves.

Little Vine Primitive Baptist Church, Highway 78, 3 miles east of Bremen, Georgia.

Haynes Creek Church, Highway 79, west of Loganville, Ga.

Fellowship Church, Alexander City, Alabama.

SAT. & 2ND SUN.   United Musical Association, moves.

2ND SUN.   Mountain Home Church, Highway 241 south, 3 miles southwest of Bear Creek, Alabama.

Hartsfield Church, 10 miles west of Moultrie, Georgia.

White Hill Church, Webster County, Mississippi.

Center Springs Baptist Church, off Highway 79, 3 miles southwest of Locust Fork, Alabama.

SAT. NGT.   Johnson School House, near Bremen, Alabama.

3RD SUN.   Blooming Grove Church, 4 miles north of Crossville Village in Lamar County, Alabama.

Choccolocco Primitive Baptist Church, North Noble Street, Anniston, Alabama.

Nix Memorial, Logan Baptist Church, Highway 11, Logan, Alabama.

Salem Baptist Church, near, Altoona, Alabama.

Shady Grove, Highway 11, Walker County, Alabama.

Second Creek Church, Highway 101, 6 miles southeast of Loretto, Tennessee.

4TH SUN.   Daniel Memorial, Cold Springs Primitive Baptist Church, 3 miles south of Winston, Georgia.

Emmaus Church, Thomaston, Georgia.

Ashland Courthouse, Ashland, Alabama.

Pleasant Hill Church, Roswell, Georgia.

Gum Pond, 18 miles northeast of Cullman, Alabama, in Morgan County.

Liberty Hill Church, 9 miles east of Boaz, Alabama.

Winston County Convention, Shady Grove Church, 3 miles north of Double Springs, Alabama.

Air Mount Primitive Baptist Church, Yalobusha County, Mississippi.

SAT. NEAREST OCT. 1   Birthday Sing, County Line Church, 10 miles west of Warrior, Alabama.

October

1ST SUN.   Old Sardis Church, 3 miles north of Lynn, Alabama.

Hopewell Primitive Baptist Church, 6 miles e. of Oneonta, Ala.

Sandy Creek Primitive Baptist Church, 1 mile s. of Flovilla, Ga.

Emmaus Primitive Baptist Church, 4 miles south of Carrollton, Georgia, off Highway 27.

2ND SUN.   Recreation Hall, Gadsden, Alabama.

Denson Memorial, Methodist Church, junction Highways 41 and 278, Addison, Alabama.

Eureka Church, 12 miles east of Sycamore, Georgia.

Alpine Baptist Church, Chilton County, Alabama.

Old Flatwoods Primitive Baptist Church, off Highway 11, 3 miles south of Nauvoo, Alabama.

Chestnut Grove Baptist Church, 3 miles southeast of Ider junction on Highway 117, Ider, Alabama.

Loyd Baptist Church, Calhoun County, Mississippi.

Muscadine Methodist Church, Muscadine, Alabama.

3RD SUN.   Fellowship Primitive Baptist Church, Highway 278, 8 miles west of Cullman, Alabama.

Rocky Mount Church, 1 mile south of Daviston, Alabama.

Little Hope Primitive Baptist Church, off Highway 82, 3 miles west of Eoline, Alabama, in Bibb County.

Little Branch Primitive Baptist Church, Albertville, Alabama.

McWhorter Memorial, Mars Hill Primitive Baptist Church, off Highway 78, Cleburne County, Alabama.

Reid Memorial, Old County Line Church, 10 miles west of Warrior, Alabama.

SAT. & 4TH SUN.   Joe Myers Memorial, New Hope Church, off Highway 69, 12 miles northeast of Jasper, Alabama.

4TH SUN.   Rice Community, 3 miles west of Arab, Alabama.

Jordan's Chapel Methodist Church, off Highway 431, Randolph County, near Milner, Alabama.

Mount Moriah Church, Highway 75, 5 miles south of Snead Cross Roads, Alabama.

November

SAT.   Social Religious Building, Peabody College, Nashville, Tenn.

1ST SUN.   Holly Springs Primitive Baptist Church, Highway 27, 2 miles south of Bremen, Georgia.

South Georgia Convention, Lebanon Church, 9 miles south of Cordele, Georgia.

Boiling Springs Primitive Baptist Church, 12 miles north of Roswell at Birmingham, Georgia.

Mount Hebron Missionary Baptist Church, Highway 25, 3 miles west of Double Springs, Alabama.

Macedonia Baptist Church, Highway 69 to Wilburn, west of Bremen, Alabama.

Pilgrim's Rest Primitive Baptist Church, Highway 11, south of Attalla, Alabama.

2ND SUN.   Harmony Church, 4 miles north of Lawrenceburg, Tennessee.

Oak Grove church, 12 miles n. of Roswell at Birmingham, Ga.

Mulberry Church, 3 miles east of Center Hill, Alabama.

Oak Hill Baptist Church, 2 miles south of Oxford, Alabama.

Shady Grove Church, Wilburn, Alabama.

SAT. NGT.   Cross Roads Primitive Baptist Church, Highway 100, 9 miles north of Tallapoosa, Georgia.

3RD SUN.   Copeland Memorial, Mount Olive Primitive Baptist Church, Highway 157, Cullman, Alabama.

Plainview Baptist Church, old Highway 100, south of Tallapoosa, Georgia.

Wehadkee Church, Highway 22, 1 mile n.e. of Rock Mills, Ala.

Banner Community Center, Highway 23, Mississippi.

THANKSGIVING NGT.   Mount Olive Primitive Baptist Church, Highway 157, Cullman, Alabama.

4TH SUN.   Mount Pleasant Primitive Baptist Church, off Highway 31, north Birmingham, Alabama.

Providence Primitive Baptist Church, Highway 35, 8 miles northwest of Cullman, Alabama.

King's School House, Mount Vernon, off Highway 278, 3 miles north of Lynn, Alabama.

Moving Sing near Lineville.

December

1ST SUN.   Liberty Community Singing, Liberty Baptist Church, 1 mile west of Highway 77, near Helicon, Alabama.

2ND SUN.   W. B. Denney Day, National Armory, Lineville, Alabama.

Rocky Mount Church, 1 mile south of Daviston, Alabama.

3RD SUN.   Zion Hill Primitive Baptist Church, 2 miles north of Snead Cross Roads, Alabama.

NEW YEAR'S EVE NGT.   Near Ider, Alabama, moves.

Other Sessions

FRI. NGT. BEFORE EACH 2ND SUN.   Little Vine Church, Oaky Hollow Road, near Empire, Alabama.

FRI. NGT. BEFORE EACH 3RD. SUN.   John Davis singing, Corinth Church, off Highway 69 at Bugtussle, 26 miles s.w. of Cullman, Ala.

3RD FRI. OF EACH MONTH   Old Folks Home, Carbon Hill, Alabama.

SAT. NGT. BEFORE EACH 1ST SUN.   Shady Grove Primitive Baptist Church, Highway 195, 3 miles north of Double Springs, Alabama.

SAT. NGT. BEFORE EACH 2ND SUN.   Keeton's Cemetery, Shady Grove, Walker County, between Nauvoo and Carbon Hill, Ala.

SAT. NGT. BEFORE EACH 4TH SUN.   Liberty Church, near Helicon, 1 mile west of Highway 77, in Winston County, Alabama.

EA. 1ST SUN. NGT.   Mount Lebanon Church, Bluff Road, 10 miles northwest of Fayette, Alabama.

Friendship Church, 12 miles southeast of Haleyville, Alabama, 2 miles west of Highway 195.

Gum Pond, 18 miles northeast of Cullman, Alabama, in Morgan County.

Liberty Church, 2 miles north of Henagar, Alabama, just off Highway 40 (Oct.–Apr.)

EA. 3RD SUN. AFTERNOON   Bethel Primitive Baptist Church, Calhoun County, Mississippi (Nov.–Mar.)

EA. 2ND SUN. NGT.   Antioch Baptist Church, off Highway 75, 5 miles north of Ider, Alabama (Sept.–Mar.)

3RD SUN. NGT., EA. 3RD MONTH   Mount Olive Primitive Baptist Church, 20th Street, Rome, Georgia.

EA. 5TH SUN. NGT.   Rice Community Church, Arab, Alabama.

EA. 5TH SUN. OF YR.   Tuscaloosa Community Center, South Side Lions Club, in Rosedale on old Highway 82 and Highway 69, Tuscaloosa, Alabama.

Liberty Church (McCormacks), north of Highway 78, 2 miles southeast of Sumiton, Alabama.

1ST 5TH SUN. OF YR.   Liberty Church, 2 miles north of Henagar, off Highway 40.

Hopewell Primitive Baptist Church, 6 miles e. of Oneonta, Ala.

Sunny Home Baptist Church, 3 miles northeast of Haleyville, Alabama, on Middle Newbury Road.

2ND 5TH SUN. OF YR.   Mount Pisgah Church, 10 miles w. of Sylvester, Ga.

(OR 5TH SUN. CLOSEST TO 2ND SUN. IN JUNE)   New Clear Creek, 2 miles east of Douglas and 1 mile south of Highway 168, Douglas to Boaz, Alabama.

3RD 5TH SUN. OF YR.   Hopewell Primitive Baptist Church, 6 miles east of Oneonta, Alabama.

Elm Grove Church, 4 miles southwest of Carbon Hill, Ala.

Pilgrim's Rest Primitive Baptist Church, Lafayette County, Mississippi.

1ST 5TH SUN. AFTER JULY 1   Union Musical Convention, Georgia, moves.

Lacy's Chapel, 2 miles southwest of Henagar, Alabama.

County Line Church, Highway 49, Mellow Valley, Alabama.

Denson-Book Singings (Black Singers)

Annual Sessions

July

SAT. & 4TH SUN.   New Home Convention, Chickasaw County, Mississippi, moves.

August

SAT. & 2ND SUN. Union Grove Convention, Webster County, Mississippi, moves.

SAT. & 3RD SUN. West Harmony Convention, Grenada County, Mississippi, moves.

SAT. & 4TH SUN. Pleasant Ridge Convention, Calhoun County, Mississippi, moves.

September

SAT. & 2ND SUN. State Convention, Mississippi, moves.

Monthly Sessions

1ST SUN. Union Grove District singing, Webster County, Mississippi, moves.

2ND SUN. Pleasant Ridge District singing, Calhoun County, Mississippi, moves.

3RD SUN. West Harmony District singing, Grenada County, Mississippi, moves.

4TH SUN. New Home District singing, Chickasaw County, Mississippi, moves.

Cooper-Book Singings (White Singers)

Annual Sessions

January

3RD SUN. Union Hill Singing Hall, Miller Cross Roads, off Highway 2, Holmes County, Florida.

4TH SUN. J. F. Helms Memorial, Carroll Primitive Baptist Church, Ozark, Alabama.

Bethesda Camp Ground, Highway 79, 7 miles southwest of Vernon, Florida.

February

1ST SUN. Central Convention Singing, moves within Geneva County, Alabama.

2ND SUN. Blair School, Highway 52, 4 miles north of Opp, Alabama.

3RD SUN. Carroll Primitive Baptist Church, Ozark, Alabama.

Traveler's Rest Primitive Baptist Church, off Highway 52, Samson, Alabama.

4TH SUN.   Davis Birthday Singing, New Hope Tabernacle, Highway 79, Washington County, Florida.

New Bethany Church, near Hinson Cross Roads, Florida.

March

1ST SUN.   Roney Memorial, Piney Grove Primitive Baptist Church, 3 miles north of Headland, Alabama.

2ND SUN.   Courthouse, Elba, Alabama.

3RD SUN.   Union Chapel, Van, Texas.

Owens Memorial, Sunny Hill Chapel, Highway 77, 3 miles south of Wausau, Florida.

Garrison Memorial, Harmony Primitive Baptist Church, off Highway 20, near Canton, Georgia.

Robbins Singing, New Hope Primitive Baptist Church, between Andalusia and Florala, Alabama.

4TH SUN.   Third District Sing, moves in Florida.

Union Singing Hall, Miller Cross Roads, off Highway 2, Holmes County, Florida.

April

EASTER   Mount Ararat Primitive Baptist Church, near Henderson, Tex.

1ST SUN.   Crenshaw County Convention, moves within Crenshaw County, Alabama.

Houston County Convention, Little Vine Primitive Baptist Church, Dothan, Alabama.

2ND SAT.   Stockholders meeting and Bassett Sing, Carroll Primitive Baptist Church, Ozark, Alabama.

2ND SUN.   Providence Primitive Baptist Church, 2 miles west of Stringer, Mississippi.

Faulk Memorial, School Auditorium in Samson, Alabama.

Barfield Memorial, Methodist Church, Highway 77, Wausau, Florida.

3RD SUN.   Bethel Church, Highway 52, between Opp and Andalusia, Ala.

Cool Springs, near Opp, Alabama.

Pilgrim's Rest Primitive Baptist Church, north of Graceville, Florida, in Geneva County, Alabama.

Pleasant Grove Methodist Church, Hinson Cross Roads, 8 miles west of Vernon, Florida.

4TH SUN. State of Alabama Convention, semi-annual session, moves in Alabama.

Gum Creek Primitive Baptist Church, 1 mile e. of Glendale, Fla.

May

1ST SUN. IBEW Union Hall, Tyler, Texas.

Collins Mill Primitive Baptist Church, Highway 2 west, 1 mile out of Graceville, Florida.

Heath Memorial, Mabson Methodist Church, 5 miles east of Ozark, Alabama.

New Mount Zion Church, south of Samson, Alabama.

Elam Church, off Highway 29, north of Banks, Alabama.

2ND SUN. New Home Church, off Highway 541, Simpson County, Miss.

SAT. Davis Memorial, Ino Baptist Church, Coffee County, Alabama.

3RD SUN. New Prospect Presbyterian Church at Scruggs Community, near Beckville, Texas.

Ramah Primitive Baptist Church, Pike County, Alabama.

South Alabama Convention, moves in Alabama.

Christian Home, Hartford-Black Highway, Geneva County, Alabama.

Baldwin County Convention, Galilee Church, near Stapleton, Alabama.

4TH SUN. Carroll Primitive Baptist Church, Ozark, Alabama.

Beda Church, between Andalusia and Florala, Alabama.

First District Sing, moves near Vernon, Florida.

June

1ST SUN. Shady Grove Church, Highway 87, Coffee County, Alabama.

First District Sing, Alabama, moves.

Pine Hill, off Highway 123, between Bonifay and Esto, Florida.

2ND SUN. Ebenezer Church, on Saco Road, near Troy, Alabama.

Harrison Grave Yard Memorial Singing, east of Highway 52, near Kinston, Coffee County, Alabama.

Second District Sing, Holmes Valley Convention, moves near Bonifay, Florida.

3RD SUN. Pleasant Home Church, Covington County, Alabama.

Zion Hill Missionary Baptist Church, Rusk County, Texas.

Memorial Sing, Live Oak Church, Live Oak, Florida.

4TH SUN. Zebulon Church, north of Banks, Alabama.

Good Hope Church, 4 miles west of Highway 29, near Dozier, Alabama.

Oak Grove Church, Washington County, near Hinson Cross Roads, Florida.

Eight-Mile Church, Geneva County, Alabama.

Valley Grove, Highway 331, 9 miles north of Opp, Alabama.

July

JULY 4   Memorial Sing, Corinth Church, 3 miles west of McCullough, Alabama.

Singing Hall at Union Hill Community, Florida, off Highway 2, near Black, Alabama.

Spring Hill Convention, Holmes County, Florida, moves.

1ST SUN.   Joquin Church, Highway 29 near Luverne, Alabama.

Old Good Hope Church, Simpson County, Mississippi.

FRI.   Enon Baptist Church, Brundidge, Alabama.

2ND SUN.   Hopeful Church, near Ozark, Alabama.

Third Quarter, Holmes Valley Convention, Florida, moves.

Wilkerson Memorial, 6 miles south of Raleigh, Mississippi.

Third District Sing, Florida, moves near Vernon, Florida.

Pine Level, Coffee County, near Elba, Alabama.

3RD WED.   Courthouse, Andalusia, Alabama.

JULY 15   Mount Gilead Baptist Church, Highway 87, 9 miles south of Elba, Alabama.

3RD SAT.   Old Union Church, Highway 331 between Opp and Florala, Alabama.

SAT. & 3RD SUN.   Escambia County Convention, moves, Alabama.

3RD SUN.   Holly Springs Methodist Church, near Canton, Texas.

Zion Chapel, Highway 87, 9 miles north of Elba, Alabama.

Underwood Singing, Liberty Hill Primitive Baptist Church, Holmes County, Florida.

THURS.   Pleasant Ridge Methodist Church, Dale County, off Highway 231, near Rocky Head, Alabama.

SAT.   White Water Baptist Church, between Geneva, Alabama and Berry Cross Roads, in Holmes County, Florida.

4TH SUN.   Cluster Springs Baptist Church, west of Glendale, Florida.

Pine Grove Presbyterian Church, Rusk County, Texas.

August

SAT. & 1ST SUN.   Coffee County Convention, Alabama, moves.

1ST SUN.   Beulah Church, Highway 277, between Graceville and Chipley, Florida.

Red Oak Church, Highway 55, northwest of Lockhart, Ala.

SAT.   Central Convention, Alabama, moves.

SAT. & 2ND SUN.   East Texas Convention, moves.

2ND SUN.   Old Center Methodist Church, off Highway 27, west of New-
             ville, Alabama.

             Fourth District Sing, Holmes Valley Convention, Sunny Hill
             Chapel, Highway 77, 3 miles south of Wausau, Florida.

             Gum Springs Church, Simpson County, Mississippi.

3RD SAT.   Five County Convention, Alabama, moves.

3RD SUN.   Asbury Methodist Church, Dale County, Alabama.

             Bethlehem Homecoming Singing, off Highway 87 between
             Samson and Elba, Alabama.

             Liberty Methodist Church, 1 mile east of Stringer, Mississippi.

SAT. & 4TH SUN.   Mississippi State Convention, moves in Mississippi.
             Denson book also used.

4TH SUN.   Pilgrim Rest Church, Rose Hill Road, 3 miles southeast of
             Dozier, Alabama.

             Cedar Grove Primitive Baptist Church, Highway 2, west of
             Graceville, Florida.

September

1ST SUN.   Butler County Convention, Mount Carmel Church, off High-
             way 10, between Greenville and Luverne, Alabama.

             Piney Grove Baptist Church, Highway 87, 4 miles north of
             Samson, Geneva County, Alabama.

             New Hope Church, Echo Road, Midland City, Alabama.

2ND SUN.   Southeastern Convention, moves, Alabama.

             County Line Primitive Baptist Church, San Jacinto County,
             Texas.

             Armstrong Memorial, Sardis Methodist Church, 6 miles south
             of Hartford, Alabama.

             Second District Sing, Alabama, moves.

3RD SUN.   Middle Creek Convention, Alabama, moves.

             Pisgah Schoolhouse, Nacogdoches County, Texas.

             Union Singing Hall, off Highway 2, Miller Cross Roads, Fla.

             Covington County Convention, Alabama, moves.

SAT. & 4TH SUN.   West Florida Convention, moves.

SAT. NGT. & 4TH SUN.   Grace Primitive Baptist Church, Hurley Street, off
             Highway 59, Houston, Texas.

4TH SUN.   South Alabama Convention, moves.

Rhodes School House, between Elba and Kinston, Alabama.

Sanford Community Center, old Highway 49, Covington County, Mississippi.

October

1ST SUN.   Chaneyhatchee Convention, Alabama, moves.

FRI., SAT., & 2ND SUN.   Holmes Valley Convention, Florida, moves.

2ND SUN.   Houston County Convention, Little Vine Primitive Baptist Church, Dothan, Alabama.

Pleasant Ridge Church, Elba-Victoria Road, n.e. of Elba, Ala.

Cold Springs Baptist Church, old Highway 49, 3 miles south of Collins, Mississippi.

Swift Missionary Baptist Church, Nacogdoches, Texas.

SAT.   Alabama and Florida Convention, alternates between Alabama and Florida, and moves.

3RD SUN.   Darin, near Luverne, Alabama.

4TH SAT.   South Main Baptist Church, Houston, Texas.

SAT. & 4TH SUN.   Spring Hill Convention, Florida, moves.

4TH SUN.   State of Alabama Convention, moves.

November

1ST SUN.   Galloway Memorial, Hurricane Creek Church, Highway 2, Florida, near Geneva, Alabama.

Little Hope Primitive Baptist Church, near Huntington, Texas.

SAT. & 2ND SUN.   Northwest Florida Convention, moves.

2ND SUN.   Carroll Church, Ozark, Alabama.

Abigail Free Will Baptist Church, Vernon, Florida.

Fourth District Sing, Alabama, moves.

3RD SUN.   Capital City Convention, Highland Park Primitive Baptist Church, Highland Avenue, Montgomery, Alabama.

4TH SUN.   Collins Mill Church, 1 mile out of Graceville, Florida, on Highway 2.

December

SAT. & 1ST SUN.   Central Florida Convention, New Hope Primitive Baptist Church, Dillard Street, Winter Garden, Florida.

2ND SUN.   Antioch Church, Barbour County, Alabama.

Sunny Hill Chapel, 3 miles southwest of Wausau, Florida.

Other Sessions

SAT. NGT. BEFORE EA. 3RD SUN.   Union Singing Hall, Highway 2, Miller
   Cross Roads, Florida.

1ST SUN. NGT., EA. 3RD MONTH   New Hope Primitive Baptist Church,
   Wintergarden, Florida.

2ND SUN. NGT., EA. 3RD MONTH   Primitive Baptist Church, off old Highway 1, Vero Beach, Florida.

EA. 5TH SUN. NGT. OF YR.   Old Bethlehem Primitive Baptist Church, Highway 29, south of Brewster, Florida.

1ST 5TH SUN. OF YR. AFTER JAN.   Middle Creek Convention, Dale County,
   Alabama, moves.

   Fairview Church, 7 miles northeast of Laurel, Mississippi.

2ND 5TH SUN. OF YR.   Seven County Convention, semi-annual, Alabama,
   moves.

   Monasna Methodist Church, 10 miles east of Quitman, Miss.

3RD 5TH SUN. OF YR.   Seven County Convention, Alabama, moves.

SPRING (MAR., APR., MAY), SAT. & 5TH SUN.   Southwest Texas Convention, Bethel Primitive Baptist Church, McMahan, Texas, in
   Caldwell County.

Cooper-Book Singings (Black Singers)

Annual Sessions

March

1ST SUN.   Dewey Williams Day, Ozark, Alabama.

4TH SUN.   County Line Church, Slocomb, Alabama.

April

3RD SUN.   Jackson Sing, Union Grove Church, No. 1, Union Grove, Ala.

May

1ST SUN.   Council Sing, Pinckard, Alabama.

4TH SUN.   Mount Sinai Church, Henry County, Alabama.

June

1ST SUN.   T. Y. Lawrence Sing, First Baptist Church, Ozark, Alabama.

2ND SUN.   Harper Sing, Old Salem Church, Ozark, Alabama.

THURS., FRI. NGTS. & 3RD SUN.   Religious Temple of Sacred Harp, Madison Avenue, Newark, New Jersey.

July

1st Sun.   Christmas Sing, Adams Street Church, Dothan, Alabama.

Sat. ngt. & 2nd Sun.   Panola County Convention, Texas, moves.

4th Sun.   New Bethel C. M. E. Church, Campbellton, Florida.

Sat. ngt. & 4th Sun.   Rusk County Convention, Texas, moves.

August

1st Sun.   Pike County Convention, Alabama, moves.

3rd Sun.   Crews Day, Church of God in Christ, Ashford, Alabama.

September

Sat. & 1st Sun.   Henry County Convention, Alabama, moves.

Thurs., Fri. ngts. & 2nd Sun.   Religious Institute of Sacred Harp, Vauxhall, New Jersey.

Sat. & 2nd Sun.   Dale County Convention, Alabama, moves.

Sat. & 4th Sun.   Alabama and Florida Union Singing Convention, moves.

October

3rd Sun.   Barbour County Convention, Alabama, moves.

4th Sun.   Tabernacle Baptist Church, Dothan, Alabama.

November

Thanksgiving   J. Humphrey Day Sing, Dothan, Alabama.

December

Christmas ngt.   Church of God in Christ, Enterprise, Alabama.

Monthly Sessions

2nd Sun. Afternoon   Religious Institute of Sacred Harp, Vauxhall, New Jersey.

3rd Sun. Afternoon   Religious Temple of Sacred Harp, Madison Avenue, Newark, New Jersey.

White-Book Singings (White Singers)

Annual Sessions

April

1st Sun.   Friendship Primitive Baptist Church, Five Forks, Gwinnett County, Georgia.

4TH SUN.   West Atlanta Primitive Baptist Church, Gordon Road, At-
             lanta, Georgia.

             Friendship Primitive Baptist Church, Highway 151, 4 miles
             north of Ringgold, Georgia (Catoosa County).

July

2ND SUN.   Hardeman Primitive Baptist Church, Glenwood Road, De-
             catur, Georgia.

4TH SUN.   Friendship Primitive Baptist Church, off Highway 41, 4 miles
             southeast of Ringgold, Georgia.

August

4TH SUN.   Friendship Primitive Baptist Church, Highway 151, 4 miles
             north of Ringgold, Georgia (Catoosa County).

September

3RD SUN.   B. F. White Interstate Convention, Hardeman Primitive Bap-
             tist Church, Glenwood Road, Decatur, Georgia.

October

1ST SUN.   Stone Mountain Convention, Camp Creek Primitive Baptist
             Church, near Lilburn, Georgia.

3RD SUN.   Head Springs Church, 4 miles south of Georgia-Alabama line
             on U. S. Highway 11 in Alabama.

Appendix B

Selected Songs from the Sacred Harp

ALABAMA

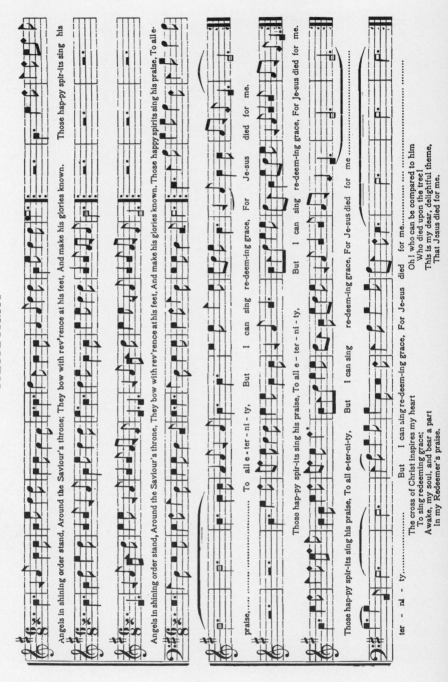

Angels in shining order stand, Around the Saviour's throne; They bow with rev'rence at his feet, And make his glories known. Those hap-py spir-its sing his

Angels in shining order stand, Around the Saviour's throne, They bow with rev'rence at his feet, And make his glories known. Those happy spirits sing his praise, To alle-

praise,.......... To all e - ter - ni - ty, But I can sing re-deem-ing grace, For Je-sus died for me.

Those hap-py spir-its sing his praise, To all e - ter - ni - ty, But I can sing re-deem-ing grace, For Je-sus died for me.

Those hap-py spir-its sing his praise, To all e-ter-ni-ty, But I can sing re-deem-ing grace, For Je-sus died for me.........

ter - ni - ty,.......... But I can sing re-deem-ing grace, For Je-sus died for me..........

The cross of Christ inspires my heart
To sing redeeming grace;
Awake, my soul, and bear a part
In my Redeemer's praise.

Oh! who can be compared to him
Who died upon the tree!
This is my dear, delightful theme,
That Jesus died for me.

ANTIOCH

Samuel Medley, about 1784

U. C. Wood, 1850. Alto by S. M. Denson, 1911

CALVARY

DANIEL READ, 1806

CHESTER

William Billings, 1770

CORONATION

REV. EDWARD PERRONET, 1779

OLIVER HOLDEN, 1793

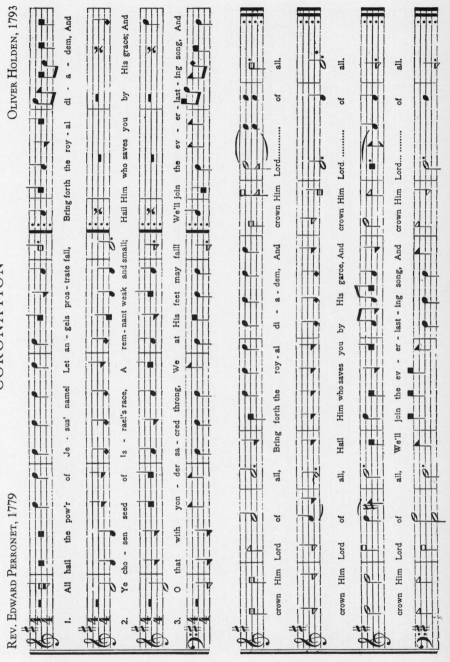

COWPER

WILLIAM COWPER, about 1779

OLIVER HOLDEN

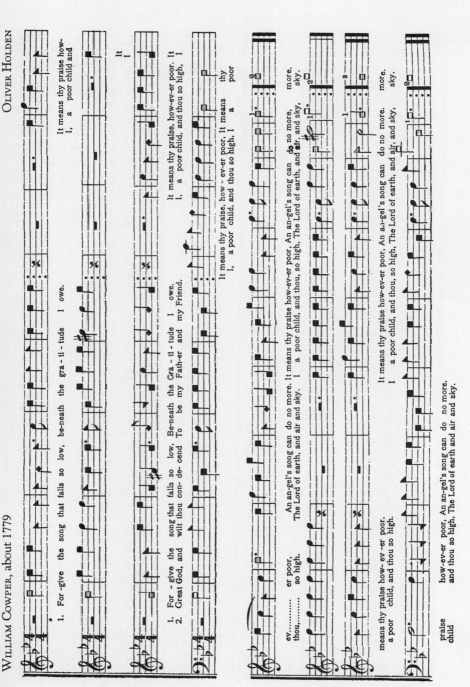

DAVID'S LAMENTATION

William Billings, about 1800

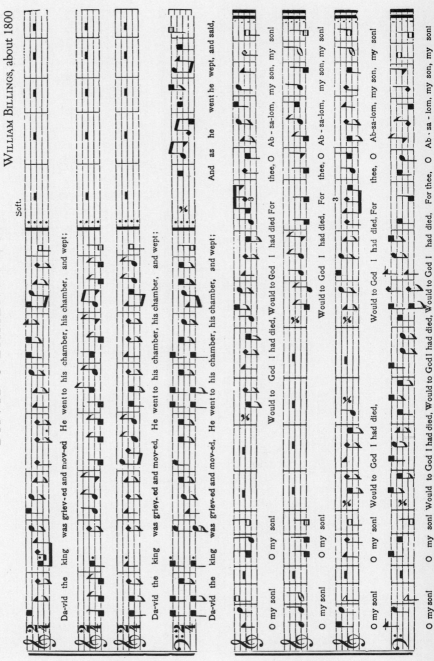

DEVOTION

ISAAC WATTS, 1719

AMARICK (?) HALL, about 1811

1. Sweet is the day of sac - red rest; No mor - tal cares shall seize my breast; O may my heart in tune be found, Like David's harp of solemn sound; sound.

2. Then shall I share a glo-rious part, When grace hath well refined my heart, And fresh sup-plies of joy are shed, Like ho - ly oil, to cheer my head; head.

3. Then shall I see, and hear, and know All I de - sired and wished be-low; And ev-'ry power find sweet em-ploy, In that e - ter - nal world of joy; joy.

THE DYING CALIFORNIAN

BALL & DRINKARD, 1859

Re-arr. and alto added by HOWARD DENSON, 1935

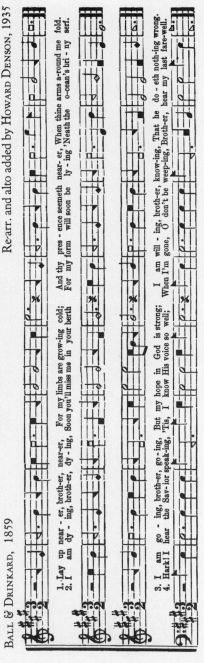

1. Lay up near - er, broth-er, near-er, For my limbs are grow-ing cold; And thy pres - ence seemeth near - er, When thine arms a-round me fold.

2. I am dy - ing, broth-er, dy - ing, Soon you'll miss me in your berth For my form will soon be ly - ing 'Neath the o-cean's bri - ny serf.

3. I am go - ing, broth-er, go - ing, But my hope in God is strong; I am will - ing, broth-er, know-ing, That he do - eth noth-ing wrong.

4. Hark! I hear the Sav-ior speak-ing, 'Tis, I know His voice so well; When I'm gone, O don't be weep-ing, Broth-er, hear my last fare-well.

EASTER ANTHEM

WILLIAM BILLINGS, 1785

nessee. For the last several years it has alternated between Georgia and Alabama.

The United Association now serves as the meeting place for the leaders of the Sacred Harp in the Denson-revision area, and it draws at least a few singers from as many as four or five states each year. At a singing where the arranging committee in a two-day session can not possibly get around to asking for a "lesson" from all the qualified leaders present, the United Convention serves also as a heartening symbol to the singers that their movement is still very much alive.

Alabama Conventions

By the late nineteenth century at least a dozen conventions had appeared in Georgia alone. But even earlier, with the two main Georgia conventions securely founded, similar musical associations began to emerge in several surrounding states as the influence of the *Sacred Harp* spread. The East Texas Musical Convention was founded in 1855, and B. F. White's paper the *Organ* reported that same year a meeting of the Alabama Musical Convention in Russell County, Alabama.[4] At least by 1869 there was a convention meeting in Florida—the West Florida Sacred Harp Singing Convention—and, by 1878, one in Mississippi as well—the Calhoun County Sacred Harp Singing.

In Alabama, particularly, the conventions fairly blossomed, as Alabama began to rival Georgia as the center of Sacred Harp activity. Perhaps the second oldest of these was the Southeastern Alabama Sacred Harp Musical Convention, which was founded, present records indicate, in 1858. Except for five years the convention has met annually for well over a century, making this the oldest Alabama singing assembly still in existence. In 1866 Oliver Bradfield, one of the founders of the Chattahoochee Convention, moved to Clay County, Alabama, and organized the Boiling Spring Sacred Harp Singing Convention. In 1873 Clay County

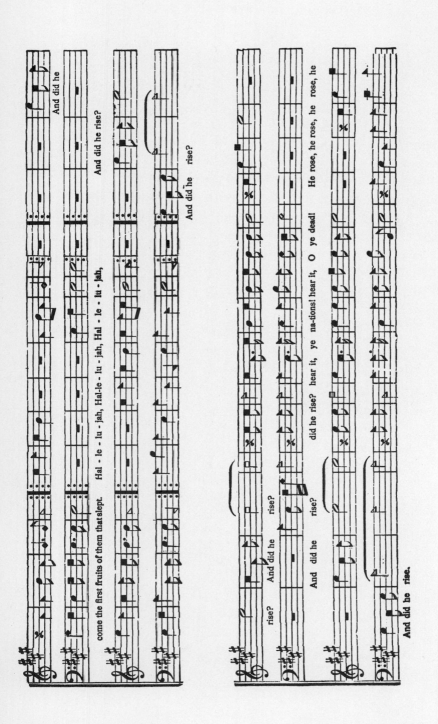

EASTER ANTHEM, *continued*

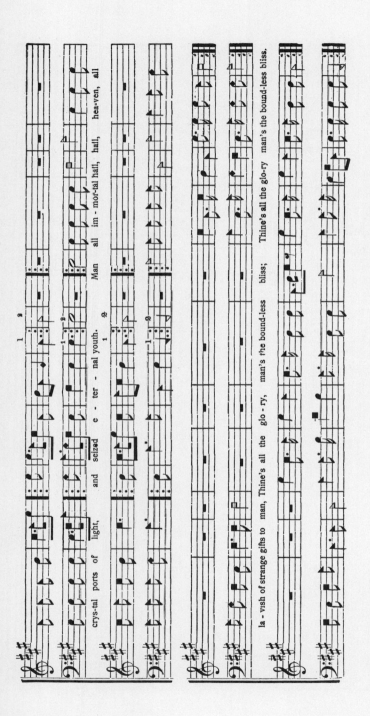

EVENING SHADE

John Leland, 1835

Alto by S. M. Denson, 1911

GREENFIELD

JOHN NEWTON, 1779

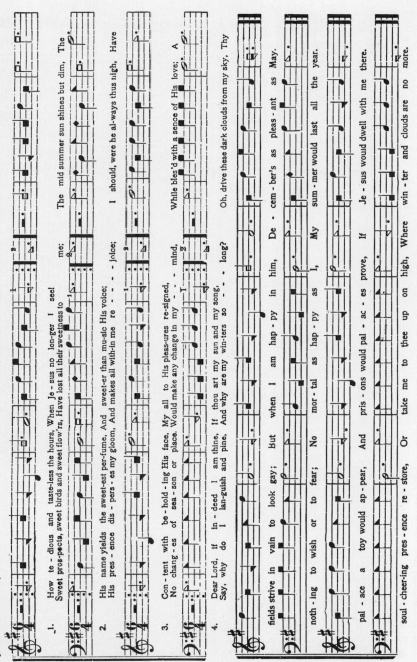

1. How te - dious and taste-less the hours, When Je - sus no lon-ger I see!
   Sweet pros-pects, sweet birds and sweet flow'rs, Have lost all their sweetness to me; The mid summer sun shines but dim, The

2. His name yields the sweet-est per-fume, And sweet-er than mu-sic His voice;
   His pres - ence dis - pers - es my gloom, And makes all with-in me re - - - joice; I should, were he al-ways thus nigh, Have

3. Con - tent with be - hold - ing His face, My all to His pleas-ures re-signed,
   No chang - es of sea - son or place. Would make any change in my - - mind, While bles'd with a sence of His love; A

4. Dear Lord, If In - deed I am thine, If thou art my sun and my song,
   Say, why do I lan-guish and pine, And why are my win-ters so - - long? Oh, drive these dark clouds from my sky, Thy

fields strive in vain to look gay; But when I am hap - py in him, De - cem - ber's as pleas - ant as May.

noth - ing to wish or to fear; No mor - tal as hap - py as I, My sum - mer would last all the year.

pal - ace a toy would ap - pear, And pris - ons would pal - ac - es prove, If Je - sus would dwell with me there.

soul - cheer-ing pres - ence re - store, Or take me to thee up on high, Where win - ter and clouds are no more.

HEAVENLY ARMOR

Wm. Walker, 1828. Alto by S. M. Denson. 1911

John Leland, 1835

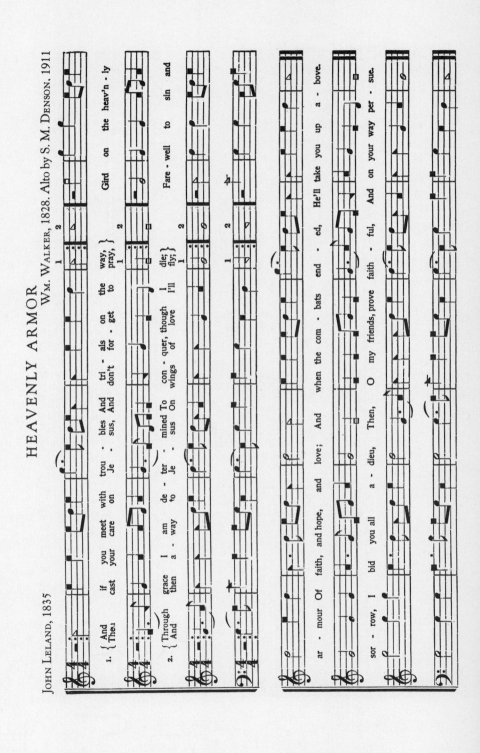

HEBREW CHILDREN

Peter Cartwright, 1820–1825. Alto by S. M. Denson, 1911

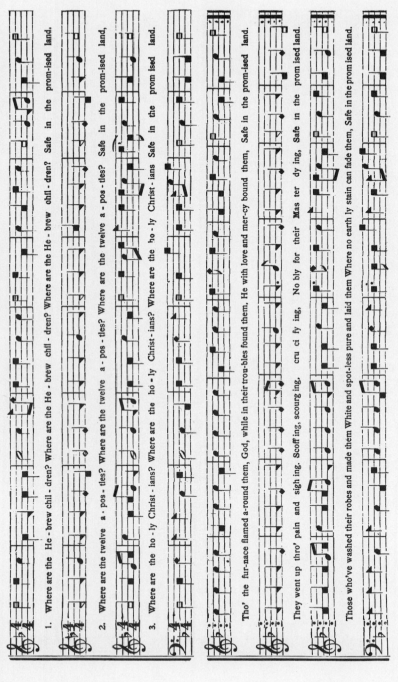

1. Where are the He - brew chil - dren? Where are the He - brew chil - dren? Where are the He - brew chil - dren? Safe in the prom - ised land,

2. Where are the twelve a - pos - tles? Where are the twelve a - pos - tles? Where are the twelve a - pos - tles? Safe in the prom - ised land,

3. Where are the ho - ly Christ - ians? Where are the ho - ly Christ - ians? Where are the ho - ly Christ - ians Safe in the prom ised land.

Tho' the fur - nace flamed a - round them, God, while in their trou - bles found them, He with love and mer - cy bound them, Safe in the prom - ised land.

They went up thro' pain and sigh ing, Scoff'ing, scourg ing, cru ci fy ing, No bly for their Mas ter dy ing, Safe in the prom ised land.

Those who've washed their robes and made them White and spot - less pure and laid them Where no earth ly stain can fade them, Safe in the prom ised land.

HOLY MANNA

"Dover Selection"

WILLIAM MOORE

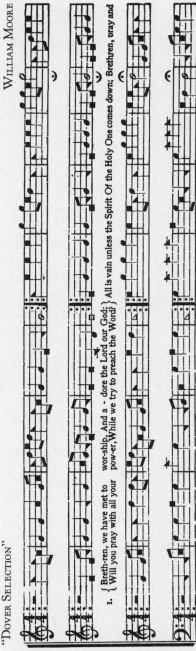

1. {Breth-ren, we have met to wor-ship, And a - dore the Lord our God; } All is vain unless the Spirit Of the Holy One comes down; Brethren, pray and
{Will you pray with all your pow-er, While we try to preach the Word? }

ho - ly man-na Will be show-ered all a - round. a - round.

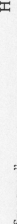

2 Brethren, see poor sinners round you,
Trembling on the brink of woe;
Death is coming, hell is moving,
Can you bear to let them go?
See our fathers, see our mothers,
And our children sinking down;
Brethren, pray, and holy manna
Will be showered all around.

3 Sisters, will you join and help us?
Moses' sisters aided him;
Will you help the trembling mourners,
Who are struggling hard with sin?
Tell them all about the Saviour,
Tell them that He will be found;
Sisters, pray, and holy manna
Will be showered all around.

4 Is there here a trembling jailer,
Seeking grace, and filled with fears?
Is there here a weeping Mary,
Pouring forth a flood of tears?
Brethren, join your cries to help them;
Sisters, let your prayers abound;
Pray, O pray that holy manna
May be scattered all around.

5 Let us love our God supremely,
Let us love each other, too;
Let us love and pray for sinners,
Till our God makes all things new.
Then He'll call us home to heaven,
At His table we'll sit down;
Christ will gird Himself, and serve us
With sweet manna all around.

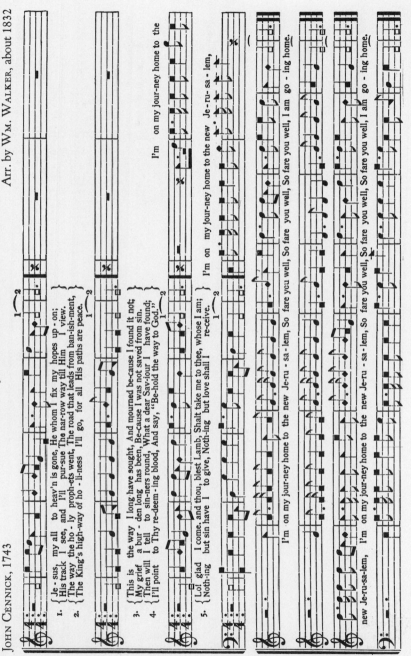

JERUSALEM

John Cennick, 1743

Arr. by Wm. Walker, about 1832

1. { Je - sus, my all to heav'n is gone, He whom I fix my hopes up - on;
     His track I see, and I'll pur-sue The nar-row way till Him I view. }
2. { The way the ho - ly proph-ets went, The road that leads from ban-ish-ment,
     The King's high-way of ho - li-ness I'll go, for all His paths are peace. }
3. { This is the way I long have sought, And mourned be-cause I found it not;
     My grief a bur - den long has been, Be-cause I was not saved from sin. }
4. { Then will I tell to sin-ners round, What a dear Sav-iour I have found;
     I'll point to Thy re-deem - ing blood, And say, "Be-hold the way to God." }
5. { Lo! glad I come, and thou, blest Lamb, Shalt take me to thee, whose I am;
     Noth-ing but sin have I to give, Noth-ing but love shall I re-ceive. }

I'm on my jour-ney home to the new Je-ru - sa - lem, So fare you well, So fare you well, I am go - ing home.

new Je-ru-sa-lem, I'm on my jour-ney home to the new Je-ru - sa - lem, So fare you well, So fare you well, I am go - ing home.

LOVING JESUS

WHITE & SEARCY, 1850. Alto by S. M. DENSON, 1911

Here's my heart, my lov-ing Je-sus, Here's my heart, my lov-ing Je-sus,—Thou who dis'st from sin re-lieve us,

Here's my heart, my lov-ing Je-sus, Here's my heart, my lov'ing Je-sus,—Thou who did'st from sin re-lieve us,

Take the purchase of thy blood, Take the purchase of thy blood! Lov-ing Je -sus, Thou hast bought a ran-som!

Take the purchase of thy blood, Take the purchase of thy blood! Lov-ing Je-sus, Thou hast bought a ran-som

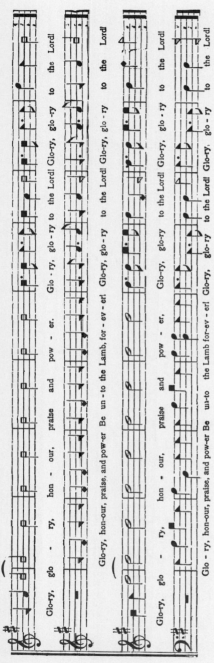

IDUMEA

A. DAVIDSON, 1817

CHARLES WESLEY, 1753

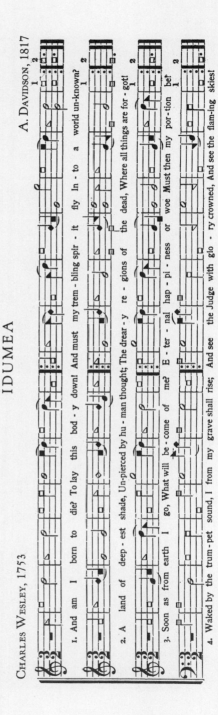

1. And am I born to die? To lay this bod - y down! And must my trem - bling spir - it fly In - to a world un-known?

2. A land of deep - est shade, Un-pierced by hu - man thought; The drear - y re - gions of the dead, Where all things are for - got!

3. Soon as from earth I go, What will be - come of me? E - ter - nal hap - pi - ness or woe Must then my por - tion be!

4. Waked by the trum - pet sound, I from my grave shall rise; And see the Judge with glo - ry crowned, And see the flam-ing skies!

THE LONE PILGRIM

B. F. WHITE, 1850. Alto by S. M. DENSON, 1911

B. F. WHITE, 1850

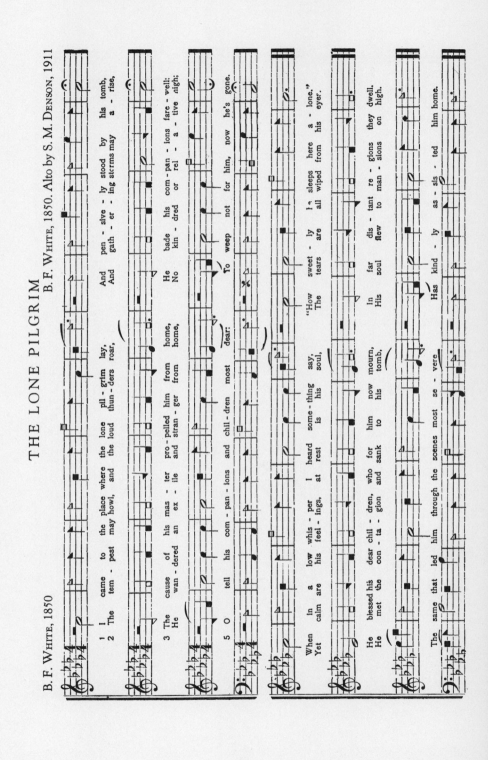

MEAR

Isaac Watts

Aaron Williams, 1760

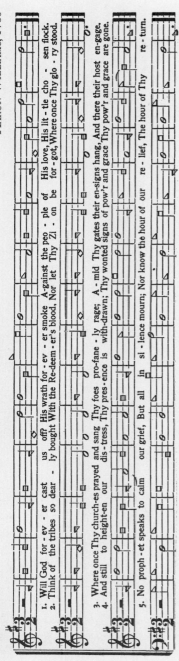

1. Will God for - ev - er cast us off? His wrath for - ev - er smoke A-gainst the peo - ple of His love, His lit - tle cho - sen flock.
2. Think of the tribes so dear - ly bought With the Re-deem-er's blood, Nor let Thy Zi - on be for - got, Where once Thy glo - ry stood.
3. Where once Thy church-es prayed and sang Thy foes pro-fane - ly rage; A - mid Thy gates their en-signs hang, And there their host en-gage.
4. And still to height-en our dis - tress, Thy pres-ence is with-drawn; Thy wonted signs of pow'r and grace Thy pow'r and grace are gone.
5. No proph - et speaks to calm our grief, But all in si - lence mourn; Nor know the hour of our re - lief, The hour of Thy re - turn.

NEW BRITAIN

John Newton, 1789

1. A - maz-ing grace! how sweet the sound, That saved a wretch like me! I once was lost, but now I'm found, Was blind but now I see. see.
2. 'Twas grace that taught my heart to fear, And grace my fears re-lieved; How pre-cious did that grace ap - pear The hour I first be-liev-ed! -lieved!
3. Thro' ma - ny dan-gers, toils and snares, I have al-read - y come; 'Tis grace has brought me safe thus far, And grace will lead me home. home.
4. The Lord has prom-ised good to me, His word my hope se - cures; He will my shield and por - tion be As long as life en-dures. -dures.
5. The earth shall soon dis-solve like snow, The sun for-bear to shine; But God, who called me here be - low, Will be for - ev - er mine. mine.

THE MORNING TRUMPET

John Leland, 1833

B. F. White, 1847

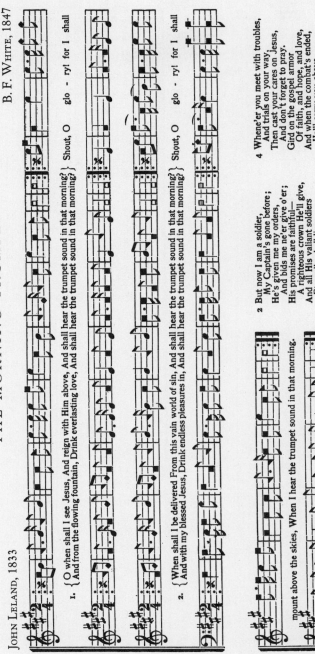

1. { O when shall I see Jesus, And reign with Him above, And shall hear the trumpet sound in that morning?
And from the flowing fountain, Drink everlasting love, And shall hear the trumpet sound in that morning? } Shout, O glo - ry! for I shall

2. { When shall I be delivered From this vain world of sin, And shall hear the trumpet sound in that morning}
And with my blessed Jesus, Drink endless pleasures in, And shall hear the trumpet sound in that morning } Shout, O glo - ry! for I shall

mount above the skies, When I hear the trumpet sound in that morning.

mount above the skies, When I hear the trumpet sound in that morning.

2 But now I am a soldier,
   My Captain's gone before;
   He's given me my orders,
   And bids me ne'er give o'er;
   His promises are faithful—
   A righteous crown He'll give,
   And all His valiant soldiers
   Eternally shall live.
      Shout, etc.

3 Through grace I feel determined
   To conquer, though I die,
   And then away to Jesus
   On wings of love I'll fly;
   Farewell to sin and sorrow,
   I bid them both adieu !
   And O, my friends, prove faithful,
   And on your way pursue.
      Shout, etc.

4 Whene'er you meet with troubles,
   And trials on your way;
   Then cast your cares on Jesus,
   And don't forget to pray.
   Gird on the gospel armor
   Of faith, and hope, and love,
   And when the combat's ended,
   He'll carry you above.
      Shout, etc.

5 O do not be discouraged,
   For Jesus is your Friend;
   And if you lack for knowledge
   He'll not refuse to lend.
   Neither will He upbraid you,
   Though often you request,
   He'll give you grace to conquer,
   And take you home to rest.
      Shout, etc.

NASHVILLE

Jeremiah Ingalls, 1800. Campbell, translator, 1804.

Alexander Johnson (?)

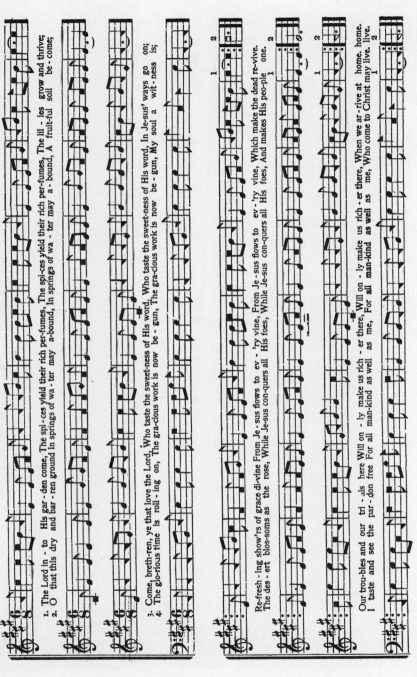

1. The Lord in - to His gar - den come, The spi - ces yield their rich per-fumes, The lil - ies grow and thrive;
2. O that this dry and bar - ren ground In springs of wa - ter may a - bound, A fruit-ful soil be - come;

3. Come, breth-ren, ye that love the Lord, Who taste the sweet-ness of His word, In Je-sus' ways go on;
4. The glo-rious time is roll - ing on, The gra-cious work is now be - gun, My soul a wit - ness is;

Re-fresh - ing show'rs of grace di-vine From Je - sus flows to ev - 'ry vine, Which make the dead re-vive.
The des - ert blos-soms as the rose, While Je-sus con-quers all His foes, And makes His peo-ple one.

Our trou-bles and our tri - als here Will on - ly make us rich - er there, When we ar - rive at home, home.
I taste and see the par - don free For all man-kind as well as me, Who come to Christ may live, live.

MURILLO'S LESSON

Alto by S. M. Denson, 1911

As down a lone val-ley with ce-dars o'er-spread, From wars dread con-fu-sion I pen-sive-ly strayed, }
The gloom from the face of fair heav-en re-tired The winds hushed their murmurs, The thunders ex-pired; }

Per-fumes as of

Fair science her gate to thy sons shall un-bar, And the east see thy morn hide the beams of her star }
New bards and new sa-ges unrival'd shall soar To fame un-ex-tin-guished, when time is no more. }

To the last ref-

E-den flowed sweetly, a-long A voice as of an-gels, en-chant-ing-ly sung,

A voice as of an-gels, en-chant-ing-ly sung,

uge of vir-ture de-sign-ed, shall fly from all na-tions, the best of mankind; shall fly from all na-tions, the best of man-

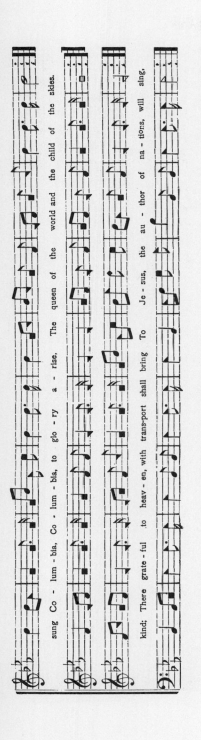

sung Co - lum - bia, Co - lum - bia, to glo - ry a - rise, The queen of the world and the child of the skies.

kind; There grate - ful to heav - en, with trans - port shall bring To Je - sus, the au - thor of na - tions, will sing,

WINDHAM

ISAAC WATTS, 1709

DANIEL READ, 1785

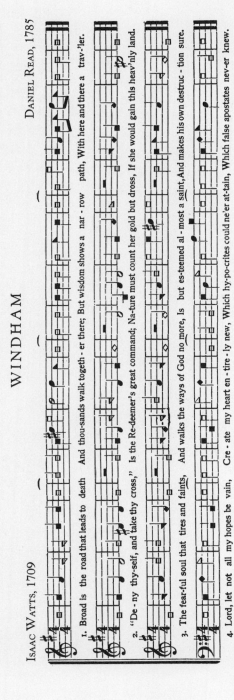

1. Broad is the road that leads to death And thou-sands walk togeth - er there; But wisdom shows a nar - row path, With here and there a trav - 'ler.

2. "De - ny thy-self, and take thy cross," Is the Re-deem'r's great command; Na-ture must count her gold but dross, If she would gain this heav'n-ly land.

3. The fear-ful soul that tires and faints, And walks the ways of God no more, Is but es-teem'd al - most a saint, And makes his own destruc - tion sure.

4. Lord, let not all my hopes be vain, Cre - ate my heart en - tire - ly new, Which hy-po-crites could ne'er at - tain, Which false apostates nev-er knew.

NEW TOPIA

MUNDAY

NINETY-THIRD PSALM

PHILIP DODDRIDGE, 1735

JEREMIAH INGALLS, 1805

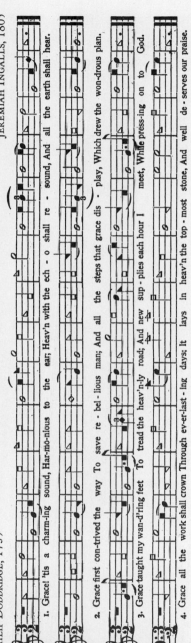

1. Grace! 'tis a charm-ing sound, Har-mo-nious to the ear; Heav'n with the ech - o shall re - sound, And all the earth shall hear.

2. Grace first con-trived the way To save re - bel - lious man; And all the steps that grace dis - play, Which drew the won-drous plan.

3. Grace taught my wand'ring feet To tread the heav'n-ly road; And new sup - plies each hour I meet, While press-ing on to God.

4. Grace all the work shall crown Through ev-er-last-ing days; It lays in heav'n the top-most stone, And well de - serves our praise.

RESTORATION

Re-arr. by T. B. NEWTON & S. W. EVERETT, 1908

REV. ROBERT ROBINSON, 1758

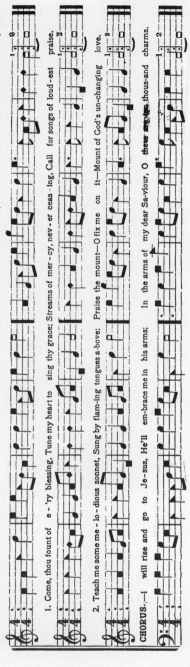

1. Come, thou fount of e - 'ry blessing, Tune my heart to sing thy grace; Streams of mer - cy, nev - er - ceas - ing, Call for songs of loud - est praise.

2. Teach me some me - lo - dious sonnet, Sung by flam-ing tongues a-bove; Praise the mount—O fix me on It—Mount of God's un-chang-ing love.

CHORUS.-- I will rise and go to Je - sus, He'll em-brace me in his arms; In the arms of my dear Sa-viour, O there are ten thous-and charms.

NORTHFIELD

ISAAC WATTS, 1701

JEREMIAH INGALLS, 1804

2 From the third heaven, where God resides,
  That holy, happy place,

3 The God of glory down to men
  Removes his blest abode;

Men, the dear object of his grace,
And he the living God.

THE OLD SHIP OF ZION

T. W. Carter, 1850

1. { What ship is this that will take us all home, glo - ry hal - le - lu - jah,
   And safe - ly land us on Ca - naan's bright shore?
2. { The winds may blow and the bil - lows may foam, glo - ry hal - le - lu - jah,
   But she is a - ble to land us all home,

3. { She land - ed all who a - ble have gone be - fore, glo - ry hal - le - lu - jah,
   And yet she is there, to land still more,
4. { If I tell them that you are com - ing up, too,

CHORUS.

'Tis the old ship of Zi - on, hal - le - lu, hal - le - lu, 'Tis the old ship of Zi - on, hal - le - lu - jah.

'Tis the old ship of Zi - on, hal - le - lu, hal - le - lu, 'Tis the old ship of Zi - on, hal - le - lu - jah.

PISGAH

REV. RICHARD BURNHAM, 1783

J. C. LOWRY, 1820

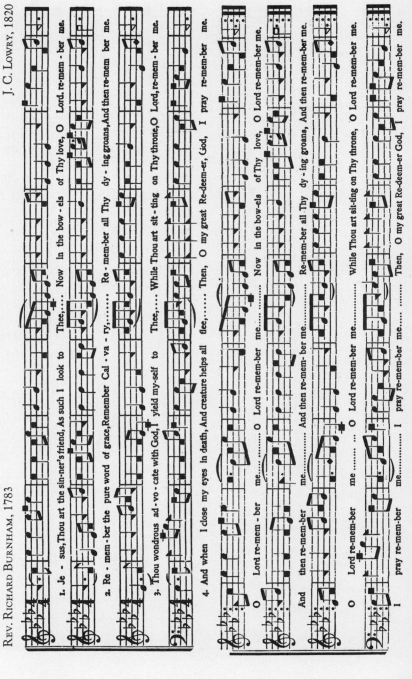

1. Je - sus, Thou art the sin-ner's friend, As such I look to Thee,.... Now in the bow - els of Thy love, O Lord, re-mem - ber me.

2. Re - mem - ber the pure word of grace, Remember Cal - va - ry,...... Re - mem-ber all Thy dy - ing groans, And then re-mem ber me.

3. Thou wondrous ad - vo - cate with God, I yield my-self to Thee,.... While Thou art sit - ting on Thy throne, O Lord, re-mem - ber me.

4. And when I close my eyes in death, And creature helps all flee,...... Then, O my great Re-deem-er, God, I pray re-mem-ber me.

Lord re-mem - ber me........ ... O Lord re-mem-ber me............ Now in the bow-els of Thy love, O Lord re-mem-ber me.

And then re-mem-ber me........... And then re-mem- ber me............. Re-mem-ber all Thy dy - ing groans, And then re-mem-ber me.

Lord re-mem-ber me .... O Lord re-mem-ber me............ While Thou art sit-ting on Thy throne, O Lord re-mem-ber me.

pray re-mem-ber me............. I pray re-mem-ber me...... .... Then, O my great Re-deem-er God, I pray re-mem-ber me.

PLEYEL'S HYMN

Helen Maria Williams, 1790

Ignaz J. Pleyel, 1831

1. While thee I seek, pro-tect-ing Pow'r, Be my vain wish-es stilled, And may this con - se-crat-ed hour With bet - ter hopes be filled.

2. In each e - vent of life, how clear Thy rul - ing hand I see! Each bless-ing to my soul more dear, Be - cause con - ferred by thee.

3. When glad-ness wings my favored hour, Thy love my thoughts shall fill; Resigned when storms of sorrow lower, My soul shall meet thy will.

Thy love the pow'r of tho't bestowed, To thee my thoughts would soar; Thy mer - cy o'er my life has flowed, That mer - cy I a - dore.

In ev-'ry joy that crowns my days, In ev-'ry pain I bear, My heart shall find de-light in praise, Or seek re - lief in prayer.

My lift - ed eye, without a tear, The gathering storm shall see: My stead-fast heart shall know no fear; That heart shall rest on thee.

THE PROMISED LAND

Samuel Stennet, 1787

Arr. by Miss M. Durham, about 1840

1. On Jordan's stormy banks - stand, And cast a wist-ful eye   To   Canaan's fair and hap-py land, Where my possessions lie.   I   am

2. O the transporting, rapt'rous scene That ris - es   to   my   sight! Sweet fields arrayed in   liv - ing green, And riv-ers   of   de - light.   I   am

3. Filled with de-light, my   raptured soul Would here no lon-ger   stay! Though Jordan's waves a-round me roll, Fear-less I'd launch a-way.   I   am

bound for the promised   land, ... I'm bound for the   promised land,   Oh,   who will come and go with me,   I   am bound for the promised land.

SARDIS

Miss Sarah Lancaster, 1869

ROCKY ROAD

J.C.B.

J. C. Brown, arr. by Paine Denson, 1935

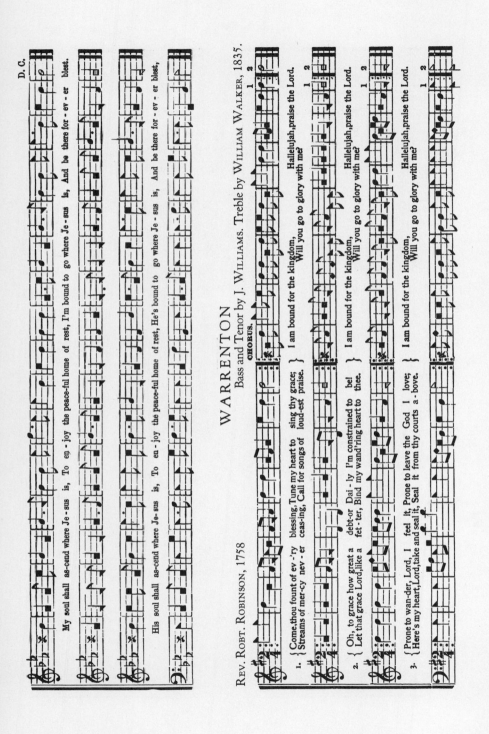

D. C.

My soul shall as-cend where Je-sus is, To en - joy the peace-ful home of rest, I'm bound to go where Je - sus Is, And be there for - ev - er blest.

His soul shall as-cend where Je-sus is, To en - joy the peace-ful home of rest, He's bound to go where Je - sus is, And be there for - er er blest,

WARRENTON

Bass and Tenor by J. WILLIAMS. Treble by WILLIAM WALKER, 1835.

REV. ROBT. ROBINSON, 1758.

CHORUS.

1. { Come, thou fount of ev - 'ry blessing, Tune my heart to sing thy grace; } I am bound for the kingdom, Hallelujah, praise the Lord,
   { Streams of mer-cy nev - er ceas-ing, Call for songs of loud-est praise. } Will you go to glory with me?

2. { Oh, to grace how great a debt-or Dai - ly I'm constrained to be! } I am bound for the kingdom, Hallelujah, praise the Lord.
   { Let that grace Lord, like a fet - ter, Bind my wand'ring heart to thee. } Will you go to glory with me?

3. { Prone to wan-der, Lord, I feel it, Prone to leave the God I love; } I am bound for the kingdom, Hallelujah, praise the Lord.
   { Here's my heart, Lord, take and seal it, Seal it from thy courts a - bove. } Will you go to glory with me?

STRUGGLE ON

H. S. REESE, 1859

H. S. REESE, 1859. Alto by S. M. DENSON, 1911

1. Our pray-ing time will soon be o'er, Hal - le - lu - jah, We'll join with those who've gone be-fore, Hal - le - lu - jah.

2. To love and bless and praise the name, Hal - le - lu - jah, Of Je - sus Christ, the bleed-ing Lamb, Hal - le - lu - jah.

Strug - gle on, strug-gle on, Hal - le - lu - jah, Strug-gle on for the work's most done, Hal - le - lu - jah.

Strug - gle on, strug-gle on, Hal - le - lu - jah, Strug-gle on for the work's most done, Hal - le - lu - jah.

WAYFARING STRANGER

Arr. by J.M.D.

Arr. by JOHN M. DYE, 1935

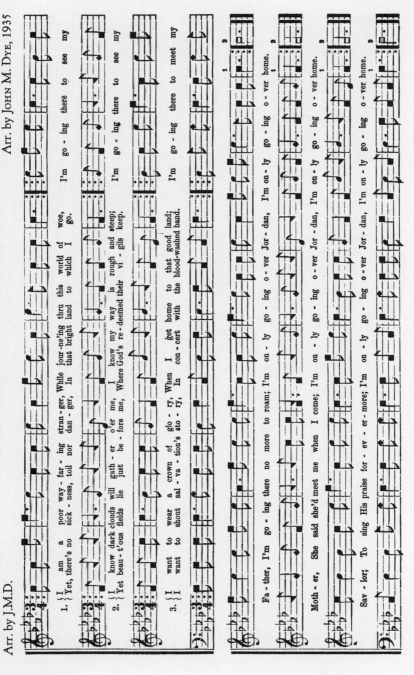

1. {I am a poor way-far-ing stran-ger, While jour-ne'ing thru this world of woe, / Yet, there's no sick-ness, toil nor dan-ger, In that bright land to which I go.} I'm go-ing there to see my

2. {I know dark clouds will gath-er o'er me, I know my way is rough and steep; / Yet beau-t'ous fields lie just be-fore me, Where God's re-deemed their vi-gils keep.} I'm go-ing there to see my

3. {I want to wear a crown of glo-ry, When I get home to that good land; / I want to shout sal-va-tion's sto-ry, In con-cert with the blood-washed band.} I'm go-ing there to meet my

Fa-ther, I'm go-ing there no more to roam; I'm on-ly go-ing o-ver Jor-dan, I'm on-ly go-ing o-ver home.

Moth-er, She said she'd meet me when I come; I'm on-ly go-ing o-ver Jor-dan, I'm on-ly go-ing o-ver home.

Sav-ior; To sing His praise for-ev-er-more; I'm on-ly go-ing o-ver Jor-dan, I'm on-ly go-ing o-ver home.

WEEPING PILGRIM

J. P. REESE, 1859. Alto by S. M. DENSON, 1911

1 You may tell them fath - er when you see them—I'm a poor mourn-ing Pil - grim, I'm bound for Canaan's land.
2 You may tell them moth - er when you see them—I'm a poor mourn-ing Pil - grim, I'm bound for Canaan's land.

3 You may tell them broth - er when you see them—1,m a poor mourn-ing Pil - grim, I'm bound for Canaan's land.
4 You may tell them sis - ters when you see them—I'm a poor mourn-ing Pil - grim, I'm bound for Canaan's land.

I weep, and I mourn, and I move slow - ly on,— I'm a poor mourning Pil - grim, I'm bound for Canaan's land.

I weep, and I mourn, and I move slow - ly on,— I'm a poor mourning Pil - grim, I'm bound for Canaan's land.

WONDROUS LOVE

Alto by S. M. DENSON, 1911

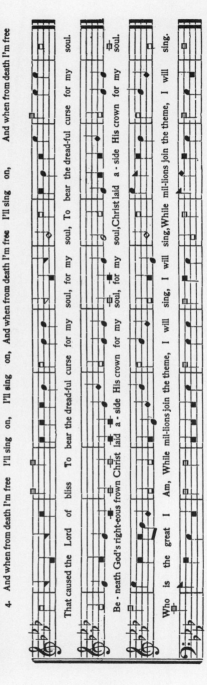

1. What wondrous love is this! oh, my soul! What wondrous love is this! oh, my soul! What wondrous love is this

2. When I was sinking down, sink-ing down, When I was sink-ing down, sink-ing down, When I was sink-ing down

3. To God and to the Lamb, I will sing, I will sing; To God and to the Lamb I will sing; To God and to the Lamb,

4. And when from death I'm free I'll sing on, I'll sing on, And when from death I'm free I'll sing on, And when from death I'm free

That caused the Lord of bliss To bear the dread-ful curse for my soul, for my soul, To bear the dread-ful curse for my soul.

Be-neath God's right-eous frown Christ laid a-side His crown for my soul, for my soul, Christ laid a-side His crown for my soul.

Who is the great I Am, While mil-lions join the theme, I will sing, I will sing, While mil-lions join the theme, I will sing.

I'll sing and joy-ful be, thro' out e-ter-ni-ty I'll sing on, I'll sing on, thro' out e-ter-ni-ty I'll sing on.

Selected Bibliography

Barfield, Louise Calhoun. *History of Harris County, Georgia, 1827–1961.* Columbus, Georgia: The Columbus Office Supply Company, 1961.

Bean, Shirley Ann. "The Missouri Harmony, 1820–1858: The Refinement of a Southern Tunebook." Ph.D. dissertation, University of Missouri—Kansas City, 1973.

Bellinger, Lucius. *Stray Leaves from the Portfolio of a Methodist Local Preacher.* Macon, Georgia: J. W. Burke and Co., 1870.

Boyd, Joe Dan. "Judge Jackson: Black Giant of White Spirituals." *Journal of American Folklore,* 83 (October-December, 1970), 446–451.

————. "Negro Sacred Harp Songsters in Mississippi." *Mississippi Folklore Register,* 5, no. 3 (Fall, 1971), 60–83.

Bronson, Bertrand Harris. *The Ballad as Song.* Berkeley and Los Angeles: University of California Press, 1969.

Bukofzer, Manfred. "Popular Polyphony in the Middle Ages." *The Musical Quarterly,* 26 (January, 1940), 31–49.

Carmer, Carl. *Stars Fell on Alabama.* New York: Hill and Wang, 1934.

Chase, Gilbert. *America's Music: From the Pilgrims to the Present.* 2nd ed., rev.; New York: McGraw Hill, 1966.

Crawford, Richard, and McKay, David P. "The Performance of William Billings' Music." *Journal of Research in Music Education,* 21, no. 4 (Winter, 1973).

Curwen, John Spencer. *Studies in Worship Music.* First Series (2nd ed.). London: J. Curwen and Sons, 1888.

Davidson, Donald. *Still Rebels, Still Yankees, and Other Essays.* Baton Rouge: Louisiana State University Press, 1957.

Ellington, Charles Linwood. "The Sacred Harp Tradition: Its Origin and Evolution." Ph.D. dissertation, Florida State University, 1969.

Etherington, Charles L. *Protestant Worship Music: Its History and Practice.* New York: Holt, Rinehart, and Winston, 1965.

Fry, B. St. James. "The Early Camp-Meeting Song Writers." *The Methodist Quarterly Review,* 41 (July, 1859), 401–413.

Harley, Rachel Augusta Brett. "Ananias Davisson: Southern Tune-Book Compiler (1780–1857)." Ph.D. dissertation, University of Michigan, 1972.

Harpeth Valley Sacred Harp News, The. Ed. William J. Reynolds, original ed. Priestley Miller. Nashville, Tennessee. Infrequent publication.

Horn, Dorothy D. *Sing to Me of Heaven: A Study of Folk and Early American Materials in Three Old Harp Books.* Gainesville: University of Florida Press, 1970.

Jackson, George Pullen. *Another Sheaf of White Spirituals.* Gainesville: University of Florida Press, 1952.

————. "The Folk Celebrates a Centennial." *Bulletin of the Tennessee Folklore Society,* 10 (1944), 1–8.

————. "The 400-Year Odyssey of the 'Captain Kidd' Song Family—Notably Its Religious Branch." *Southern Folklore Quarterly,* 15 (December, 1951), 239–248.

————. *Spiritual Folk-Songs of Early America.* Locust Valley, New York: J. J. Augustin, 1937.

————. *The Story of the Sacred Harp, 1844–1944.* Nashville: Vanderbilt University Press, 1944.

————. *White and Negro Spirituals: Their Life Span and Kinship.* Locust Valley, New York: J. J. Augustin, 1943.

————. *White Spirituals in the Southern Uplands.* Chapel Hill: University of North Carolina Press, 1933.

James, J[oseph]. S[ummerlin]. *A Brief History of the Sacred Harp and Its Author, B. F. White, Sr., and Contributors.* Douglasville, Georgia: New South Book and Job Print, 1904.

Lomax, Alan. Commentary on *All Day Singing from "The Sacred Harp"* Prestige International 25007. Southern Journey series, ed. Carlo Rotolo. Prestige Records Inc., Bergenfield, New Jersey.

Lowens, Irving. *Music and Musicians in Early America.* New York: W. W. Norton and Co., 1964.

Lytle, Andrew. "The Hind Tit." *I'll Take My Stand: The South and the Agrarian Tradition.* Twelve Southerners. New York: Harper and Brothers, 1930.

Rourke, Constance. *The Roots of American Culture and Other Essays.* New York: Harcourt, Brace and Company, 1942.

Seeger, Charles. "Contrapuntal Style in the Three-Voice Shape-Note Hymns." *The Musical Quarterly,* 26 (October, 1940), 483–493.

Sharp, Cecil J. *English Folk-Song, Some Conclusions.* London: Simpkin and Co., 1907.

————. *English Folk Songs from the Southern Appalachians.* 2 vols. Ed. Maud Karpeles. London: Oxford University Press, 1932.

Simkins, Francis Butler. *A History of the South.* 2nd ed., rev.; New York: Knopf, 1953.

Steinberg, Judith T. "Old Folks Concerts and the Revival of New England Psalmody." *The Musical Quarterly,* 59 (October, 1973), 602–619.

Stevenson, Robert. *Protestant Church Music in America: A Short Survey of Men and Movements from 1564 to the Present.* New York: W. W. Norton and Co., 1966.

Symmes, Thomas. *The Reasonableness of Regular Singing, or Singing by Note.* Boston, 1720.

Wolf, John Quincy. "The *Sacred Harp* in Mississippi," *Journal of American Folklore,* 81 (October-December, 1968), 337–341.

Work, John W. "Plantation Meistersinger." *The Musical Quarterly,* 27 (January, 1941), 97–106.

Yasser, Joseph. *A Theory of Evolving Tonality.* New York: American Library of Musicology, 1932.

Notes

Chapter 1

1. Although the singers have reduced the hours from in the early twentieth century when the sessions often lasted from eight to four, the vocal stamina evident at almost any singing today is extraordinary.

2. The formal titles of these revisions are as follows: (for the White book) *The Sacred Harp, B. F. White and E. J. King, A Collection of Tunes, Odes, Hymns and Anthems. Fourth Edition, with Supplement.* Copyright 1911, by J. L. White; (for the Cooper book) *The B. F. White Sacred Harp, As Revised and Improved by W. M. Cooper and Others.* The Sacred Harp Book Co., Inc., Troy, Alabama. Most recent edition, 1960; (for the Denson book) *"Original Sacred Harp"* (*Denson Revision*), *1971 Edition.* Sacred Harp Publishing Co. Copies of the Denson book can be ordered from the publishing company, Box 185, Bremen, Georgia 30110.

3. "The *Sacred Harp* in Mississippi," *Journal of American Folklore*, 81 (October-December 1968), 340.

4. *The Story of the Sacred Harp, 1844–1944* (Nashville, 1944).

5. *A Brief History of the Sacred Harp and Its Author, B. F. White, Sr., and Contributors* (Douglasville, Georgia, 1904). This short rare work, obviously written for those already familiar with the Sacred Harp tradition, is faultily paged and not always reliable generally. It has nevertheless proved an indispensable aid to subsequent researchers of the movement. Further references in the text will not be cited.

6. In 1952 Thurman completed "The Chattahoochee Musical Convention: 1852–1952," a history of the rural Georgia institution. A copy of the unpublished work is owned by Hugh McGraw, Bremen, Georgia. Subsequent references will not be cited.

7. "The Sacred Harp Tradition of the South: Its Origin and Evolution" (Ph.D. diss., Florida State University, 1969), p. 75.

Chapter 2

1. *The Roots of American Culture and Other Essays* (New York, 1942), p. 183.

2. *Southern Folklore Quarterly*, 15 (December 1951), 239–248. See also Bertrand H. Bronson, "Samuel Hall's Family Tree" in *The Ballad as Song* (Berkeley and Los Angeles: University of California Press, 1969), pp. 18–36.

3. George Pullen Jackson, *Spiritual Folk-Songs of Early America* (New York, 1937), pp. 147–148.

4. Jackson, *Spiritual Folk-Songs*, pp. 104–105.

5. George Pullen Jackson, *Another Sheaf of White Spirituals* (Gainesville, Florida, 1952), p. 52.

6. *Another Sheaf*, p. 82.

7. *Spiritual Folk-Songs*, p. 15.

8. *White Spirituals in the Southern Uplands* (Chapel Hill, 1933), pp. 161–163.

9. *White and Negro Spirituals: Their Life Span and Kinship* (Locust Valley, N. Y., 1943), p. 240.

10. *Sing to Me of Heaven* (Gainesville, Florida, 1970), p. 98.

11. Quoted by Joseph Yasser, *A Theory of Evolving Tonality* (New York, 1932), p. 347.

12. Seeger, "Contrapuntal Style in the Three-Voice Shape-Note Hymns," *Musical Quarterly*, 26 (October 1940), 483, and Lowens, *Music and Musicians in Early America* (New York, 1964), p. 284.

13. *Music and Musicians*, p. 48.

14. *White and Negro Spirituals*, p. 247.

15. "The Sacred Harp in the Land of Eden," *Still Rebels, Still Yankees, and Other Essays* (Baton Rouge, 1957), pp. 148–149.

16. *A Theory of Evolving Tonality*, p. 56.

17. *English Folk-Song, Some Conclusions* (London, 1907), p. 71.

18. *White Spirituals*, p. 69.

19. "*Sacred Harp* in Mississippi," 340.

20. In this instance, another parallel can be drawn between the singing style of the Sacred Harp and religious music of the eighteenth century. An elderly interviewer told John Spencer Curwen, nineteenth-century authority on English church singing practices, that "in the old times the people liked the tunes pitched high; the women especially enjoyed screaming out high G. It made the psalmody more brilliant and far-sounding." See Curwen's *Studies in Worship Music* (London, 1888).

21. *Journal of Research in Music Education,* 21, no. 4 (Winter 1973), 318.

Chapter 3

1. *Protestant Worship Music: Its History and Practice* (New York, 1965), p. 188.

2. *White Spirituals,* p. 4. For fuller explanation of this system, derived from the Guidonian Hexachord system, see Dorothy D. Horn, *Sing to Me of Heaven,* pp. 5–7.

3. This and the two following quotations from *Music and Musicians,* p. 282.

4. *White Spirituals,* pp. 19–20.

5. *Protestant Church Music in America: A Short Survey of Men and Movements from 1564 to the Present* (New York, 1966), pp. 85–86.

6. "Old Folks Concerts and the Revival of New England Psalmody," *Musical Quarterly,* 59 (October 1973), 605.

7. Steinberg, p. 619.

8. Steinberg, p. 611.

9. pp. 284–85.

10. *Sing to Me of Heaven,* p. 7.

11. This and other background information on E. J. King and his family was found by Kenneth H. Thomas, Jr., a descendant of the King family. The facts surrounding King's death appear in the Talbot County court records.

12. (October 1844), p. 154, col. 1.

13. This information is from Louise Calhoun Barfield's *History of Harris County, Georgia, 1827–1961,* privately published in Columbus, Georgia, in 1961 (available in the Atlanta Public Library). James, it might be pointed out, had referred to White as clerk of the superior court.

14. *America's Music: From the Pilgrims to the Present* (New York, 1966), p. 223.

15. *History of Harris County.* I am indebted to William J. Reynolds in vol. 4, no. 2, of the *Harpeth Valley Sacred Harp News* for pointing out this fact.

16. For list of songs see Steinberg, "Old Folks Concerts," *Musical Quarterly,* 616–617.

17. *White Spirituals,* p. 93.

18. The edition of the *Christian Harmony* now available in Georgia, Alabama, and Mississippi is a 1958 revision by John Deason and O. A.

Parris. Its many new songs are considerably more modern than Walker's original tunes.

19. This letter was reproduced by T. H. Mosely, the son of W. J. Mosely, in a privately printed book, *Humorous Travels: From Ridiculous to Sublime, from Laughter to Weeping* (ca. 1961). A copy is owned by Hugh McGraw of Bremen, Georgia. Edmonds and Pound, mentioned in the letter, were prominent figures in the early days of the Sacred Harp movement. Pound, who contributed several songs to the *Sacred Harp,* was listed by James as having received musical instruction from B. F. White. He is discussed further in chapter 4. Edmonds is honored in the Sacred Harp volume by Elder Dumas's tune "Edmonds," a contribution to the 1869 edition.

20. 41 (July 1859), 407, 413.

21. *White and Negro Spirituals,* p. 86.

22. (Macon, Georgia).

Chapter 4

1. "Popular Polyphony in the Middle Ages," *Musical Quarterly,* 26 (January 1940), 35.

2. "All-Day Singing" (New York, 1934), p. 51.

3. The convention ledgers quoted in the text are passed each year from the secretary of each convention to his elected successor. The original ledger containing the minutes of the Chattahoochee Convention dating from 1866 has now been preserved in the Georgia Department of Archives and History.

4. *White Spirituals,* p. 99.

5. Two copies of this revision have only recently surfaced in the Atlanta area. This study made use of the copy owned by Philip Daniel Brittain.

6. In her unpublished dissertation "*The Missouri Harmony, 1820–1858:* The Refinement of a Southern Tunebook," Shirley Ann Bean describes a similar remaking of the popular *Missouri Harmony* in 1850. Bean cites this revision, undertaken at the request of the publishers by Charles Warren, "Professor of Music," as a reverse of the common process of "southernizing" tunes, by which the voice parts of songs originating in the North or East were changed into "dispersed harmony," or were at least enlivened melodically, by southern tunesmiths. The discovery of White's 1909 revision of the *Sacred Harp* demonstrates that the *Missouri Harmony* was not the only volume of popularity in the rural South to be scrubbed up to meet citified standards of "correct harmony."

7. "Ananias Davisson: Southern Tune-Book Compiler (1780–1857)" (Ph.D. diss., University of Michigan, 1972), p. 121.

8. *Story of the Sacred Harp,* p. 39.

9. *White Spirituals,* p. 108.

10. *Musical Quarterly,* 27 (January 1941), 97–106.

11. *Journal of American Folklore,* 83 (October-December 1970), 446–447.

12. "Judge Jackson," 449.

13. "Plantation Meistersinger," 103.

14. "Judge Jackson," 448.

15. "Sacred Harp in the Land of Eden," p. 143.

Chapter 5

1. *English Folk Songs from the Southern Appalachians.* 2 vols. Ed. Maud Karpeles. London: Oxford University Press, 1932.

2. "The Hind Tit," *I'll Take My Stand* (New York, 1930), p. 232.

3. This and the two following quotations from *White Spirituals,* pp. 102–104.

4. See Barfield, *History of Harris County,* p. 231.

5. *White Spirituals,* pp. 105–106.

6. New York, 1963, p. 403.

7. *White Spirituals,* p. 109.

8. "The Sacred Harp in the Land of Eden," p. 142.

Chapter 6

1. *Story of the Sacred Harp,* p. 37.

2. *Music and Musicians,* p. 155.

3. *Music and Musicians,* p. 284.

4. "Current Attitudes Toward Folklore" in *Still Rebels, Still Yankees,* p. 136.

5. "All-Day Singing," pp. 54–56.

6. "The Folk Celebrates a Centennial," *Bulletin of the Tennessee Folklore Society,* 10 (1944), 7.

7. "The Sacred Harp in the Land of Eden," p. 145.

Index

Titles of songs from the various editions of the *Sacred Harp* are listed under "Songs from the *Sacred Harp*."

Powell's Chapel Church, Ga., 133

Presbyterian Church, 19

Primitive Baptist Church, 5, 10, 19–20

Providence Baptist Church, Talla-poosa, Ga., 144

Psalm-singing, 58

Quartal harmony, 35

Raised sixth, 33–34

Read, Daniel, 33, 62, 64, 73, 85

Reasonableness of Regular Singing, The (Symmes), 58

Record albums, Sacred Harp, 50, 114–15, 116, 158

Reese, H. S., 23, 74, 86, 109

Reese, J. P.: as singing master, 15; the composing of "Weeping Pil-grim," 74; as "musical corre-spondent," 133; his children, 152; mentioned, 23, 83, 86

Religious nature of Sacred Harp: of tradition, 17, 18–21, 149, 155; theology in songs, 26–27

Revival spirituals. *See* Camp-meet-ing spirituals

Reynolds, William J., 114

Rhythm, Sacred Harp, 47–48

Rock Creek Mountain Home Con-vention, 140

Rogers, Lonnie, 18

Roopville, Ga., 18

Rourke, Constance, 30

Rudiments, Sacred Harp: as source of information on chord struc-ture, 14; on major and minor chords, 40–41; on beats to the measure, 48; J. L. White's rudi-ments, 99, 100, 109; Denson Re-vision's, 113; mentioned, 16, 157

Russell County, Ala., 139

Ryan's Creek Convention, 140

Sacred Harp Book Co., 7, 233

Sacred Harp Publishing Co.: or-ganized, 7–8, 112–13; record albums, 50, 114–15, 158; publi-cations, 113–14; how it functions, 115–16; Hugh McGraw, execu-tive secretary, 116–17; address to order books, 233

St. Joseph, Tenn., 153

Sand Mountain, Ala., 50, 93, 140

Sawyer, Rev. S. B., 27

Seating arrangement at singings, 8, 10

Seven-shape music: surviving sys-tems, 5–6; different from Sacred Harp, 9; four beats to measure, 48; use of in Mississippi Sacred Harp, 51–52; threat to four-shape music, 67; *Christian Harmony* as sturdiest example, 75; Sacred Harp singers and *Christian Har-mony*, 76; mentioned, 1, 2

Shaped notes: origin and use, 4, 6, 9, 65–66; surviving shaped-note traditions, 5–6; Walker's and Aikens's seven-shape systems, 75. *See also* Seven-shape music

Sharp, Cecil, 46, 129

Shell, I. M., 137

Shenandoah Valley, Va., 5, 66

Shumway, Nehemiah, 85

Singing school: early New England, 4, 58, 59–61; vestiges in Sacred Harp tradition, 8; discussed, 13–16; movement south, 65–67; role of Southern Musical Convention, 132–33; older participants, 156; mentioned, 5, 99, 117, 157

Smith, William, 66

Social Harp (McCurry), 53, 67, 70, 94

Solmization, 2–3, 4, 9, 51–52, 58, 59; mentioned, 13, 40, 114

Songs from *The Sacred Harp*

"Abbeville," 29; "Adoration," 24; "Alabama," 29, 35, 38, 116, 188; "Amazing Grace" ("New Britain"), 3, 37–38, 43, 53, 54, 209; "The American Star," 32; "Antioch," 28, 29, 189; "Arkan-sas," 29

"Babel's Streams," 26; "Balls-town," 20; "Bear Creek," 15; "Be Saved To-Night," 93; "Blind

INDEX 243

Bartimeus," 26; "Bound for Canaan," 69; "The Bower of Prayer," 70; "The Bride's Farewell," 26

"Calvary," 55, 190; "Can I Leave You?," 25, 55; "Chester," 191; "The Child of Grace," 55, 69; "Christmas Anthem," 110; "Claremont," 152; "Cleburne," 29; "Columbiana," 29; "Columbus," 37; "The Converted Thief," 26, 37; "Corinth," 29; "Coronation," 192; "Coston," 29; "Cowper," 193; "Cusseta," 29

"David's Lamentation," 26, 194; "Delight," 35; "Devotion," 195; "Dull Care," 70; "Dumas," 29; "The Dying Boy," 26; "The Dying Californian," 195; "The Dying Christian," 70

"Easter Anthem," 39, 64, 196–99; "Edmonds," 236; "Evening Shade," 200

"Farewell," 25; "Farewell Anthem," 25, 39; "Farewell to All," 25; "Fleeting Days," 27, 146; "Florida," 29; "Florida Storm," 119, 120–21, 122; "Frozen Heart," 70

"Georgia," 29; "Gospel Trumpet," 69; "The Great Roll-Call," 97; "Greenfield," 201; "Greenwich," 29, 33, 91; "The Grieved Soul," 23; "Guiding Spirit," 93

"Happy Day," 99; "Heavenly Armor," 101, 102, 202; "Hebrew Children," 26, 203; "Holly Springs," 29; "Holy Manna," 204; "Horton," 29

"Idumea," 104, 105, 207; "Invocation," 76

"Jackson," 23, 29; "Jerusalem," 205; "Jester," 29; "Jordan's Shore," 34

"The Last Words of Copernicus," 28; "Lenox," 64; "Life Is the Time to Serve the Lord," 90; "Living Hope," 117; "The Lone Pilgrim," 72, 208; "Louisiana,"

29; "Loving Jesus," 72, 206–7

"Majesty," 64; "Manchester," 94; "Mear," 77, 209; "Mercy's Free," 27; "The Midnight Cry," 28; "The Minister's Farewell," 25; "Montgomery," 22–23; "Morgan," 29; "Morning Sun," 27; "The Morning Trumpet," 43, 72, 210; "Murillo's Lesson," 3, 212–13; "My Native Land," 43; "My Span of Life," 43

"Nashville," 29, 211; "Never Part," 25; "Never Turn Back," 55; "New Britain," see "Amazing Grace"; "New Harmony," 29; "New Hope," 29; "New Jerusalem," 91; "New Topia," 214; "Ninety-Third Psalm," 66, 101, 103, 215; "Northfield," 38, 216

"Ode on Science," 39; "Ogletree," 29; "The Old-Fashioned Bible," 32; "The Old Ship of Zion," 43, 217

"Parting Friend," 25; "Parting Friends," 25; "The Parting Hand," 25; "A Parting Prayer," 25; "Pisgah," 218; "Plenary," 31; "Pleyel's Hymn," 219; "Primrose," 66; "Primrose Hill," 31; "The Prodigal Son," 26; "The Promised Land," 27, 35, 220; "Prospect," 29

"Ragan," 4, 43; "Raymond," 94; "Red Sea Anthem," 111; "Restoration," 215; "Reverential Anthem," 70; "The Road to Life and Death," 90; "Rock of Ages," 90, 99; "Rocky Road," 3, 222–23; "Rose of Sharon," 15

"Saints Bound for Heaven," 55; "Sardis," 29, 221; "Sawyer's Exit," 27; "Seaborn," 29; "Sharon," 55; "Sherburne," 64; "Sister's Farewell," 25; "Struggle On," 224; "Sweet By and By," 93, 97; "Sweet Canaan," 14; "Sweet Morning," 43

"Talbotton," 68; "The Teach-